"Stories of 32 Coaches Who Helped Lay the Foundation of What the Strength and Conditioning Profession is Today."

THE

GOLDEN

AGE

OF STRENGTH
AND CONDITIONING

FOREWORD BY

BOYD EPLEY

CORE

Published by The Core Media Group, Inc., P.O. Box 2037, Indian Trail, NC 28079.

Cover Design: Kayla Owle
Interior Design: Nadia Guy

Printed in the United States of America.

Foreword
by Boyd Epley,
Hall of Fame Strength Coach

For the first 100 years of college football, almost every coach told athletes not to lift weights, afraid they would become muscle-bound and lose coordination. We now know that there is no faster way to improve athletic performance than through strength training and conditioning. When looking at the strength and conditioning profession today, it's hard to believe that a football player at Marquette University was kicked off his college football team in 1967 because he refused to stop lifting weights after being told by his coach to stop.

On August 15, 1969, Bob Devaney, Head Football Coach at the University of Nebraska, took a chance and hired me as the first paid collegiate strength and conditioning coach. At that time, there was no in-season lifting, no summer conditioning, and no performance testing combines. Only a few athletes sprinkled across the country were lifting in basements or garages out of sight from their coaches because coaches at the time thought lifting weights would make their athletes slower. When Coach Devaney hired me he said, "We're going to give lifting weights a try because [Assistant Football Coach] Tom Osborne thinks it's a good idea, but if anyone gets slower you're fired."

The national perception of strength training changed quickly once football coaches saw the turnaround at Nebraska with back-to-back National Championships in 1970 and 1971.

In this book, 32 college and professional strength coaches share their story of how and why they became part of the first 50 years of strength and conditioning and how and why strength and conditioning became important to almost every athlete in every sport in the world.

Introduction
by Chip Sigmon,
CSCS* D, RSCC*E, CISSN, USAW

How This Book Came to Be

I was on my way to work on a cold rainy Monday morning in November 2017 when I picked up the phone to call legendary strength coach Mike Gentry. Mike had just retired from Virginia Tech and I wanted to catch up with him and see how he was doing. I knew he would be up, because it was slightly before 7:00 a.m., and a strength coach sleeping past 5:30 a.m. is sleeping in!

We started talking about how we started out in the profession. I recalled the time when Mike did one of my first strength & conditioning clinics while I was at Appalachian State in 1986. Mike asked me what I started off making (money wise) when I got the head strength coach job at ASU in 1984. I told him I went there for free, just training table and a place to lay my head down at night, which was a small room under the Field House where the officials dressed during game day!

Mike responded by saying "Well, you've got me beat. When I went to East Carolina in 1982 I started out making $12,000."

We continued to talk about how things were back then in the infancy of the profession. I then said something to the fact that "Yes, those were the Golden Years for sure!"

And Mike said without hesitation, "That sounds like a good book!"

Therefore, with that being said, one year and many conversations later, we would like to present to you,

THE GOLDEN AGE OF STRENGTH AND CONDITIONING.

This book is a compilation of autobiographies of strength & conditioning coaches who helped lay the foundation of the strength & conditioning profession.

We being the Core Group of this project:
- Mike Gentry: former Strength Coach, Virginia Tech
- Jerry Palmieri: former Strength Coach, NY Giants, NFL
- Bill Foran: Strength Coach, Miami Heat, NBA
- Allan Johnson: Strength Coach, East Tennessee State University
- Chip Sigmon: former Strength Coach, Charlotte Hornets, NBA
- Robert Walker: Publisher of "The Core Media Group, Inc." and NFL agent

Each one of us worked tirelessly each week for a solid year making this book a reality.

On a personal note, it took months and long conversations to come up with a list of strength & conditioning coaches to select for this book. Our requirements were that they had to be a Head Strength Coach of a collegiate, university, or professional team in the late 1970s or in the decade of the '80s. Our publisher only allowed us so many coaches and he was kind enough to extend the list to even more. Some coaches, who were invited to contribute to this book, graciously declined for one reason or another.

The hard part is leaving out another 25 or so coaches who also played a role in the growth of the strength and conditioning profession. You know who you are. We just could not include everyone. Although we could not include every coach, we greatly respect you and your role in the establishment of our profession.

Finally, we would like to thank our three sponsors—Woodway, CYTO-SPORT™, and Total Strength and Speed/Williams Strength—for their support. Their financial contribution made this book possible. These leaders in athletic performance will tell their stories of the establishment and growth of their companies and the role they played in the profession of strength & conditioning.

Table of Contents

CHAPTER 1

The Mike Arthur Story

Looking back on my life and reviewing all the experiences, now seems as if my life had a written script. Growing up in Nebraska during the fifties and sixties, I had an ambition to play football at Nebraska. When I was old enough to participate in midget football, I had one big problem. I did not weigh enough. The cut-off limit was 100 pounds and I weighed 80. The next year, the same thing. Somehow I had to gain weight. One day, strolling through the sports department at Montgomery Wards I spotted a picture of Bruce Randall, a former Mr. Universe, curling a barbell. He looked muscular, so I figured that was my ticket to putting on bodyweight. At that time, most coaches, including my dad, were not receptive to lifting weights. They believed adding excessive muscle would restrict your joint mobility and speed of movement, negatively affecting physical performance. I did not care, I was going to do whatever it took to gain weight. Furthermore, besides gaining muscle mass, the side effect of strength could only but be a positive. How could it not be?

My dad reluctantly purchased the 110-pound barbell set for my Christmas present. The program that came with the barbell set included only upper body exercises. No squats, no bench-presses, no power cleans. Consequently, I did not gain much weight. Nevertheless, the veins in my forearm started sticking out noticeably from all the curls. A few months later, while at a local drug store, my eyes spotted a magazine cover of a very muscular man bending a thick piece of steel rebar. The magazine was *Mr. America*, published by Joe Weider. Then I spotted other muscle magazines, *Iron Man*, published by Peary Rader, *Muscular Development and Strength & Health*, published by Bob Hoffman. Useful information, which I could apply to my personal workouts, packed these magazines. I fervently read them all, from cover to cover numerous times, enhancing my lifting expertise in bodybuilding, powerlifting, and Olympic weightlifting. I constructed my own lifting equipment (bench and power rack), and this subsequently led to other boys in our neighborhood training in my basement weight room. They all benefited by building muscle and getting stronger. Unfortunately, I did not gain much weight, but I developed phenomenal strength. I played three years of high school football, but never played enough to letter. On the other hand, some of the neighborhood boys who lifted with me, later made the all-state football team and played in the senior shrine bowl. That verified, in my mind, nevertheless, the positive benefits of lifting weights were irrefutable.

During the spring of 1969, I entered and won the Nebraska State Powerlifting Meet at the age of 17, weighing 120 pounds. Because of my success in powerlifting, I decided to shift my focus to lifting instead of football. As destiny would have it, I saw a NFL documentary that highlighted a person named Alvin Roy. It featured him coaching the San Diego Chargers on how to lift weights. Deep inside, I knew this was my calling, the reason I was alive. I envisioned myself becoming an athletic trainer, and, as a spin-off, developing a weight-training program for the football players. The combination of two fascinations that I loved, lifting and football. Alvin Roy was showing the way.

One thing led to another. I learned about a small weight room at the University of Nebraska. It was in the Schulte Fieldhouse with the purpose to rehab injured athletes. Everything was lining up with a weight room already in place. It just needed the right person (me) to implement a lifting program for the football team. During the fall of 1969, I started sneaking workouts in at fieldhouse after school while the football team was out practicing. The room provided an Olympic bar, a bench press bench, and the squat rack needed for powerlifting. To enter the weight room, I first had to go through the training room. One afternoon, the head trainer happened to be in the training room. He noticed me entering the weight room and followed. In a snappy authoritative way, he told me that I could not lift there. As this transpired, another person approached us. He told the trainer that I was Mike Arthur, state powerlifting champion, that it was okay.

I recognized this person as Boyd Epley, who I had previously witnessed as a talented pole-vaulter at track meets I had attended. It impressed me that he knew who I was. He informed me that Bob Devaney had recently hired him as the strength coach for the Nebraska football team. I was disappointed that he beat me to the punch, but on the other hand, I sensed that Boyd was a good fit, with his physical appearance and outgoing personality. I immediately became good friends with Boyd. Nebraska football got their money's worth hiring Boyd. Football took a sudden leap forward winning the NCAA football championships in both 1970 and 1971. This quickly transformed the way football operated in a radical way and on a national level. The belief of becoming muscle bound quickly vanished.

I enrolled at the University in the fall of 1970. I took pre-med classes, so that I could gain acceptance to physical therapy school. I never was fond of going to school and sitting in classrooms. I could not figure out the importance of Chemistry, it bored me to death, and I started skipping classes. The consequence was bad grades. After two years, the university put me on academic probation. I had to take a class and get a B or better to continue my college education. That summer I took a history class and received a B+. The next semester, I cut the number of credit hours I took so that I could get things figured out. I landed a part-time job at a local health club geared towards competitive lifters and bodybuilders. I enjoyed my new job setting up programs for serious lifters and dropped out of school for one semester. The following semester I took only six hours. One of the classes I took was exercise physiology. I completely enjoyed the subject, studied rigorously and received an A. I switched majors to physical education, went back to school full-time and received good grades.

Subsequently, I met a beautiful girl. Looking back, I was merely infatuated with her, but I thought it was love. We shared an apartment, and the bills started pouring in. Instead of dropping the girl, I dropped out of school. I quit my part-time health club job and worked full-time as a construction laborer. After about a year, we broke up. Earning a good salary, I continued to work construction. During the summer of 1976, I was offered a job at University of Oregon, not as a strength coach, but as a construction laborer to help build dormitories. The pay increase was substantial, and I decided to go. Before leaving, I stopped by the weight room to say good-bye to Boyd. He told me that I was making a serious mistake; instead, I should finish my degree. He added, when I received my degree, he would hire me as his assistant. This definitely caught my attention, but I felt obligated to go to Oregon. I told him I would think about it.

I went home and thought it over. After taking exercise physiology, I saw two drawbacks related to strength training. (Note: Boyd Epley deliberately used the phrase strength training to differentiate it from competitive lifting, bodybuilding and weight training for fitness.) First, the lack of strength research; though a limited number of scientists were conducting strength research, the unscientific acceptance of the condition known as being "muscle bound" was still prevalent. Second, muscle magazines covered the only worthwhile programming information, which did not relate to the strength training of football players. There was a gigantic gap between strength research and the practical application of strength science for football players. I wanted to bridge the gap I observed between science and strength application. I met with Boyd and told him I did not want to spend all my time in the weight room. Instead, I wanted to devote some time to keeping up-to-date with strength and conditioning research and then develop training systems and methodologies based on new scientific insights. Boyd responded positively. Without any hesitation, "OK."

During the summer of 1978, just before I graduated, the first NSCA convention was held under the guidance of Boyd Epley in Lincoln. It seemed like a reunion of sorts, of a team called the Lincoln Lifters. Going back to the summer 1969, three former Lincoln Lifters teammates and I had taken a trip to Denver, Colorado to participate in regional powerlifting competition. I reflected how incredible it was that this trio of former teammates influenced the strength and conditioning profession.

In the spring of 1978, Jim Williams, who at that time was the strength coach at the University of Wyoming, and Pete Martinelli, strength coach at the University of New Mexico, discussed the possibility of a strength coach's convention. They decided Boyd had the resources and the know how to pull it off, so Jim called Boyd with the idea. I happened to be at Boyd's house when he got the call. Boyd and I discussed all the potential outcomes, and that night the NSCA became a vision of strength training in the future.

Tom Baechle was the chair of the physical education department at Creighton University. He developed the certification examination for strength and conditioning specialists. Tom also organized several experts to write chapters providing the most up-to-date information and cutting-edge material in strength training in book call the "Essentials of Strength Training and Conditioning." Tom also recommended me to Human Kinetics, to write the book "Complete Conditioning for Football."

Ken Kontor was hired by NSCA in August 1978, as Assistant Executive Director, and eventually named Executive Director in 1983 to run the NSCA office. Ken was instrumental in publishing the Strength and Conditioning Journal providing the much-needed unbiased practical applications of cutting-edge strength and conditioning. Later, with the assistance of William Kraemer, published the peer-reviewed Journal of Strength and Conditioning Research, to "bridge the gap" from the scientist to the strength specialist.

The NSCA is now the world leader in sports conditioning, with over 45,000 members.

Looking back to the first days of the NSCA, I have a bone to pick, because I experienced the time when most coaches scorned strength training. Reading what many strength coaches and sport scientist are writing today, the consensus is that the Soviet Union invented modern sports training. I disagree, though being a baby boomer who grew up during the height of the cold war might have something to do with it. From an American football point of view, training today consists of many components that prepare the athlete, divided between the football coach (fundamentals, strategies, formations, and plays), athletic training staff (injury rehabilitation), the strength and conditioning coach (physical readiness), and, most recently, the sports nutritionist (energy needs). The acceptance and implementation of strength training was the paradigm shift, not the Soviet Union's theory of sports training. Strength training made the single, most positive contribution in developing the size and speed of football players, and later affected how other sports trained, especially where optimal power is essential.

Soviet material started to surface in the late '70s and early '80s. At that time, Soviet information written by scientists and sports coaches was more theoretical than scientific or practical and did not make much sense to me. There was nothing relevant to training football players. One concept used by the soviets was periodization, a common term today among strength coaches, but an expression scarcely used by American sport coaches, and sports writers have no idea what it means. To me, periodization was just a word for annual plan where periods represent seasons. Strength coaches began using the term back in 1982, after John Garhammer and Mike Stone popularized it in the *NSCA Strength and Conditioning Journal.* I am not saying that I did not learn something from the article, I learned a lot. John and Mike took a tedious theory, related it to the "General Adaptation Syndrome," scientifically researched it, and rendered it into a simplified plan of action.

We must remember that the Soviets predominantly train athletes involved in individual sports (Olympic weightlifters), where the goal is to peak for world or Olympic competitions. This does not apply very well to football, where the athletes must report to fall camp in top condition and maintain endurance and strength levels for the entire season. They cannot physically peak as the season progresses to win the bowl game at the end of the year. The teaching of specific game fundamentals, learning plays and gaining playing experience during the course of the season are primary, strength and conditioning, though extremely essential, is secondary. The planning is different in an essential way.

The trademarks of Boyd's programming were detailed planning, a git 'r done attitude, and the ability to adjust the plan as needed. He definitely had an annual training plan, with conditioning objectives for each season. Here is a passage from one of the first manuals he wrote in 1972.

"The University of Nebraska has developed a year-round program for all sports with specific training programs for different periods of the year."

Boyd adjusted his program to how football coaches prepared by breaking the year down into seasons. Football coaches, long ago, instinctively had the basics of periodization in place, meticulously planning every detail.

Here is my short-history version on how this paradigm shift took place:

Thomas DeLorme, an American doctor, rehabbed injured soldiers after World War II and demonstrated the benefits of weight training. He coined the term "progressive overload" in 1945. Athletic trainers were the first to make

Conditioning Period	Explosive Strength	Muscular Strength	Muscular Endurance	Muscle Bulk	Motor Ability	Speed (of movement)	C-V Endurance	Game Fundamentals	Injury Rehabilitation
Summer	M	D	M	D	D	D	M	M	D
Pre-Season	D	R	D	R	R	D	D	M	R
Fall Camp	M	M	M	M	D	D	M	D	M
In-Season	M	M	M	M	M	M	M	D	M
Off-Season	M	D	M	D	M	M	M	M	D
Winter Conditioning	D	D	D	D	D	D	D	M	D
Spring	M	M	M	M	M	M	M	D	M
Off-Season	M	D	M	D	M	M	M	M	D

D - Develop
R - Refine
M - Maintain

The Strength of Nebraska – 1972, Boyd Epley, Page 2

TABLE II
University of Nebraska
Football Training Schedule

MONTH	FOOTBALL TRAINING SCHEDULE	RECOMMENDED TYPE OF WEIGHT TRAINING
MAY	Spring Game	In-Season (Maintenance)
JUNE	Summer Conditioning (No scheduled Football Practice)	Off-Season (Development)
JULY		
AUGUST		Pre-Season (Refinement)
	Fall Camp (2 practices a day)	None
SEPTEMBER	Regular Football Season	In-Season (Maintenance)
OCTOBER		
NOVEMBER		
DECEMBER	Bowl Preparation	
JANUARY	Off-Season (No scheduled Practice)	Off-Season (Development)
FEBRUARY		
MARCH	Winter Conditioning (Six Weeks)	
APRIL	Spring Football Practice	In-Season (Maintenance)

The Strength of Nebraska – 1972, Boyd Epley, Page 3

weight training acceptable purely as a method of rehabilitation.

It was around this time that bold individuals understood the importance of strength and began to weight train. In 1951, American shot putter Parry O'Brien included strength training as major part of his training. He became the first to throw over 60 feet in 1954. Consider that the 50 feet barrier was first done in 1912 and it took 42 years to get to 60 feet. 13 years later in 1967, over 50 men topped 60 feet and Randy Matson broke the 70-foot barrier, throwing 71'51/2" (Track and Field Omnibook, Ken Dogherty, 1971).

"This means that weightlifting for shot putting success almost seems to be an end in itself, lifting for its own sake." (Joe Henderson, "Weight Training Yields Power," Track and Field News, 1969.)

Alvin Roy, in 1954, began strength training with a high school team that went undefeated and won the state championship in Louisiana. In 1958, the LSU football team won the National Championship, with Alvin's help. In 1963, he helped the San Diego Chargers win the American Football League Championship. His prize athlete was Billy Cannon, 1959 Heisman Trophy winner and first pick in the 1960 NFL draft (Paraphrased from "Iron Game History," January 1992, by Terry Todd).

With Alvin Roy showing the way, and the hiring of Boyd Epley in 1969, along with the formation of the NSCA, strength training reached a tipping point. Boyd came along at the right time and responded to the opportunity.

"The paradigm shift from an athletic world with only a few isolated barbell men, to a professional organization (NSCA) of strength coaches with national reach happened suddenly, and the reason for that shift is best encapsulated in five words: Boyd Epley and Husker Power." Journal of Strength and Conditioning Research. 26(12):3177-3188, December 2012. Jason Shurley and Jan Todd.

Enough said, back to my story.

I finally graduated in August of 1978. I was so glad to get that behind me. I had my degree, and now I was the first paid full-time collegiate assistant strength coach. A dream come true, the script was playing itself out. I never continued my education, though that does not mean I quit learning. I consider strength training an art, and science as the foremost tool. It seems as I come to gain a better understanding of strength training the more questions I have. Look how complicated strength coaching is today. We now have incredible investments of money and time spent collecting and analyzing data in an effort to predict how athletes will respond to the demands of sport performance. The perpetual search for the next paradigm shift continues.

Mike Arthur's Coaching Bio

- 1976 to Present - University of Nebraska, Director of Strength and Conditioning
- 1976 - World Record, 540.25 lb. Deadlift, 132-pound weight class (International Powerlifting Federation)
- 1995 - National Collegiate Strength and Conditioning Coach of the Year (Professional Strength and Conditioning Coaches Society)
- 1998 - Complete Conditioning for Football (Human Kinetics)
- 2003 - Inducted into USA Strength & Coaches Hall of Fame
- 2018 - NSCA Impact Award

CHAPTER 2

The Mike Clark Story

In 1978, while enrolled in graduate school at the University of Kansas, I met a man who would change my outlook on the future of my life. I had always wanted to become a high school coach because those men had such an impact on my life. But while I was at Kansas studying Perceptual Motor Development (working with physically handicapped children) and Exercise Physiology, I had the chance to meet Coach Keith Kephart. Coach Kephart was the strength and conditioning coach at KU, and he showed me that I could put my love of lifting and exercise physiology to good use as a strength coach. I had never heard of such a thing and was blown away by the thought that I could actually make a career out of my natural interest in training for athletics. Coach Kephart had opened my eyes to the possibility of a different direction for my life, but at the time I had no idea where that path would take me.

After attending grad school, I was teaching and coaching at Topeka High School in Topeka, KS. I had taken a trip at the start of summer to visit a friend in Dallas, TX. While I was there, a college teammate tracked me down and left a message on my friend's answering machine. "Call this number; they have a strength coaching position open," is all it said. I called the number, and a lady named Jo Kraemer answered. She started telling me about the job, and that her husband is helping with the search. Jo talks to me for about five minutes before I finally interrupt her and ask, "Just where is this job?" She goes silent, finally saying it is at the University of Wyoming. I say okay and she asks me "Are you still interested?" Later that day, I get the chance to talk with her husband (Bill) who was a PhD student studying Exercise Physiology. I was hired for my first S&C position by Bill Kraemer. What an experience, getting to know and hang out with Wild Bill the Boy Scientist, as he was known around the athletic department. I was privileged to be a part of a blood lactate study Bill was doing that proved that high intensity circuits were not appropriate for the training of college football players. That study is still referenced today when speaking about training specificity for sport.

While I was at Wyoming, I had no idea of the relationship bond that I would build and still enjoy with Bill. We don't talk every day, but when we do it is as if we have been together the day before. Wyoming would provide me with another relationship that I still enjoy today. When I went to the high plains of Wyoming, the last thing I was looking for and the last thing that I wanted was to find a wife. However, God had a different idea. After our loss to Hawaii, our staff got together at the apartment of one of our GA's (Steve Rondeau). It was there in a tiny apartment that I met the woman of my dreams. I tried to tell myself that it was not real, and that the thin air must be getting to me, but deep down I knew she was the one. As it has turned out, I found the perfect coach's wife, and I can truly say that I would not have had the success I enjoyed in my career without Kris. She has always had a way of making things better and more enjoyable, no matter through the good times or bad.

After spending just one year at the University of Wyoming, I left to return to the University of Kansas, to what I thought would be my dream job. I did not go into coaching to get rich but to make a difference in the lives of all those that I coach. When I went to Wyoming from Topeka High school I took a substantial pay cut, from $16,000 to $11,000, so when Kansas offered me $19,000 to come back to Lawrence, I thought I had really made it big. Our football season and basketball season did not meet expectations, and the three men who had made the decision to hire me were let go. As it turned out, I was fired from my dream job the day I got back from our honeymoon. I was in the office at 7:00 a.m., had a meeting at 8:30 a.m., and was home without a job and with my last paycheck already in the bank by 10:00 a.m.. That was an extremely stressful time, with a new wife and no job, however it turned out to be one of the best things that has ever happened to me.

After several weeks of wondering if I had made a mistake by becoming a strength coach, I received a call from Pete Martinelli telling me that the University of Oregon needed a Strength Coach. Pete gave me the phone number of the head football coach, Rich Brooks, along with some other information about the job. As I was writing some notes from our conversation, the phone rang, and it was Rich Brooks. I was given an interview and eventually offered the job. "Honey, what do you think about the west coast?"

As it turns out, Oregon was a great place to be a young strength coach. It seemed like every other month a foreign track team would come over to train in Eugene, especially throws coaches. They came to visit with our hammer coach. Sometimes they would come and use our weight room. Watching them train and getting a chance to talk with some of the coaches was quite informative.

While at Oregon, I had the pleasure to coach numerous stand-out athletes, but one of them was unique. Gary Zimmerman, who played offensive guard on our team, was already an all-Pac 10 player and a projected high draft pick. He was receptive to my coaching and threw himself into everything he did. His willingness to work at the things I was teaching gave me instant credibility with the rest of the team. Gary went on to a long successful NFL career and ended up in the Hall of Fame.

After leaving Oregon I went to The University of Southern California. The first player I met was Junior Seau. He had managed to get into the weight room while I was signing my contract. When I finished and went to the weight room, he was there training. He came over, introduced himself, and asked me what I could do to help him become a great player. I asked him if he'd ever done power cleans. "Not really," was his response, so we put bumpers on a bar and went to work. To say he was a natural does not truly describe him. Junior was ruggedly built and very explosive; once he learned the basics of the exercise, which happen after about four or five sets, he began going up in weight. His last set of two that day had 315 pounds on the bar. Needless to say, I felt pretty good about my coaching that day. The truth is, if Junior had watched a video he would have been able to do the same thing just by mimicking what he saw. From that day on, Junior was a big proponent of my program, and, like Gary Zimmerman, once he was on board, the team was on board.

When I went to USC, Larry Smith was our head coach. Coach Smith told me that since he had been a head coach at Arizona, and now USC, that he had a really poor record in his opening games. Something like four wins and 12 loses. He asked me to make sure we trained hard in the summer and to be ready for the season. Needless to say, he wanted to make sure our team was in really good condition for our first game of the season against a very good Syracuse team in the Carrier Dome. So, on the first day of training camp, Coach Smith had the team do a conditioning drill called four corners. The team was divided up into four groups and put into the four different corners of the end zones. Half the group in each end zone would run around the field about 325 yards while the other half stayed in their corner and did sit ups, pushups, body weight, squats and such. The team ran 5 reps of the four corners drill. This was Coach Smith's favorite conditioning drill and one he had done every year he'd been a head coach.

Needless to say, I was a bit nervous at the staff meeting that night when I brought up the subject of our conditioning. Some of the staff looked at me like I'd been dropped from Mars when I explained that although the four corners drill was a very good general conditioning drill, it was not specific to the metabolic needs of a football team getting ready to play their first game. It took some convincing, but Coach Smith allowed me to run the conditioning for the team after practices from that point on. We began running much shorter and much faster runs, scramble start 15s and 20s. Also drills that had short change of direction, jingles, jangles, and much less running volume overall. Coach Smith and some of the other staff would question me, asking if we were truly running enough. I must say, I was a little nervous about the outcome, but I could see our players were practicing faster and harder.

About five days before the game my father in law passed away unexpectedly, so when the team traveled to New York for the game I was in Wyoming for his funeral. John's funeral was in the afternoon, and we played that evening, so after the service we sat down to mourn and watch the game. USC got after Syracuse and dominated from the very start, and I was pleased, but also conflicted. About an hour after the game was over, the phone rings and my mother-in-law answers, "Mike it is for you!" Larry Smith was on the other end informing me that he had given me a game ball in the locker room. He felt that our team was in the best condition of any team he had ever coached for the first game. Normally, things we do as Strength Coaches don't show up until much later because training is such a long-term process. This, however, reminded me that we do have an effect that can be felt for the good or bad in the short term. What we do today *matters*.

While at USC, Angel Spassov, a strength and conditioning coach from Bulgaria, had defected, and was on a speaking tour of the US. His last stop was a clinic we hosted at USC. A very dynamic and authoritative speaker, he captivated the audience as we all strained to understand him in his heavy Bulgarian accent. After the clinic he had no place to stay, so he stayed with us. What an education, riding to and from work with him in the car and having the privilege watching him coach our players.

The decision to leave USC after just two years was difficult; I loved coaching at USC. All the athletes on all the teams were fun to coach, and they truly were appreciative of the time and effort to help them. The only things I did not like were the traffic and the earthquakes. We had just had a quake that was centered very close to our house; I was at work 33 miles away and did not feel a thing because I was out on the field running the team. Kris was okay, but she was getting tired of feeling like a single mom of two boys. So when Texas A&M called, I listened. After much thought and prayer, we left Southern Cal for College Station, TX. What a culture change, from surfer dudes to squared away Texans.

The ground work for the profession of strength and conditioning had been laid in the '80s, but I personally saw the effects of that foundation take place in the '90s. When I first went to A&M, I had one full-time assistant but four graduate assistants. During the '90s at A&M, my staff grew and changed to five full-time assistants and up to eight graduate assistants. While there, we started a graduate program for S&C, and those graduate students took a class from one of my assistants, Raychell Ellsworth. We had a wealth of man power in the mid to late '90s that we used to assess athlete readiness through periodical vertical jump testing and perceived exertion surveys. We performed body comps by underwater weighing and max VO2 testing in the lab connected to our weight room. We were able to do heart rate studies that included football strength and conditioning workouts, practices, and games. This led to the development of a refined program designed to train our athletes in a sport-specific manner.

By this time, I had developed strong feelings about how I wanted to train our team. I was mainly working football, so my focus was on developing an explosive, fast football team. Our head coach, RC Slocum, always wanted a fast team, so this was a very good match. Football speed is not just about running fast in a straight line. In fact, it is more important to be able to accelerate, stop, and reaccelerate. With that in mind, I felt it was important to train for power while on our feet. So Olympic lifts, squats, jumps and towing sleds for speed were important in our program. I had realized early on that bench press was not the corner stone of training it had been made out to be when I first started coaching. The more we trained on our feet, the better we became. At that point, A&M was known for the Wrecking Crew on defense and running the ball on offense. It was a fun time, filled with good wins and good players.

Like Oregon and USC, when I first arrived at A&M I was blessed with a player who had already had great success and embraced me and my program. Quentin Coryatt, who became the second player picked in the draft and was best known for "The Hit," became the hardest worker and the biggest proponent of our program. Without him, I'm not sure if I would have had the same success I was able to enjoy at Texas A&M. The culture of "hard work pays off" became the backbone of the Strength Program at A&M and it permeated to other sports as well.

As I write this today, I am reminded that none of us have become successful on our own; I was blessed with great opportunities to learn from some of the best minds that have formulated the principles we all use today. I am merely a combination of great minds, including the minds of Bill Kraemer, Jimmy Radcliffe, Angel Spassov, Allen Kinley, Rob Graf, Vernon Banks, Larry Jackson and Robb Rogers. I was blessed to hire one of the first female assistants, and one of the best strength coaches in Raychell Ellsworth. All of these people and more have shaped me, and in many cases they taught me more than I taught them. I hope the strength coaches of today and beyond will honor the legacy that so many have strived to leave behind. A legacy of professionalism and a genuine desire to do what is the very best for the athletes they coach.

Mike Clark's Coaching Bio
- 1979-1980 - Topeka High School, Assistant Football Coach, Head Swimming Coach
- 1981-1982 - University of Wyoming, Head Strength Coach
- 1982-1983 - University of Kansas, Head Strength Coach
- 1983-1988 - University of Oregon, Head Strength Coach
- 1988-1990 - University of Southern California, Head Strength Coach
- 1990-1998 - Texas A&M University, Head Strength Coach
- 1998-2004 - Texas A&M University, Assistant Athletic Director for Sport Performance
- 2004-2010 - Seattle Seahawks, Strength & Conditioning Coordinator
- 2010-2013 - Kansas City Chiefs, Head Strength Coach
- 2013-2015 - Chicago Bears, Strength & Conditioning Coordinator
- 2015-2017 - Washington Redskins, Head Strength & Conditioning Coach
- 2017- Present - Trinity University, Head of Football Performance

Achievements & Honors
- 1993 - National Strength Coach of the Year NSCA
- 1996 - Inducted into Kansas University Athletics Hall of Fame
- 1998 - Big XII Strength Coach of the Year NSCA
- 2001 - Strength Coach of the Year, NFL Strength Coaches Society
- 2001 - President of the Collegiate Strength & Conditioning Coaches
- 2003 - USA Weightlifting Hall of Fame induction as a Coach
- 2006 - NFL Strength Coach of the Year
- 2010 - Sampson NFL Strength Coach of the Year

Personal
Married to Kris Clark since 1983. We have three children:
- Matthew Clark married to Jane Clark
- JJ Clark married to Samantha Clark
- Alicia married to Chris Kragthorpe

CHAPTER 3

The Jeff Connors Story

I grew up in Western Pennsylvania. My grandfathers both started working in the coal mine when they were twelve years old and together put in exactly one hundred years underground. Coal mining communities in Western Pennsylvania were referred to as "the Patch" because all of the houses were exactly the same, with a mining-company owned store where miners purchased the necessities of life. Miners possessed an incredible amount of work ethic and an undying loyalty to their families. I believe that the descendants of these individuals were heavily influenced to also work very hard. Any success that I've had in my profession must be attributed chiefly to an acquired work ethic and the power of blue-collar values.

My father was my high school football coach. His teams won WPIAL Championships in 4A and 2A and were runners-up in 3A. He was inducted into the Washington-Greene Chapter of The Pennsylvania Sports Hall of Fame along with many other accomplishments in athletics as an athlete and a coach. The greatest honor in my life was being inducted into the same Hall of Fame with my father in 2011. His influence on my life could only be expressed by declaring that it is part of who I am every day. I am proud beyond words to be his son and his quarterback.

When I was in high school, I met a man named Tom Domen who played with the famous Chuck Howley, Fred Wyatt, Bruce Bosley and that group was coached by Pappy Lewis at West Virginia. Tom introduced me to several people who were experts and enthusiasts in developing strength. I met people who promoted the use of free weights and also Nautilus equipment, which was relatively new to the scene. I was introduced to the concept of variable resistance provided by the special Nautilus "cam" which facilitated the strength curve. Only wealthy individuals could afford Nautilus equipment, but Tom knew a wealthy chiropractor who owned a line of Nautilus and he would take me there on occasion. I always looked forward to it, but I haven't seen one of those machines in quite a number of years.

I played defensive back in college and developed an intense interest in speed development in 1976. I was always looking for ways to get faster so I did a ton of hill training. Looking back, my training was very effective even though I didn't have a strength coach. We played a lot of zone coverage in college and I played a position referred to as strong corner. My college coach, Larry Blackstone had a 24-station circuit that we went through four days a week with the coaching staff in our face. One of the stations was 10 power cleans with metal plates on a concrete floor. Every station was maximum reps in 30 seconds with a 30 second rest. We did two rounds which of course was 48 sets. It was tough, and scientifically a little nuts, but we got stronger and developed a high level of muscular endurance as well. I captured the dip record with 90 reps. I started to become very strong for my 190-pound body weight, and I became obsessed with lifting. I would lift weights twice a day when I was home on breaks. If I went somewhere for spring break, the first thing I would do in the morning was find a place to lift. I definitely became addicted to training.

Upon graduation from college, with a degree in hand, I went job hunting. Because of the recession, my first job was a nighttime janitor at a school in Tennessee. I don't know if young folks were different back then, but I would have rather attempted to climb one of those mountains in West Virginia than to ask my family for money. I went on to work as a tennis court paver, sewing factory worker, tobacco farmer, and dug huge holes for bridge pilings in Knoxville, Tennessee. I met a coach from Cleveland, TN named Rusty Clayton and he got me interested in powerlifting. I started to enter some meets and did well in the 181-pound weight class. I entered a meet in Nashville one weekend that was being conducted by Doc Kreis. It was good to meet Doc, and the meet was very well run. There were some real characters who entered powerlifting meets in Tennessee during that time. I remember the Hood brothers from Chattanooga, Joe and Jody Cummins from Knoxville and UT's full back Doug Furnass would also frequently compete. I remember Doug at a clinic squatting 500 for ten reps in a pair of gym shorts as a demo.

I really enjoyed powerlifting, but I desperately missed football and the smell of that fresh-cut grass in the summer. I thought I might give powerlifting a shot because it might help me de-program my intense love for football. Our "gear" was terrible. I think I used a wresting singlet to squat in for a while until I discovered the magic super-suit. I chose to compete in ADFPA meets for the most part and I ended up ranked in the top five in the nation for a couple of my lifts. Sumo deadlift was my best lift, and I lived by "the meet don't start 'til the weight hits the floor." I loved to get juiced for those last three attempts and I convinced some lunatic out of the stands to slap me in the face at the combined North and South Carolina State meet one year. He almost knocked me out, but I pulled the weight and won the meet. That was a good day.

One of the most interesting experiences I had as a powerlifter was competing at the Pittsburgh Federal Penitentiary. Everybody I talked to was in there for murder. We competed in the middle of the yard. The audience was very unique. My life might have been in jeopardy, but the prisoners treated me well and I took second in the 198-pound class. That trophy is one I will keep for the memory. I also entered the Pennsylvania State meet one year and took second to Richie Wenner who I think had me by 20 pounds. Richie was a great lifter.

I made the cut in Delray Beach to become a police officer. They picked seven of us out of 140 applicants. I could have sworn I failed the face to face psychological interview because I didn't like the guy, but he passed me. I proceeded to chase many individuals on steady midnight shift because I could still run pretty well. I became the fitness director for the department and won a Florida State Police Olympic meet. The chief gave me a commendation. They eventually returned me to the streets. Over time, I knew it was in my heart to coach. I moved back to Tennessee, coached post graduate football and ran a Nautilus fitness facility at TMI Academy. I also had a little powerlifting team.

In the mid-1980s I returned to Florida and coached at the high school level. I brought Bob Ferraro in from Bucknell University to teach at my wrestling clinic. He convinced me to come to Bucknell and start a strength and conditioning program. I quit my teaching job and moved to Pennsylvania after speaking to the Athletic Director there. I worked at Bucknell initially with wrestling and football. Joe Susan was the offensive line coach and also was handling strength and conditioning. I think he was happy to give me a shot. I was also a Resident Director over about 12 Resident Assistants in the dorms. I worked part time at the local high school teaching life skills. Bucknell was also paying for my master's degree, so I was in school as well. Earning a M.S. from Bucknell was not something I was going to miss out on.

I had a great time there. The place was immaculate, and the area had the lowest crime in the nation. We ended up with four All-Americans in wrestling while I was there, and I think Bucknell had the first winning football season in about twenty years. My wife became the first female water meter reader in Pennsylvania. She was also pregnant with our second child by then. We lived in thirteen different dorms and finally bought a little row house for $50,000. We planted a garden and attempted to settle into the simple life. I swear I would be nowhere without that woman.

I met Ronnie Jones from the Eagles during my time with the Bison. He was Buddy Ryan's strength coach. Ronnie brought Kevin McNair to Philadelphia to teach speed development and we all became friends. I brought Kevin to East

Carolina University later on in my career. I also spent time visiting Bill Kraemer and Dr. Andy Fry during my time at Bucknell. Those guys were great about sharing information and getting me involved with the National Strength and Conditioning Association (NSCA). These coaches are still very highly respected in the field of research, and Dr. Kraemer is legendary. I was fortunate to have them in the area at the time. I also met Doug Lentz, who has been involved with the NSCA for many years and remains a fixture at the National Conference.

ECU - Getting ready for the 1992 Peach Bowl.

Ronnie Jones called me one day and told me that ECU needed a strength coach. Ronnie had been hinting with me that he was moving to linebacker coaching and I might have a shot to come to the Eagles if he did. Then they all got fired. Ronnie was friends with Steve Logan who was the OC at ECU. Long story short, Bill Lewis offered me the job and I move to Greenville, N.C in the spring of 1991.

I ran those guys into the next universe that summer. I was there for business. I signed for $35,000 and I had to teach three physical ed. classes every morning. I had 400 athletes in a 5,000 square foot space. I had one assistant and two GA's. I hired Tom Howley as my assistant. Tom has done well at Cornell University since then. We started winning and kept winning. We ended up with an 11-1 season and defeated N.C. State in the Peach Bowl. Bill Lewis left and then Steve Logan stepped in. I stayed with Steve until 2001, and we had a lot of success. He became the ECU coach with the record for most wins. We had some great wins over Miami, Stanford, Texas Tech, Virginia Tech, South Carolina, Pitt, West Virginia, Syracuse and many more. It was a great 10 years. I became very close with Steve. I had tremendous respect for his intelligence and moral compass. He took care of me and I would have jumped in front of a car for that guy and that is no exaggeration.

ECU - Preparing for the Liberty Bowl.

I fell into a very unique responsibility there when I was asked to prepare the Friday

night emotional prep speech. It
took a lot of thought and a lot
of work. Steve was not known to
believe in emotion over intellect
so he chose me to be the resident nut case. I brought in war
veterans, martial artists, former
coaches, former players, a police
dog, drill instructors and the
handicapped. They told their
stories. I loved every minute. I
believe very strongly in Marine

*Preparing to run the Pirates on to the field with
Coach Steve Logan.*

Corp leadership principles and esprit de corp. The emotional prep speech was
a great opportunity to influence our athletes with something I hope they will
always remember.

We defeated Texas Tech in the Gallery Furniture Bowl in 2000 but Steve and
the Athletic Director were not getting along. I got a call from UNC Chapel
Hill, so after the team and I flew back to Greenville, I then drove to UNC at
11:00 p.m. to interview for the job that same night . I took the job but didn't
want to give up my vacation, so the next day I'm in the Virgin Islands on a small
boat wearing a UNC hat. That's how fast it happens. This is a brutal business,
make no mistake. I have kept a steady paycheck since 1988. I've made it to age
62. I've worked for seven head coaches and sold out every day for every one
of them. My ferocious sense of loyalty is the reason I was never fired through
three decades. If you want a steady paycheck, you better work for a winner or
get ready to find one. Don't be sensitive. Nobody cares about what you know or
don't know. It's not about that.

My time at UNC was bittersweet. John Bunting hired me, and he is another
great human being. He got it right, but it took him too long. Six years is a
good run. He passed on some great recruits to Butch Davis and Butch Davis
continued hitting home runs on the recruiting trail. When Bunting left, I had
an opportunity to go with Jeff Jagodzinski at Boston College. I really appreciated the call but Butch told me to stay. I was a bit surprised because I had
turned down the Miami job previously after interviewing with Butch and Greg
Schiano. I very much appreciate the four years I spent on his staff. He had
incredible insight and knowledge of the way to build a total program and of all
aspects of the game.

I had a very unexpected opportunity to return to ECU. My kids grew up
there. I had been living away from my family for almost three years because
I moved them to the coast to avoid the turmoil around the UNC program. I
missed them desperately, but I had to provide for them. When you coach, that's

all you know. It was tough, but we were under one roof again when I came back to Greenville to work for Ruffin McNeill. However, Butch had just negotiated a contract for me at UNC so coming home required bridge burning. That's just the way it went. Butch had success but somehow got fired the next year. I made a good decision.

I've coached some great players and coached with a whole list of rock star coaches. They all impacted my life and provided me with wisdom and satisfaction. There are too many to thank but I honor their successes.

I want to express my appreciation to Duane Ledford, Steve Logan, Robert Jones, George Koonce, Vonta Leach, Dave Huxtable, Steve Shankweiler, Bob Slowick, Larry Coyer, Bob Babich, David Garrard, Marcus Crandall, Bert Hill, Ronnie Jones, Bill Lewis, Willie Parker, John Bunting, Butch Davis, Sam Pittman, Scottie Montgomery, Ruffin McNeil, Garrett Reynolds, Chase Rice, Kyle Jolly, Jason Brown, David Thornton, Quincy Monk, Emmanuel McDaniel, Chuck Pagano, Art Kauffman, Jim Fleming, David Blackwell, Kirk Doll, Julius Peppers, Ronald Curry, Bruce Carter, Danorris Searcy, Deunta Williams, Sylvester Williams, David Thornton, Robby Caldwell, Kenny Browning, Jim Webster, Hal Hunter, Charlie Williams, John Lovett, David Crumbie, Rod Coleman, Paul Jette and many, many more.

Finally, I want to thank Boyd Epley, Chuck Stiggins and Scott Caulfield for promoting our profession.

Jeff Connors's Coaching Bio
- MS, MSCC, RSCC, +E
- 1988-1991 - Bucknell University, Strength and Conditioning Coach
- 1991-2001 - East Carolina University, Director of Strength and Conditioning
- 2001-2011 - UNC Chapel Hill, Assistant Athletic Director for Strength and Conditioning
- 2011-Present - East Carolina University, Assistant Athletic Director for Strength and Conditioning

Achievements & Honors
- 2011 - Inducted into The Pennsylvania Sports Hall of Fame
- 2016 - Inducted into the USA Strength and Conditioning Coaches Hall of Fame
- 2017 - Named Collegiate Strength Coach of the Year by The National Strength and Conditioning Association

CHAPTER 4

The John "Mother" Dunn Story

In the immortal words of Yogi Berra, "If you don't know where you're going, you might wind up somewhere else." This statement applies to many of the men in this book. There wasn't a curriculum or blueprint to follow, only a passion regarding weight lifting and fitness which has led us to today's current strength and conditioning coaches. This is my story.

I'm a division one football player. I expected numerous challenges. However, the one challenge I didn't expect was being told, "We do not lift weights here. We don't want musclebound players. Weight lifting is for bodybuilders or power lifters, it's not for team-oriented sports. You're here to be an athlete, not for standing in front of a mirror." In the back of my mind, they had to be wrong. Bench pressing made me bigger and stronger; it was the main reason for my athletic success and what got me here. But it was my freshmen year at Penn State University, and my goal was just to fit in. Welcome to the early '70s.

To understand the importance of the bench press and its impact on my life we have to start at the beginning. I grew up on the same small dairy farm where my father was born and raised in upstate New York. My mother was killed in a farming accident when I was 12. The farm continued on a smaller scale. My father was my hero. His relentless work ethic made him my ultimate role model. My father had a full-time job in the department of social services in Albany, New York. He would wake up feed the cows, leave the house at 7:30 in the morning then drive 40 miles to Albany. Returning home at 6 in the evening he'd finish his farm work. Growing up, my younger brother Mark, my two older sisters, Mary and Diane, and I had chores to do on the farm; however, it was the summers in the hay fields that resonated the most with me. Whoever could throw the hay bales the furthest or highest held a certain level of prestige to me. Throwing hay bales lead to throwing the shot put, and that lead to the bench press which eventually lead to my strength training career.

As a freshman in high school, throwing hay bales gave me an edge and I won the county shot put championship. That fall I visited Springfield College and was introduced to the school's shot putter, a burly Irish exchange student. He told me "You have to bench press to get better." I started benching and it paid off. My sophomore year, my distances improved significantly in the shot put and discus, and I placed fifth at the New York Track & Field State Championships. My junior year, I drifted away from benching and my track results were disappointing. The conclusion I came to for the lack of improvement was I stopped benching! My senior year, I was focused and constantly benching and my strength improved dramatically, I won first place in the shot put at the New York Indoor and Outdoor State Championships, and placed sixth at the High School National Championships in Sacramento, CA.

The reason I talk about my track accomplishments is because Penn State never saw me play football. We had no game film. I was recruited by Penn State because my friend Damian Farley's father wrote a letter to his friend who happened to be Joe Paterno's high school football coach about my track accomplishments. Mr. Farley was a two-time Olympic athlete and captain of a Navel Destroyer in WWII. That letter got me to Penn State, and in my mind, the bench press was the reason for all of this. So as a freshman football player, to be told weight lifting was bad for you didn't make sense. I was proof that it did.

The conditioning program at Penn State consisted of push-ups, sit ups, climbing a rope, and travelling the length of a 16-foot ladder using hand over hand technique suspended nine feet off the ground. Before the eighth game of my freshman year, newspaper articles were written about the University of Maryland instituting a weight lifting program. It stated they had 30 players benching over 300 pounds and Randy White, their All-American defensive lineman, could bench 450 pounds. We won the game, but no one realized that game was the impetus for the birth of Penn State's first weight room.

Penn State's first weight room was a converted storage room under the bleachers in Rec Hall. We had two bench presses, two squat racks and one platform. The room was open from 1:00 to 4:00 p.m. Lifting wasn't mandatory. My sophomore year, there was an expansion of our locker room, and an area approximately 1500 square feet was created for a weight room. They hired Frank Ahrenhold, a former player, as the first strength coach. The decision to move the weight room into the locker room so they were together under one roof was the beginning of the evolution toward today's amazing training facilities, now the epicenter for recruiting. The summer heading into my senior year,

Frank left the program and Penn State hired Dan Riley, the man who would become my mentor and change my life forever.

Dan had worked at West Point and supervised a ground-breaking strength training study with Author Jones and its cadets. Author Jones was the inventor of the Nautilus machine, which got its name from the shaped cam which resembled the shape of a Nautilus sea shell. The cam gave the machine variable resistance throughout the full range of the exercise. It was ground breaking in the evolution of weight lifting equipment. At the time, Jones's principles of strength training were against the accepted norms; he professed short, single sets with maximum intensity to maximize muscle growth. He was among the first researchers to incorporate the eccentric phase of the exercise. When Dan arrived at Penn State things changed dramatically. Most of the weights and racks were removed and replaced with Nautilus machines. This was very unsettling, and I thought "how are we going to get better with machines?"

My first workout with Dan was memorable. I spent 15 minutes arguing, "You have to bench press to get stronger, and you can't get bigger doing one set." The workout lasted 42 minutes. I had no idea what happened. I couldn't walk, and my hands shook uncontrollably. I had to lie down so I didn't throw up. After years of strength training experience, I now understand the physiological responses that caused the body to respond that way. After that workout I was Dan's shadow. I picked his brain, I wanted to learn everything he knew. I assume because I was a senior and an offensive captain, Dan indulged me in my quest for knowledge. I had a new belief in strength training and it wasn't the bench press.

Our season was a success. We finished ranked fourth in the country. I graduated, spent the summer with the Philadelphia Eagles, was cut, and then returned to Penn State as a graduate assistant with the offensive line. That year I was able to spend time with Dan as a peer rather than a player. Our friendship grew as well as my knowledge of his methodology. That's when I realized I didn't want to be an offensive line coach. Though at the time there really wasn't a path to become a strength coach, I had a passion for a career in fitness.

It was the late '70s. Discos were dying, and health clubs were becoming popular, so I opened up my own fitness center, Mother Dunn's Nautilus in York, PA. I owned and operated the center for four years. The name Mother Dunn's stems from the nickname I received in college my freshman year. Penn State's first All American William Thomas Dunn's picture hung in our locker room, and his name tag read W.T. "Mother" Dunn. Not related to William Thomas Dunn, yet having the same last name the senior started calling me Mother Dunn for laughs, and the rest is history.

In the '70s, fitness and exercise weren't a part of our American culture. There was no such thing as jogging. There were no food labels. People didn't realize there were proteins, fats and carbohydrates. If you had an injury, there weren't physical therapy clinics, but times were changing. The Movie "Pumping Iron" starring Arnold Schwarzenegger took the underground world of body building and weight lifting mainstream. This trend, combined with My Nautilus Facility and others like it, led to the acceptance of strength training for the average America. Our new approach to strength training provided a clean, safe environment for men and women, young and old. People didn't have to spend hours in the weight room to experience the health benefits. There were two memorable moments during my time in York. The first came from training a girl for a body building competition who would later become my wife. Her name was Julia DiBerardo. The second came from a phone call from Dan Riley asking me if I wanted to join him at the Washington Redskins to become his first full-time assistant.

The NFL was vastly different in the early '80s. The two main factors for the differences were there was no free agency and no salary cap. No free agency resulted in players playing their entire career for one team. This created loyalties similar to their college experiences. No salary cap meant your back up players were older veterans making it more difficult for younger players to make a roster. The initial challenge for strength coaches was convincing players who never lifted a weight in their careers to strength train even though they had been successful for years in the league without lifting. When I arrived at Washington, it was Dan's third year. He had spent the two previous seasons educating the players of the benefits so in my first year I met little resistance from veterans during workouts. Dan's program was very organized. We schedule 45-minute time blocks for workouts, with two players per coach. With 15 time blocks a day, Dan ensured that every player received one on one training. As crazy as it sounds, if you could get the majority of your team lifting consistently, you were considered successful at the time. Many head coaches viewed the weight room and strength coaches as a necessary evil. It wasn't till the mid '80s when every team hired full-time strength coaches.

Washington Redskins weight room in 1984;
Head Strength Coach Dan Riley in the front and
myself in the back.

The calendar year was vastly different for players in the '80s. The Regular season ended in December unless you made the playoffs. During the off-season, players were only required to show up in May for a three day minicamp. My second year, Dan decided we needed a way to monitor a player's fitness level. Joe Gibbs didn't like conditioning tests at training camp, so we purchased three treadmills and designed our own fitness protocols to determine our players conditioning level. Using the Bruce Protocol, we made each player run to their Vo2 max although, looking back, running players until they collapsed wasn't the safest idea. After gathering all the data, we determined the cardiovascular standards that players were required to achieve. This was the beginning of integrating cardiovascular exercises with the strength program. Initially, we were only known as a strength coaches, but now, the title is Strength and Conditioning Coach. My third year, the program was running on all cylinders and as a result I was offered and accepted my first head coaching position with the L.A. Raiders.

I was in the mafia, the Raider mafia. Al Davis was the "Dark Vader" of the NFL. I feel privileged to have worked for him and taken part in their storied history. My challenge with the Raiders was building a program from ground zero. Our facilities were located in a converted Jr. High school and the weight room was the old boys and girls locker-room. It was approximately 2000 square feet. There were four shower bays, each housing a piece of equipment. A bench in one, a squat rack in another, abdominal equipment and low back in the other two. The main floor had a complete line of Nautilus equipment with a rack of dumbbells against a wall. Success came in baby steps. Convincing one

Photo of myself stretching Bo Jackson before the 1987 Monday night game in Seattle. In that game, Bo ran 90-yds for a touchdown and ran over Brian Bosworth to score a second touchdown.

veteran that the program had value was a victory. By the end of my first year, I had a core of believers. My second year, they hired Mike Shanahan. At the time, he was the youngest head coach in the league. He represented the future for strength coaches because he had lifted weights as a player and strongly believed in the weight room. He put pressure on players to lift. Some of Mike's ideas clashed with Al's and he was fired after one year and replaced by Art Shell. At the end of my third season I had three different head coaches. That off-season the former General Manager of the Redskins, Bobby Beathard became the General Manager of the San Diego Chargers. Julia and I just had our first daughter Jessica, and Bobby was a friend, so when he offered the opportunity to join him in San Diego, I did.

It was 1990, and the NFL was changing. Computers became an everyday tool. The science of exercise was growing exponentially. Head coaches now viewed the weight room as essential and strength coaches as peers. The players achieved a limited form of free agency from the league. It was called Plan B. Plan B allowed teams to protect 35 players, leaving the remaining players as free agents. This had an effect on strength coaches because for the first time you had players in your program coming from different teams with different training philosophies. Back then training philosophies were clear cut. You were either a "machine guy" or "free weight guy" and head coaches hired accordingly. As more free agents changed teams, strength programs began to change, and strength coaches

Photo of myself and my Dad on the sidelines of the San Diego Chargers game (1990).

began mixing free weights with machines. I spent seven years in San Diego with three different assistants: Chris Clawson, Chip Morton, and John Hastings. All three went on to become head strength coaches in the NFL: Chris with the Rams in '92, Chip with the Carolina Panthers in '95 and John with the Chargers in '97. San Diego was a special stop in my career. My second daughter Taylor was born, and we went to the franchise's first Super Bowl XXIX. Growing up in New York, I dreamed of someday working for the New York Giants, and in 1997 that dream came true.

While working for the Giants I had the privilege of knowing Wellington Mara. Wellington was the NFL. By the mid '90s, head coaches were putting pressure on players to attend off-season programs. Nutrition and speed training were making their presence felt; the Giants had their own nutritionist on staff, Heidi Skolnik, and I brought in Bill Parisi to teach speed acquisition during the off-seasons. In our fourth year, we went to Super Bowl XXXV. Like most coaches, you're hired to get fired, and my seven-year run with the Giants came to an end. After the Giants, I spent two years at Washington, four years at Baltimore and finished with The Green Bay Packers in administration.

I had a charmed career. I was involved in the evolution of fitness in America. I was mentored by one of the greatest pioneers in strength training, Dan Riley. While at Washington, I became friends with a Hall of Fame inductee, general manager Bobby Beathard, who helped guide my career. Throughout my career I trained 86 pro bowlers. I also trained 13 Hall of Fame Players who would call me a friend. They are John Riggins, Morten Anderson, Art Monk, Darryl Green, Russ Grimm, Howie Long, James Lofton, Mike Haynes, Tim Brown,

Marcus Allen, Jr. Seau, Michael Strahan, and Ray Lewis, as well as the iconic Bo Jackson. It was a great life for someone who started out throwing hay bales and liked to bench press.

John "Mother" Dunn's Coaching Bio
- 1980-1983 - Mother Dunn's Nautilus Fitness Center, Owner and Operator
- 1984-1986 - Washington Redskins, Assistant Strength Coach
- 1987-1989 - Los Angeles Raiders, Head Strength Coach
- 1990-1996 - San Diego Chargers, Head Strength Coach
- 1997-2003 - New York Giants, Head Strength Coach
- 2004-2006 - Washington Redskins, Head Strength Coach
- 2007-2008 - West Point, Assistant Strength Coach
- 2008-2011 - Baltimore Ravens, Assistant Strength Coach
- 2014-2015 - Green Bay Packers, Administrative Assistant

Achievements & Honors
- 1974 - 1st Place in New York State Indoor Shot Put Championship
- 1974 - 1st Place in New York State Outdoor Shot Put Championship
- 1974 - 2nd Place in New York State Outdoor Discus Championship
- 1977 - Offensive Co-Captain, Penn State Nittany Lions
- 1978 - Philadelphia Eagles Training Camp
- 1994 - Super Bowl XXIX, San Diego Chargers
- 1994 - NFL Strength Coach of the Year
- 1994 - San Diego Hall of Champions Achievement Award
- 1999 - President's Council Physical Fitness
- 2000 - Super Bowl XXXV, New York Giants
- NFL Strength Coach for 27 years

Education
- 1978 - Pennsylvania State University, Bachelors of Sciences in Physical Education

CHAPTER 5

The Boyd Epley Story

A New York Times article credited Nebraska as the birthplace of the modern strength and conditioning program. Bob Ley's report on ESPN's Outside the Lines, went even further by stating, "Nebraska is the home of off-season conditioning. No college has made a greater commitment to such programs and this is where it all started."

Bob Devaney joined Nebraska in 1962 as the Head Football Coach and immediately established his football program as a force in the Big Eight Conference. Prior to Devaney's arrival, Nebraska had seven consecutive losing seasons in football. Devaney engineered an immediate turnaround with a 9–2 record in 1962. The following year, Devaney coached an even better 10–1 season and claimed the conference title and an Orange Bowl victory. His success continued through 1966, with records of 9–2, 10–1, and 9–2. However, during consecutive 6–4 seasons in 1967 and 1968, Devaney became the subject of a whispering campaign about whether he had peaked. In response, the coaching staff started looking for something to help them get back on track.

"Alabama looked at us as a bunch of big, slow guys from the North, and they were fast, quick guys from the South," said former NU linebacker Adrian Fiala. "After the 1966 season, the next few weeks before conditioning got under way, Bob Devaney

Fig. 1 - Coach Bob Devaney served as Nebraska Athletic Director from 1967 to 1993.

told us we had to lose in terms of weight. Everybody was put on a program to lose weight." This weight loss might have ranged from 10 to 15 pounds. Fiala said that after the weight loss, Nebraska couldn't enforce its will anymore on offense. Its offensive line lacked power and its skilled players' lacked strength. When you are playing in the Big Eight and you are undersized, things happen, and they are not good.

For the first time since Devaney's first season in 1962, Nebraska would not lead the Big Eight in total offense. Looking back, it was clear that Nebraska was headed in the wrong direction physically. Nebraska was shoved around, and the point production fell off. In in 1965, their average was 32.1 points per game and ranked second in the country, but 1967 their average was down to 12.7 points a game. Nebraska scored more than 17 points just once in 1967 and tumbled to a 6-4 record. The 1968 season was nearly a mirror image. Devaney was concerned about job security at that point, especially after Oklahoma posted a 47-0 victory over Nebraska in the 1968 season finale in Lincoln on national television. It was the worst loss during the Devaney era at Nebraska and the low point of his regime.

Nebraska had a weight room in 1968, but it was only for injured athletes. The Schulte Fieldhouse Weight Room was a modest 416 square foot room which included a Universal Gym (see Fig. 2), a few dumbbells, one 400-pound Olympic set, an additional Olympic bar, a leg extension machine and a squat rack. (Fig.3). Most of this equipment was purchased when a health club in Lincoln failed. At the time, lifting weights was not recommended for healthy athletes.

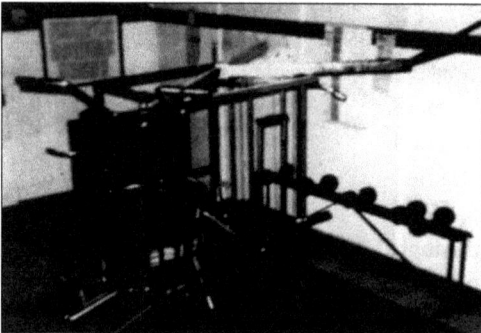

Fig. 2 - Schulte Fieldhouse weight room looking West.

Fig. 3 - Schulte Fieldhouse weight room looking East.

In 1968 Devaney asked Offensive Line Coach Cletus Fischer, Assistant Track Coach Dean Brittenham, and Athletic Trainer George Sullivan to create a winter conditioning program for football. The program aimed to recreate physical dominance. They created a very demanding eight station circuit of drills and running stations. Football coaches ran most of the stations. Unfortunately, with 40 minutes of continuous work, the result was more endurance than strength.

I was a pole vaulter who spent a lot of time in the weight room rehabbing a back injury. Coach Fischer saw me and asked me to help him make a film to show the football players what to do at each station. Then he asked if I would run a lifting station. I oversaw a station where the players lifted 47.3-pound bars with cement cans on each end continuously for five minutes. I was happy to do so but I knew the lifting station and several other stations were too much endurance with not enough rest built into the stations. One of the stations was continuous running for five minutes. The new winter program was very demanding for the players and even though it had a heavy focus on endurance it was better than anything they had done before because the players showed a good work ethic.

I was not a football player at Nebraska, but I had been in high school and was now focused on pole-vaulting. In my sport I ran as fast as I could carrying a 16' long pole 40 yards before vaulting over a crossbar. I increased my bodyweight from 160 to 180 pounds in two months by lifting weights at a health club and I knew endurance running was not what the Nebraska football players needed. I was surprised that only a handful of athletes were lifting weights at Nebraska to get stronger and faster. I was stronger than all of the Nebraska football players and just a couple years later would win the Mr. Nebraska physique title and set state lifting records.

Strength and conditioning historian and author Dr. Ken Leisner has stated that, when Nebraska Athletic Director and Head Football Coach Bob Devaney responded to the urging of Assistant Football Coach Tom Osbourne and hired me as the first paid collegiate Strength and Conditioning Coach, history was made. Devaney decided to take a chance and give strength training a try but first he looked me in the eye and said, "If anyone gets slower you're fired."

I was hired to create a strength program and put in charge of the winter conditioning program. It took me a couple of years to convince the coaches to build rest intervals into the stations and install rest periods between stations. With test data I was able to prove the focus needed to be on building muscle to improve strength and speed which would then improve on field performance.

Nebraska had an incredible turn around in one year going from a 47-0 loss to Oklahoma to a 44-14 win over them in Norman the next year. The HUSKER POWER strength

Fig. 4 - Nebraska football players in Schulte Fieldhouse.

and conditioning program had a modest beginning in the Schulte Fieldhouse. Devaney approved an expansion by removing the wall between the weight room and a film room (Fig. 5). The strength and conditioning concepts, along with innovations in lifting equipment, impacted millions worldwide.

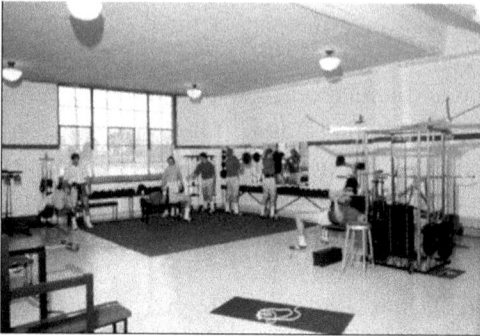

Fig. 5 - Schulte fieldhouse weight room expansion.

As a result of Coach Devaney's statement regarding what would happen if any players got slower, Nebraska players were tested on a variety of performance tests to be able show Coach Devaney their progress. Testing the players before and after the season provided me with the facts we needed to change attitudes toward strength training for athletes forever. Mike Beran, #62, an offensive guard, was one of the most dedicated to lifting weights in Husker history, shown here doing the Incline Press (Fig. 6). As a freshmen Mike was 180 pounds and ran 5.5 seconds for 40 yards. The Nebraska football coaches encouraged him to go to a smaller school because he was too small, not strong enough or fast enough to play in the offensive line for the Huskers. Mike (Red) Beran proved everyone wrong. He worked so hard lifting weights that he gained everyone's respect and started at guard for Nebraska's 1971 National Championship team. His senior year, Beran was 230 pounds, ran a 4.9 second forty, and had a 360-pound bench press. His remarkable progress and work ethic set a standard for all Nebraska athletes. No one could believe athletes

Fig. 6 - Mike Beran – a walk-on who set the standard for what is called work ethic.

could actually gain 50 pounds and yet run faster. It was his improvement in speed like his that changed everyone's mind about lifting weights.

In 1970 the average bench-press for Husker players was 212.2 pounds. The average bodyweight was 212.17 pounds Linebacker John Pitts became the first Husker to bench press 300 pounds Offensive Center, Doug Dumler was the first to power clean 300 pounds In October of 1970, Carl Johnson a junior college transfer from Arizona bench pressed 375 pounds which set a new record for football. Along with Carl, Keith Wortman, Dick Rupert and Bob Newton were also junior college transfers from California that made a huge impact in the development of Husker Power. They had lifted weights at their junior colleges and quickly helped create a culture for Nebraska that lifting was an important part of preparing to play football. Offensive Tackle Bob Newton was the first player to incline press 300 pounds. At 6'5" and 275 he overpowered his opponents. He was one of the toughest players and loved to lift. Nebraska did not have carpet in the weight room at that time and Bob had a bad habit of spitting on the floor. I asked him to stop spitting on the floor, but Bob continued. I stood up to him and asked him not to come back for two weeks. Carl Johnson later told me that he gained a lot of respect for me that day for standing up to one of the toughest players and a leader on the Nebraska team. Newton and I then became best of friends and he became my first All-American offensive linemen.

A 35-31 win in the game of the Century against Oklahoma in 1970 put Nebraska in position to win its first national title against LSU.

Nebraska won the National Championship in football again with a win over Alabama and Legendary Coach Bear Bryant in the Sugar Bowl. After 125 years of college football, Sporting News magazine announced that the 1971 Nebraska Football team was the best football team of all-time. Johnny Rodgers, Heisman Trophy winner, is shown on the cover of Sporting News.

In 1971 Larry Jacobson became the first Husker to win the Outland Trophy Award recognizing the Outstanding Lineman in

Fig. 7 - Bob Newton – one of the toughest linemen in Nebraska history.

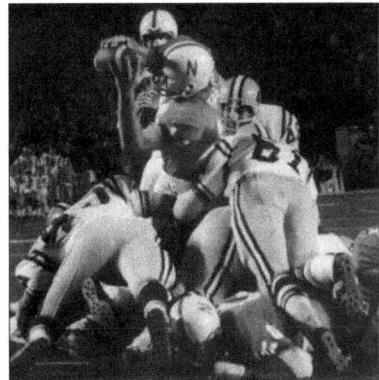

Fig. 8 - Jerry Tagge crosses the goal line against LSU for Nebraska's first National Championship.

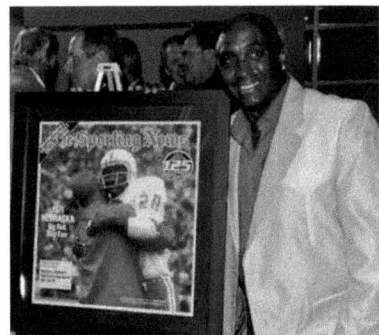

Fig. 9 - Johnny Rodgers – Nebraska's first Heisman Trophy winner.

the nation.

In 1972 a 1400 square foot Circuit Room was opened in the new South Stadium at Nebraska. This room provided a different type of training where the athletes would move from one station to the next until their circuit was complete. Circuit Training with the correct work/rest ratio proved to be a great way for athletes to build muscle.

Fig. 10 - South Stadium Circuit Room.

In 1973 at age 35, Tom Osborne was named Nebraska's Head football Coach. His 25-year career then generated 255 wins and three more national championships, a Hall of Fame Induction and more. While Coach Devaney is credited with hiring the first strength coach it was Tom who recognized the need and convinced Coach Devaney to give strength training a try. Tom Osborne in 2005 said, "I remember a time when everyone believed in distance running and endurance training which was the mind-set toward training football back in the '60s and '70s. Boyd did not agree with that philosophy at all and didn't believe that was what it took to make a great football player." Osborne would tell you, "What the strength program did for Nebraska was give us something we didn't have before and that was the ability to develop the player's size and strength." It was Osborne that first recognized that players who were lifting weights were also improving their speed.

Fig. 11 - Tom Osborne, who first recognized the need for strength training to improve speed for Nebraska.

Jim Williams became my first non-paid assistant strength coach; however, he was hired away by Arkansas in 1973 before he could be offered a paid position at N.U. Jim was later hired away from Arkansas by Wyoming before going to the New York Giants, New York Jets, and Philadelphia Eagles.

Also, in 1973, Donn Swanbom, my second non-paid assistant, was hired away by SMU then later worked for UCLA.

The Lifter of the Year Award was created for Football in 1974. Center Rik

Bonness won this award the first two years. Bonness was 188 pounds as a freshman and 220 pounds as a senior, with a 4.6 forty-yard dash. His dedication showed as he drove 50 miles from his home in Omaha each workout all summer to train at Nebraska. His hard work paid off being named an All-American Center twice.

Nebraska became the first school to lift weights in an organized summer program in 1974. A conditioning manual was created for the athletes that could not be in Lincoln.

In July 1975 - Dr. Aleen Swofford was hired as the first Women's Athletic Director at Nebraska and I was asked to introduce strength training to all women's sports. Title IX opened the door for female athletes to lift weights in the facilities that were previously for men only. Also, in 1975, the University of Miami hired me to design their first football weight room. Steve Bliss, my third non-paid assistant, was then hired by Miami to run it. Bliss was later hired by the legendary Woody Hayes to be Ohio State's first strength coach.

Fig. 12 - Steve Bliss of Miami (right) with his mentor, Boyd Epley, at the Nebraska vs. Miami game in Lincoln.

Mike Arthur, my first assistant to be paid in 1976 set the world record deadlift 540.25 pounds at 132 pounds bodyweight. Arthur would become one of the top strength coaches in the nation, including being inducted into the USA Hall of Fame. Mike has stayed with the Huskers his entire career and has become one of the most respected strength coaches in the country for his expertise in researching the best ways to improve performance for student-athletes. Mike has worked his entire career as the "Bridge" between research and application.

In 1976 Rod Horn wins the Football Lifter of the Year as a 260-pound freshman. He power cleaned 342 pounds, snatched 237 pounds, squatted 560 pounds, at 6'4.5". Rod was

Fig. 13 - Mike Arthur shown setting the world record deadlift.

known for eating a loaf of bread and drinking a gallon of milk each day. Also, in 1976, Head Coach Rick Forzano of the Detroit Lions hired me as their first strength and conditioning coach, but a week later Tom Osborne convinced me to stay with the Huskers. Tom said, "If you stay with me here at Nebraska, I will always be there for you." That was all I needed to hear.

Husker Power celebrated 100 wins in football with a victory against Penn State 42-17 in 1977 and in that same year Offensive Guard Lawrence Cooley became the first Husker football player to bench press 400 pounds He was using the "Jack Bench". This bench featured an adjustable bar catch to adjust the bar height based on arm length. Two tractor jacks donated were mounted in the frame. The Jack Bench is now at the Lutcher Stark Museum in Austin, Texas. The search for adjustable bar height led Nebraska to develop several other adjustable products leading to the invention of the Transformer in 2002.

Fig. 14 - Rod Horn won the Lifter of the Year Award as a Freshman.

Husker Power Club purchased an Apple computer as the first computer for the strength program in 1977 which changed how strength programs were printed for athletes.

In 1978 Offensive Tackle Kelvin Clark set the Incline Press Record for football at 350 pounds at a bodyweight of 270 pounds

July 28-29, 1978 - The National Strength and Conditioning Association was founded in Lincoln, Nebraska at the Nebraska Continuing Education Center (fig. 17). The University of Nebraska had a big influence on the success of the NSCA. My staff at the time, Mike Arthur, Bill Allerheiligen, and Gary Wade helped host the event. Nebraska AD Bob Devaney was the featured speaker and Husker All-American tackle Kelvin Clark provided singing entertainment to the 76 charter members.

Fig. 15 - Larry Cooley records the first 400-pound bench press for a football player in Nebraska history.

Fig. 16 - Kelvin Clark shown on the Incline Press.

Note: Nebraska won five National

Fig. 17 - Nebraska Continuing Education Center.

Fig. 18 - Nebraska strength coaches who help start the NSCA – (l to r) Jim Williams, Gary Wade, Mike Flynt, Dave Redding, Mike Arthur, Boyd Epley, Steve Bliss and Bill Allerheiligen.

Championships and 356 football games in my 35 years as Head Strength Coach. I credit Mike Arthur for his innovative research and program development Randy Gobel for his innovation in facility development and David Ellis for his innovation in nutrition. We paved the way in the early years for others to have success in the field of strength and conditioning.

Boyd Epley's Coaching Bio

- 1969-2004 - University of Nebraska, Head Strength and Conditioning Coach
- 2004-2006 - University of Nebraska, Associate Athletic Director for Facilities
- 2006-2014 - National Strength and Conditioning Association World Headquarters, Senior Director of Coaching and Special Projects
- 2014-Present - University of Nebraska, Assistant Athletic Director and Director of Athletic Performance

Achievements & Honors

- 1980 - National Strength Coach of the Year Award presented by the National Strength and Conditioning Association
- 1993 - Nebraska Football Hall of Fame Lyell Bremser Special Merit Award
- 1993 - Lifetime Achievement Award from the National Strength and Conditioning Association
- 2003 - Hall of Fame Induction, USA Collegiate Strength Coaches
- 2004 - National Associate Athletic Director of the Year,

All-American Football Foundation
- 2007 - Legends Award, College Strength and Conditioning Association
- 2008 - Presidents Award, Professional Football Strength and Conditioning Coaches Society
- 2010 - Carey E. McDonald National Citation from the National High School Athletic Coaches Association.
- 2011 - Distinguished Alumni Award, University of Nebraska
- 2014 - President's Council on Fitness, Sports & Nutrition Lifetime Achievement Award
- 2016 - Inducted into the Mr. America Hall of Fame
- 2016 - Inducted into the Phoenix Union High School Hall of Fame

CHAPTER 6

The Bill Foran Story

My career started in 1977 as a teacher and coach at a small high school in Michigan. I taught elementary P.E. and coached at the high school. We were the smallest school in the conference and had not had a winning football season in years. I knew that these were our athletes and we had to make them better, so I started a strength and conditioning program. We started winning and that is when I knew that I liked developing athletes more than the x's and o's.

That took me to Michigan State University as their first ever grad assistant in strength and conditioning. I received my master's degree in exercise physiology in June of 1981. That summer there were two openings for head strength and conditioning coach at the college level, Mississippi State and Washington State. This type of jump doesn't happen these days, but I went from a grad assistant at Michigan State to the Head Strength and Conditioning Coach at a Pac 10 school, Washington State University.

Washington State's football team had not been to a bowl game in 50 years. It is amazing what can happen when you incorporate a basic, fundamentally-sound strength and conditioning program and the players buy into it. We had three winning seasons in four years and a bowl game. In January of 1985, the Head Strength and Conditioning Coach position opened at the University of Miami and I was fortunate to get that position. I was with the Miami Hurricanes for four seasons, and prepared the football team for the fifth season, leaving before the season for the Miami Heat. During those five seasons, the Miami Hurricane football team was 55-5 with two National Championships and two number-two rankings.

The Miami Heat's first season was 1988-89. They practiced that first season at the University of Miami, and the university allowed me to work with the Heat as their Strength and Conditioning Consultant. I became the Heat's full-time strength and conditioning coach for their second season, and just finished my 30th season.

Washington State University

I was thrilled to become the Head Strength and Conditioning Coach at Washington State University with a starting salary of $18,000. I had a fulltime assistant and a few student assistants for 18 different sports. The weight room was about 4,000 square feet. We got a lot of work done in that weight room.

The Power Quotient: An Indicator of Athletic Success

In 1983, while at Washington State we came up with The Power Quotient as a way to rank all our athletes. We wanted to know who is generating more power: for example, a 270 pound athlete with a 28" vertical jump or a 220 pound athlete with a 34" vertical jump?

The Power Quotient is the square root of the vertical jump in inches times the square root of the body weight in pounds. The 270 pound athlete had a power quotient of 86.9 and the 220-pound athlete had a power quotient of 86.4, very similar power output.

The first time we tested the Power Quotient, the results were very interesting. Of the top 15 male athletes, seven were on the track team, six were on the football team, one was on the basketball team, and one was on the wrestling team.

The seven track athletes were the best athletes on the track team that won the last two outdoor Pac 10 Championships and finished third in the NCAA indoor championship and second at the NCAA outdoor championship. The six football players were all starters, and four of them were first team all PAC 10. The basketball player was the starting power forward and the wrestler was the PAC 10 heavyweight champion.

This really opened the eyes of our athletes on what was important for athletic success.

I was impressed with all the coaches at Washington State, but one stood out: The Head Basketball Coach George Raveling. What a motivator Coach Raveling is! He had a library of motivational books at his home and he allowed me to borrow his books on a regular basis. I am forever grateful.

University of Miami

When I arrived at the University of Miami, the weight room was about 3500 square feet, but they were in the process of building a new 6000 square foot weight room! How times have changed! Another change is salaries. When we won the National Championship in 1987, I was making $30,000. Again, I had one full time assistant and a few student assistants and 18 different sports.

As part of the *30 for 30* series, ESPN featured the "U", the Miami Hurricane

Football Team in the 1980s. It showed all the hype, but it did not show the preparation and work behind the scenes. Vinny Testaverde, All American quarterback and Heisman trophy winner would work out in the weight room with the offensive lineman. All American wide receiver Michael Irvin was a beast in the weight room. These are just two examples of the work ethic these athletes had. I wish I could name all of them. This work ethic became contagious. The young freshmen would come in and see the work ethic and would follow suit. These athletes understood: If you want to be great, you have to put in the work.

In October of 2017, the University of Miami held the 30th anniversary reunion to honor the 1987 National Championship Football Team. What an

Myself with Head Coach Jimmy Johnson - 1988 Orange Bowl

awesome evening! It was great to reminisce and catch up with so many people. Coach Jimmy Johnson gave an inspirational talk with lots of the old stories. Although I had not seen most of these men for over 25 years I recognized most and was amazed and proud of how successful they have become. Many are now teachers, coaches, lawyers, businessmen, and doctors.

Miami Heat

In March of the first season, Head Coach Ron Rothstein approached me to join the Heat full-time. I met with Billy Cunningham, the Heat's Managing Partner, to discuss the Strength and Conditioning Coach position. During the meeting, there was a knock on his office door. Wilt Chamberlain was in Miami for a volleyball tournament and he wanted to stop by and see his former teammate. When Wilt heard what we were talking about he told us that when he attended the University of Kansas he was a basketball player and a track athlete. At the time, basketball players were not allowed to lift weights, but track athletes lifted weights. Wilt said that everyone thought he dominated because of his size. He said he dominated because he was stronger than every basketball player he played against. He told Billy, "You have to have a strength and conditioning coach." Thank You Wilt! When I was hired that summer, Miami became only the sixth NBA team to have a full-time strength and conditioning coach. It initially was a tough decision for me to leave the college setting, but the thought of going from about 350 athletes to 15 was very enticing. I could be hands on with every athlete.

Rony Seikaly- Miami Heat's First Ever Draft Pick

In 1988, Rony Seikaly became the first ever draft pick for the Miami Heat. He was a 6'10" 230 pound center out of Syracuse. As a first year expansion team, the Miami Heat went with a youth movement, and Rony started as a rookie.

He came in for his first workout with me and said, "I am here to work out, but I don't squat." I told him that we are doing a four-day split routine and we will do an upper body workout today. Tomorrow is the lower body workout, and we squat differently here. The next day Rony came in and the first thing he said was, "How do you squat differently?" I said, "We squat correctly."

Rony really struggled as a rookie. At 230 pounds, he was not physically prepared to battle veteran NBA centers. The next summer, he stayed in Miami and went to work. Rony trained for 16 weeks and did not miss a workout. He progressed through four four-week Phases of a four-day split routine.

Monday- Thursday: Upper Body Strength Training, Conditioning

Tuesday-Friday: Lower Body Strength Training, Plyometrics, Agilities

He went from 230 pounds to 252 pounds while staying at 8.0% body fat and increased his vertical jump by 3 inches. His Power Quotient improved from 78.8 to 86.9. The next season, Rony was voted the most improved player in the NBA...and he became a very good squatter!

Proper strength training improves your speed, power, and agility and makes you a more durable. When you are strong and powerful, your true ability comes out.

Keith Askins-Undrafted Miami Heat Player

In 1990, after his college career, Keith had a tryout with the Miami Heat as a courtesy to his college coach, Wimp Sanderson at the University of Alabama. He was 6 feet, 8 inches, and came in at 185 pounds. Yes, 185 pounds! He proceeded to out-work everyone in fall camp and made our team on a one-year contract through pure effort and work ethic. The next summer, he did not miss a single workout, came into camp at 198 pounds and had to prove himself again. Keith had to prove himself on one-year contracts for five straight seasons before he got a multi-year contract. His weight steadily increased from 185 to 198 to 208 to 215 to 220. Each summer, Keith would ask for my vacation schedule so he could take his vacation at the same time; He was so dedicated and driven that he would not miss a workout. He became a tremendous perimeter defender with his effort and work ethic and developed a solid three-point shot. He had a fine nine-year career with the Miami Heat, which at the time was an NBA record for an undrafted player.

Pat Riley comes to Miami

Pat Riley arrived in Miami in September of 1995 as the new Head Coach and President of the Miami Heat. In our first meeting, he told me he is into two things: "Fundamentals and Conditioning: If you have those, you have a chance." It was amazing to have a basketball coach that valued the importance of strength and conditioning. I got to work with another master motivator. When it comes to motivating athletes, Pat Riley is second to none. In the 23 years under Pat's leadership the Miami Heat has been Division Champions 13 times, Eastern Conference Champions five times, and have won three NBA Championships. It has been an amazing journey.

During 2017 there were many articles about the first 30 years of the Miami Heat. One article was titled "The 10 Most Influential People in Franchise History." Of course, number one was Pat Riley. At number 10 was the Strength and Conditioning Coach, which is an awesome honor for our profession.

A Career Highlight

A unique part of my journey has been working with my son Eric. For the last six years we have been working together as the strength and conditioning staff of the Miami Heat. He has upgraded the program with his knowledge, creativity, and elite training.

In middle school, he wanted to start lifting weights. He started with an age appropriate basic program. Eric enjoyed training and continued to progress in to high school. The strength, power, and speed he developed made a huge difference in his new-found passion: the pole vault. As a high school senior, Eric was the State Champion, an All American and signed with the University of Florida. At Florida, he was an All SEC pole vaulter and a member of two National Championship teams.

While at Florida, he went on to get his master's degree in applied physiology and kinesiology. Eric needed an internship, and Pat Riley allowed him to be my intern even though we do not have an internship program. One semester turned into two years, and then the Miami Heat offered Eric a full-time position as the Assistant Strength and Conditioning Coach. In Eric's sixth season with the Heat and my 30th, I became the Strength and Conditioning Consultant just like my first season, and Eric has taken over. I did not see this happening, but it has been amazing.

Strength and Conditioning Principles

My strength training principles: Multi planar, total body balanced strength with an emphasis on the hips and core.

My main conditioning principle for the NBA is: World-class athletes need to be in world class shape.

This is accomplished through interval training, court drills, and playing basketball. This includes being at their optimal body weight and body fat.

The worst way to lose is to an inferior team because your team fatigued in the second half.

Work Hard and Dream Big!

Bill Foran's Coaching Bio
- MS, CSCS, RSCC*E
- 1977-1980 - Ovid-Elsie High School, Physical Education Teacher, Assistant Football Coach
- 1980-1981 - Michigan State University, Graduate Assistant, Strength and Conditioning
- 1981-1985 - Washington State University, Head Strength and Conditioning Coach
- 1985-1989 - University of Miami, Head Strength and Conditioning Coach
- 1988-2018 - Miami Heat, Head Strength and Conditioning Coach

Achievements & Honors
- 1989 - NSCA Presidents Award
- 2009 - NBA Strength Coach of the Year (Inaugural Year)
- 2014 - USA Strength and Conditioning Coaches Hall of Fame
- 2017 - NSCA Professional Strength and Conditioning Coach of the Year

Published Books
(Main author of books credited to National Basketball Conditioning Coaches Association)
- 1994 - NBCCA, *Condition the NBA Way*, Cadell & Davies
- 1997 - NBCCA, *NBA Power Conditioning*, Human Kinetics
- 2001 - Foran, B., *High-Performance Sports Conditioning*, Human Kinetics
- 2007 - NBCCA, *Complete Conditioning for Basketball*, Human Kinetics

Education
- 1977 - Central Michigan University, B.S. Education, Double Major: Physical Education, Health Education
- 1981 - Michigan State University, M.S. Exercise Physiology

CHAPTER 7

The Chet Fuhrman Story

How Coaching in High School Prepared Me to Be a Strength & Conditioning Coach

Winning championships at three levels of coaching is the biggest accomplishment of my coaching career. In 1978, I coached at Steelton-Highspire High School and we won a Pennsylvania High School State Championship; in 1982 and 1986 at Penn State University we won Collegiate National Championships; in 2005 with the Pittsburgh Steelers we won a Super Bowl World Championship; and in 2011 with the Virginia Destroyers we won the UFL Championship, giving Head Coach Marty Schottenheimer his first professional championship. Those who have coached or played for him in the past know the feeling I had for Marty that night. Winning a championship at *any* level is the ultimate goal each year for any coach or team.

Each place I coached, I was blessed to work with the greatest coaches and coach some of the greatest players in the country. Many coaching experiences I had at the high school level taught me how to become a better college and professional-level coach.

How I Got into the Profession of Strength & Conditioning

As a high school football coach in 1977, I first became interested in working as a Strength and Conditioning Coach after hearing Dan Riley, then Head Strength Coach at Penn State, give the best clinic talk I have ever heard at the Coach of the Year Football Clinic in Allentown, PA. After his clinic talk, I walked up to ask Dan where he was going to speak next so I could listen to him speak again. I wanted to learn more about his strength program. He told me he was going on a speaking tour at five more clinics throughout the state.

After I attended his third clinic talk, Dan reminded me that he was giving coaches the same clinic material he used at the Allentown Clinic. My response to Dan was, even though it was the same material, I learned something new each time he spoke. I asked Dan if he would do a clinic at our high school for our players, their parents, and local coaches. He accepted the invitation, and our players got to see firsthand what we were going to bring into our strength and conditioning program. Dan wrote a book, *Strength Training the Penn State Way*. I read the book three times front to back, and each time I read the book I learned something new.

After the second year of using Dan's strength program, our team was ranked the number one football team in the state of Pennsylvania (Pennsylvania did not start a playoff system until 1980). After the season was over, our team rode around town on fire engines with sirens blasting through Steelton and Highspire like we just won the Super Bowl. The next day, I wrote Dan a letter, thanking him for helping our team achieve our number one goal of winning the 1978 State Championship. Two months later, out of the blue, I received a letter back from Dan, asking me if I would accept a position to be his Assistant Strength and Conditioning Coach at Penn State University.

My number one value in coaching is trust. My relationship with Dan Riley put me in a position where he trusted that I could do the job of being his assistant. I'll always remember that my strength training career all started with that first question to Dan Riley at the Allentown Clinic. My message to any individual who wants to break into the coaching profession is this: over time you have to build a relationship with coaches, schools, or organizations you might want to work for one day.

How to Build a Weight Room When You Don't Have One

When we started coaching at Steelton-Highspire High School in 1977, we had a major problem; we did not have a weight room. There was a large storage closet above the gym that we asked the administration if we could use as a weight room. Surprisingly, they said yes. Coaches and players were excited to start this project together.

The first thing we wanted to do is carpet the cement floor. I went to a carpet dealer in town and he said we were in luck. A lady who lived in a big house in town got new carpet every three years and had just ordered new carpet. We could have her old not-so-used carpet for free. Next, we wanted to put mirrors on the walls. My mom had two dresser mirrors in her attic I knew we could use. I asked the players to ask their parents and check their own attics for mirrors, and we ended up with eight mirrors on the walls of the weight room. Next, we needed music to lift to. One of the players donated his eight-track stereo to the weight room. I had the art students come in and paint murals on the wall. We were on a roll.

It was starting to look like a weight room, all we needed was equipment. A universal gym, a set of dumbbells up to 70 pounds, and one bench press were stored in the stadium field house. We asked the administration if we could buy one bench press, one incline bench press, and two York Olympic barbell sets. We were looking for any equipment that would apply a force for resistance. Then I found a bonus—in the Physical Education storage room they had four old Exergenie units with ropes that apply resistance. Before I knew it, our weight room was complete.

When I built the Steelers new weight room, I built it the same way I did the high school weight room. The only difference was I didn't have to ask for hand-me-downs, I bought everything brand new. True story, Kordell Stewart, our starting quarterback, asked me why we didn't have a running Exergenie exerciser. I blew him away when I went to a box I had in storage and pulled out a running Exergenie. I had kept one of those old Exergenie units I found in the gym storage room at Steelton-Highspire many years before Kordell was even born.

How I Put Together My Lifting Routine

After we knew what equipment we had, we put together a total body lifting routine. We broke the body into five different muscle groups: Neck, Legs, Upper Body (Pectorals, Latissimus Dorsi, and Deltoids) Arms, and Abdominals. The players worked together with partners. One player was the lifter and went through the workout while the other player was the spotter. After the first lifter completed his routine they reversed roles. Total time for both lifters to complete the routine was about an hour and ten minutes.

For our neck routine we would perform front and back manual resistance neck exercises, which I learned from Dan Riley when I attended his spring clinic talk, and shoulder shrugs with dumbbells.

For the lower body exercises we used the universal gym to do leg presses, leg extensions and leg curls. We also did calf raises using a weighted belt on the weight room steps as well as the good morning exercise for the lower back.

For upper body exercises we did the barbell bench press and dumbbell pectoral flies for the pectoral muscles; lat pull-down on the universal gym and chin-ups for the latissimus dorsi muscles; side lateral raise and seated press using dumbbells for deltoid muscles. For variety, sometimes we did incline bench press, body weight or belted dips, or manual resistance exercises for the three upper body muscles.

For the arms Dan Riley showed us a number of ways to exercise our biceps, triceps, and forearms using manual resistance. For the abdominal muscles we did a group sit-up/core routine. Our total body lift routine was complete.

A coaching point to remember when putting together your lifting routines, the exercises you perform will be determined by what equipment you have in your weight room. Use whatever you can that provides resistance, and remember, the muscle doesn't have a brain in it to know what resistance is being applied to the muscle (i.e. barbells, dumbbells, kettle bells, machines, cinder blocks, logs, sand bags, tires, etc.)

How to Get Your Player to Participate in Your Program

Now all we needed to do was get athletes to come, be dedicated, and believe in our new strength and conditioning program. When I started our strength and conditioning program at Steelton-Highspire High School, attendance was not mandatory. In order to build a winning program, I felt I needed a strategy in place with an emphasis on attendance. Later on in my career, with the Pittsburgh Steelers, I had the same challenge. Some of the tactics I used on the high school level I also used when I started the Steelers program.

I went to the Art teacher and asked for sheets of large construction paper. I made a large attendance chart for each class: seniors, juniors, and sophomores. I spaced the names and dates of our workouts on lines one inch apart. When a player attended a workout session, I would color in the date box with a red marker. The goal was for each player to have a solid red line the whole way across the chart. If there were blank spaces under workout dates next to a player's name, I would have the leaders of each class talk to their peers about the importance of attending our program for the betterment of our team. I used myself as a last resort.

The charts were posted at the door where the players entered the weight room. When the players entered through the doors, the first thing most of them did was check the attendance chart to see if their dates were filled in red for the pervious workout. I did the same thing with attendance charts when I coached at Penn State and the Steelers.

Sometimes, and on purpose, I would not color in the box for one or two players who did previously workout. It took about two seconds for the players to come see me to make their plea that they did attend the workout session. It's a funny sight, to see a pro player react to this tactic. In the end, all was good, and we got a few laughs from the situation.

At the end of the conditioning program, I would look at the charts to see which class of players had the most complete chart. It told me which class attended most often, but it also told me which class was the strongest. If you are just starting a program, attendance will usually be higher with younger players than older players. In a year or two though, those younger players will be older, and your program will be off and running at full capacity.

How to Reward "All" Players for Their Effort

From the time I was a high school coach, I was not big on giving awards or posting names of players on the wall for being the strongest lifter for a certain strength training exercise. Here is my reasoning for not rewarding a chosen few. During my first year of coaching in high school, I gave awards and posted the names of players on the weight room wall who were the strongest in eight different exercises. True story, one player won the award for lifting the most weight in seven of the eight exercises. At the end of the off-season program, I ask players if these awards were important to them. All the strong players said yes, but about 70% of the players responded they could never win an award and the awards were not important to them. In that 70% were players we were counting on starting for us in the upcoming season.

The next off-season, I wanted to reward players for their hard work, effort, and sacrifice to make us a better team. I wanted to give out awards that everyone could achieve. After having a staff discussion, we came up with the idea of giving out awards for attendance. I know many coaches will think this idea is not that exciting. There are two reasons why we came up with this idea: It was something that everyone could achieve and we knew the more often a player attended workouts, the stronger, better conditioned, and more confident they would become. We wanted to give everyone a chance to get an award, not just 30% of the team.

If a player attended 70% of the workouts, they received a logo t-shirt; if they attended 80% of the workouts they received a t-shirt and a logo sweatshirt, and if they attended 90% of the workouts they received a t-shirt, sweatshirt, and logo windbreaker jacket. The booster club had a fund-raising project to help pay for the awards.

This type of award encouraged players to attend workouts more often, even those players who had not attended at all. Players who had the highest number of attended dates were put into leadership roles within the team. We chose leaders in each class; seniors, juniors, and sophomores. As our attendance got stronger, so did our team.

How Sometimes You Must Listen to Your Players

Many strength and conditioning coaches get the physiological term, Specificity of Training, totally confused, or don't understand this physiological principle. Today in the field of Strength and Conditioning, there are many gimmicks with the use of training equipment to improve one's skill. Many coaches also have their athletes do movement drills that have no carryover to what the athlete needs to perform his skill on the field, but it is a waste of a player's time, and, more importantly, a player's energy, to perform drills that have no skill carryover to what a player does on the field.

I was coaching linebackers at Steelton-Highspire High School. There were several drills I had the players perform in our warm-up period before we started practice. First, the players performed a shuffle drill going right and then left for 15 yards. Next, I had the players perform the carioca drill for the purpose of loosening up their hips. The last warm-up drill, the players perform a lateral run drill, keeping their shoulders and hips square to the line of scrimmage. Note: a coaching point was to never cross your feet behind the opposite leg when running laterally, because if a player got hit in this awkward position with his leg behind the other leg, most likely they would lose their balance and fall down to the ground.

Here is a lesson I learned from one of my high school linebackers on the principle of Specificity of Training. I had the players perform the first two warm-up drills: shuffle right and shuffle left and carioca right and left. Last, I had the players perform the lateral run drill. The third player in line crossed his leg behind, and I yelled out that a few seconds earlier I told him not to cross his legs behind. Well, he yelled back at me and said, "If I didn't do the carioca drill before the lateral run, I would not have crossed my leg behind when I did the lateral run." His nerves and muscles performed an automatic response to something he performed a minute or two before, the carioca drill.

I stopped and thought for a second and admitted to the player he was right. If I don't ever want him to cross his leg behind when performing a linebacker skill, why would I have him practice a skill I never want him to perform on the field? Performing the carioca drill would only promote bad habits for my linebackers. From that moment on, including my time coaching at Penn State and with the Steelers, I have never used the carioca as a drill again for football.

How to Make Your Conditioning Program Fun

Having your players lift and run for three or four days a week in a eight to ten week off-season program benefits your athletic program. However, if lifting and running is the only thing you have your players do for that length of time, some of your players may lose interest in the program. At the start of our 1978 off-season, our staff decided to add some fun and excitement into the program. We decided to use the last ten to fifteen minutes of our allotted time to have what we called a "fun period."

Our thought process was this: if we ended a workout with players running gassers, distance running, or repetitive sprints; the first thing the players would think of as they walked to the next workout would be—what they did last in the previous workout. Example: "Oh no, the dreaded workout at the end, do I give a 100% or do I pace myself through this workout, or do I even want to go to the workout?" Instead, ending with the fun period, we wanted the players to have the attitude of positivity and excitement as they walked to he next workout. Knowing that after they worked hard through the workout, at the end they will have some fun and leave with an upbeat attitude.

We organized our conditioning into the fun session. We broke the team down into small groups and did relay races. The losers had to do pushups. We did every relay we could think of: sprinting, bear crawl, wheel barrel, crab walk, body carry, etc. We had the players play team sports like soccer, basketball, or razzle-dazzle football. We even let the players think of or create new things to do in the fun period.

As coaches, we made sure the fun period ended with excitement and enthusiasm. All the coaches made it a point to go into the locker room and tell each of their players what a great effort they put into their workout and the fun session.

The fun session is something we also did at Penn State and with the Steelers. After one spring workout with the Steelers, we had the players play ultimate frisbee football. We played ten-minute games, single elimination, and two teams played for the Frisbee Football Super Bowl. It was a sight to see these amazing athletes make acrobatic moves on the field catching a frisbee instead of a football. At the end of the fun session, when everyone came together to break as a group, there was a lot of excitement and enthusiasm. Everyone was giving high fives, and they were excited to do this again.

Just like when I was coaching in high school, after the fun session all of the coaches went into the locker room to tell each of their players what a great effort they put into their workout and the fun session. Coaching never ends, so coach players up, and not down, everyday!

Finale

I have been fortunate to experience coaching on three different levels in my career: high school, college, and professional. I was blessed to work for eight of the greatest coaches that ever coached at any level. I would like to thank these great leaders for helping me to have such an amazing coaching career: High School–Joe Makosky, Harrisburg High School, Mickey Minnich, Steelton-Highspire High School; College–Mike Price, Weber State University, Joe Paterno, Penn State University; Professional–Bill Cowher, Pittsburgh Steelers (NFL), Marty Schottenheimer, Virginia Destroyers (UFL), Terry Shea, Boston Brawlers (UFXL).

I would like to give a special thanks to Dan Riley (United States Military Academy, Penn State University, and Washington Redskins). Dan is one of the greatest Strength and Conditioning coaches of all time. If Dan hadn't given me an opportunity to join his staff in 1979, I never would have had the career I had. He taught me so much, not only strength and conditioning information, but more importantly, how to communicate that information to my players. Someone once said: "To be the best, you must learn from the best." D-Boy –

YOU'RE THE BEST!

Last, I would like to give thanks my wonderful wife Lisa. She allowed me to work long days for 25 of my 36 years in coaching, travel to away games on many, many weekends, and be away for recruiting weekends during my years coaching in college, while raising and taking care of our three amazing children: Erica, Michael, and Maria. To my family, I love you all.

Earl "Chet" Fuhrman's Coaching Bio

- Harrisburg High School, Health Education Teacher/Football Coach
  » Head Freshman Football Coach
- Steelton-Highspire High School, Physical Education Teacher/ Football Coach/Strength Coach
  » Awarded the 1978 State Championship for being the Number One ranked team in the state of Pennsylvania
  » Offensive/Defensive coordinator for football and Strength Coach
- Penn State University, Assistant Strength and Conditioning Coach
  » Provided leadership for the overall management for 28 varsity team sports both men and women
- Weber State University, Strength and Conditioning Coach
  » Our first year, team had the first winning season in 14 years
- Penn State University, Strength and Conditioning Coach
  » Team won the 1982 and 1986 NCAA Collegiate National Championship
  » Team played in three National Championship games, eight bowl games, and had nine winning seasons
- Pittsburgh Steelers, Conditioning Coordinator/Football Operations Coordinator
  » Team won the 2005 NFL Super Bowl World Championship
  » Team had 10 winning seasons, 9 playoff appearances, 8 division titles, played in 5 AFC Championship games, and 2 Super Bowls appearances
  » Coached 28 different players that made the Pro Bowl Roster 66 times
  » Received the following awards: 2002 Presidents Award for contributions to the Field of Strength and Conditioning, 2005 National Football League Strength Coach of the Year
- Virginia Destroyers, Strength and Conditioning Coach/Tight

Ends Coach
» UFL - United Football League
» Team won the 2011 UFL Championship
- Boston Brawlers, Strength and Conditioning Coach/Defensive Line Coach
» FXFL - Fall Experimental Football League

Education
- University of Central Oklahoma, Bachelor of Science in Health and Physical Education

CHAPTER 8

The Mike Gentry Story

I've always wanted to improve myself, and when a friend in high school took me to a small, brick building that was the private gym for some accomplished bodybuilders, powerlifters, and other hard-training iron heads, I found a home. I don't remember my friend really lifting there, and I don't remember me ever not training there until I left Durham, North Carolina for college. I left this little back yard gym, but I never left the iron. For many years, when I'd visit my parents, I'd go to this little gym with the homemade equipment and the rusty weights and get a workout. This 155-pound, average high school athlete saw that these weights and this discipline offered a way of change, of hope and a path for self-determination. If I couldn't have articulated it then, I felt it. The gym became my personal Iron Dojo. I learned a lot from the iron warriors and the training, and I've been able to share my love and continued knowledge of training with thousands of collegiate athletes during my strength and conditioning coaching career.

It was at Western Carolina University, where I earned an undergraduate degree in Health and Physical Education, that I read a book by the late, great, pioneer strength and conditioning coach Bill Starr. This book, *The Strongest Shall Survive*, has become a "bible" for strength training for football and opened my eyes to the possibility of a career path in my area of passion. This book had a major influence on my life.

I was fortunate to teach and coach a year after college at the high school where I did my student teaching. I coached three sports and taught all the ninth-grade boys' physical education. I learned more that year at Owen High School in Swannanoa, North Carolina than I did during my college years. One thing I learned was that if you had the "shop class" build a power rack for the weight room, always measure the door to the weight room first!

UNC 1980-82

I decided that if I was going to be a high school teacher and coach, I should get a master's degree and make a thousand more dollars a year. I was very fortunate to enroll in the graduate program at the University of North Carolina at Chapel Hill in the fall of 1980, where I joined the Tar Heel Strength and Conditioning Staff as a part-time employee for five dollars an hour and the opportunity to eat at the training table.

The athletic program at UNC was top tier, the football program was strong, with Lawrence Taylor and Amos Lawrence and a host of All Stars. Michael Jordan had just joined the basketball team, and baseball, the women's soccer, women's field hockey, men's lacrosse, men and women's tennis, etc. were all very strong and nationally competitive. The strength and conditioning program was ahead of its time due to the leadership of former football player and then current administrator Paul Hoolihan. I learned so much, from the dynamics of coaching large groups of athletes to how hard to push the conditioning of football players in the summer and the importance of training the Olympic lifts for most explosive athletes.

I really enjoyed my two years in "Blue Heaven." I was busy, teaching two physical education activity classes and working with collegiate athletes in the afternoons and at a local Nautilus Center part time. I took a full academic load and continued to train and compete in powerlifting. I even had a social life! One more year of this would have killed me!

East Carolina University 1982-1986

Thankfully, I was able to land the Director of Strength and Conditioning position at East Carolina University (ECU) in the fall of 1982. At the time, I was 24 years old and the youngest Division 1A Head Strength and Conditioning Coach in the country. I was paid $12,000 a year and was provided a car, a four door Chevette, to drive. I was responsible for the strength training for all of the athletes at ECU. The initial Pirate Strength and Conditioning staff consisted of myself and a football medical redshirt assigned to me. Fortunately, this young man turned out to be a godsend and has become a lifetime friend.

ECU was where I grew up as a coach. My mentor was the late, iconic Head Football Coach Ed Emory. Coach Emory was unforgettable, with the most dynamic, larger-than-life personality that I've met on this planet. He was a rolling ball of razor blades! A former ECU Offensive Linemen and journeyman assistant football coach, he was absolutely determined to make the Pirates national contenders. He was a master motivator and tireless worker. His commitment to strength and conditioning was complete, and his expectation of effort from his players and assistant coaches was total. I was very well supported as a coach, and I had a good coach to model.

The East Carolina Strength Complex was a most unique and functional facility. The building was massive and located a few blocks off campus. This brick, warehouse-looking structure had a fine and varied history. The Union Carbide Battery Company created the structure during the 1940s and made batteries there. Later, the building became a landmark nightclub featuring groups such as the Allman Brothers band. Before becoming the strength training home of the Pirates, the facility was a combination ice rink and roller skating facility. During my tenure at ECU, the facility, leased from a former Pirates athlete, was dual-purposed as a training center and part-time Bingo Parlor! Fortunately, the two functions rarely overlapped.

Pirate Power Poster, circa 1983 – This poster was an educational/recruiting poster sent out to high schools. The poster highlighted our core lifts for football and team lifting results.

The facility offered me the two most important components for functional use: plenty of open space, and enough free-weight barbells and racks to train large groups of athletes. I actually had a large area, the old ice rink floor, available for warm up, functional movement, and stretching, and another large area dedicated for strength training in the space previously used for roller skating. The ice was gone, and the rink floor was level.

I arrived at ECU at a great time. The football program had a great combination of talent and leadership among the players. In 1982 the team was 7-4, and in 1983 the record was 8-3. 1983 was the first year that East Carolina University's Football team was included in the AP Top Twenty. In those days there were much fewer Bowl game opportunities and the Pirates weren't invited to a Bowl. However, I did receive a frozen turkey from a local grocer as a bonus after the 1983 season!

Terry Long "History's Strongest Football Player

I'd be remiss if I didn't honor the 1983 Consensus All American Offensive Guard, Terry Long. When I interviewed for the job, Coach Emory said that the Pirates had one of the strongest football players in the country. He was right. Terry Long was a former Army Airborne veteran who was off-the-charts strong. I trained Terry for the 1983 North Carolina Powerlifting State Championship and he shocked the powerlifting world with a 2202 total made from an 837-pound squat, 500-pound bench press and an 865-pound deadlift. Terry's strength was

1985 East Carolina University Super Buc Award Winners. These were our most accomplished football lifters. Notice the wood splitting mauls that were donated and then painted by the Strength Staff and used for awards.

complete and legendary. *Bigger Faster Stronger Journal* featured Terry and named him "History's Strongest Football Player." Terry played nine seasons at offensive guard for the Pittsburgh Steelers. Tragically, Terry Long took his life soon after his professional career ended. An autopsy of his brain revealed evidence of post concussive syndrome (PCS) that was attributed to his football career and possibly influenced his death. Devastating loss.

Virginia Tech 1987-2016

In February 1987, I was named the Director of Strength and Conditioning at Virginia Tech. I was interested in this job for location, size of the school, and perceived chance to win. My starting salary was $30,000, but I didn't realize that the Virginia Tech football was going on NCAA probation as punishment for the previous Athletics Director's indiscretions. The football team had several years of reduced new scholarship numbers. Virginia Tech was also not in a football conference, which had become important, since no conference meant less television revenue and scheduling stability.

The strength and conditioning facility was on campus, within the athletics department footprint, but it was only 2500 square feet, a real challenge when charged with the mission of training all 500 plus Hokie athletes.

First year Head football Coach Frank Beamer was a young, positive, well organized leader that ran a quality program. He was supportive of the strength and conditioning program without micro management, which is about as good as it gets in this business.

Eventually, we got off probation and restricted scholarships and joined the Big East Football Conference in 1991. We were successful in this league, and the proceeds helped all sports and facilities at Virginia Tech. When we joined the Atlantic Coast Athletic Conference in 2004, the athletics program was fully vetted and on solid ground.

Our little 2,500 square foot strength facility morphed into three different strength and conditioning facilities: the Merryman Center with over 17,000 square feet of usable space, the Olympic Sports Training Facility with 7,500 square feet, and the Hahn Basketball Training Facility Weight Room which is 3,000 square feet.

The strength and conditioning mission grew along with our facilities, and number of strength and conditioning staff increased. We became more wholistic with our training approach with all sports, and included more speed and agility training as well as team conditioning during the off-season for many sports.

The Virginia Tech Iron Palace Poster featured the Merryman Center Strength and Conditioning Facility created in 1999 at Virginia Tech. It was a giant leap forward.

Under Coach Beamer's leadership, the football program was second in the nation for active Bowl streaks, with 23 consecutive bowl appearances. Coach Beamer's overall record of wins and losses during his 29 seasons at Virginia Tech is 238-121-2. Frank Beamer was inducted into the National Football Coaches Hall of Fame upon his retirement in 2016.

I was able to grow the strength and conditioning program into an organization called "Athletic Performance" in 2001. The Athletic Performance model included sports nutrition, sports psychology, and strength and conditioning. Virginia Tech was one of the first universities in the nation to create full-time departmental positions in both sports nutrition and sports psychology. I am very proud of this accomplishment, and I was happy to be the administrator for Athletic Performance as well as directly responsible for football strength and conditioning from 1987 through the 2015 season.

I was named the National Collegiate Football Strength and Conditioning Coach of the Year in 2004 and was inducted into the USA Collegiate Strength and Conditioning Hall of Fame in 2011.

Training Principles

The roots of my training principles for most explosive sports included the use of multi-joint exercises trained using undulating periodization models. The exercises and the training model specifics were determined by the sport, specific athlete needs, and the time of the training year relative to the competitive schedule. As I matured, and the tools and expectations of the industry grew, a more wholistic training approach was created with the inclusion of functional movement, pre-habilitation exercises, specific speed and agility training, and recovery methods included in the overall training model.

The ability of the strength and conditioning coach to understand the basic science of training is essential. The ability to properly apply the scientific principles to different situations such as sports and individual athletes is also critical.

I believe that training teams together builds team unity and offers leadership opportunities. Shorter, intense strength training sessions of one hour or less are preferable and most profitable.

Coaching Principles

"Coach the Kid, Not the Weight." Legendary Strength and Conditioning Coach Johnny Parker's great advice. This simple yet profound statement is critically important to me.

"Nothing is special if you don't make it special." It is our job to make our program special. Special requires accountability.

Be active and positive in your coaching but coach your own personality. Be authentic.

A Career of Significance - Beyond the Sets and Reps

For me, my career in Collegiate Strength and Conditioning was everything I could have imagined. The good fortune of having been involved in the earlier days of the profession allowed all of us to be more creative in how we interpreted our mission. We had a common purpose: to train kids and teams to win. How we approached this goal was largely up to us. If we envisioned a larger mission beyond getting athletes bigger, faster, and stronger, we were allowed to embrace it.

The same reasons that I connected to the small backyard gym in high school fueled my reasoning when physically training athletes. I knew that the discipline of training would teach them about themselves and offer a path of self-determination, self-improvement, and hope for a brighter future. I believed that the principles of organization, consistency, and effort could transcend the physical training and athletic goals and could be applied to life goals and objectives. I reasoned that the Iron Dojo could offer guidance that some may have missed from parents and role models.

I further observed and embraced how a group of athletes training hard together toward common goals builds team unity and commitment. As the individuals improved and worked together side by side, the team also improved. You have a higher degree of trust when you've seen your teammate fight through the fires of training.

Now that this career path is over, I've had the blessing of personal reflection and the priceless gift of the feedback from the hundreds of athletes that I've trained over a thirty-four-year career. Success is measured in many ways. For me, having the opportunity, the God-given ability, and the love to impact as many athletes as I did is both humbling and gratifying. To those I failed to reach for various reasons, I apologize. Maybe I wasn't skilled enough in different ways, or maybe the timing wasn't right for the student or the teacher.

At the end of the day

I can't adequately thank the staff of men and women who made our strength and conditioning programs special over the course of my career. Each one of them brought so much and asked for so little. Many were former athletes, and some went on to captain their own programs. It was an honor to work together and become friends. God Bless you all.

To the athletes who we were attempting to inspire and educate, let me assure you that we coaches were the ones that received the education and inspiration. Thank you for all of your sweat equity.

The relationships and life-lasting impressions we had on the young people under our direction made this career significant beyond our expectations. That has become our real and lasting compensation, and I hope our legacy.

The ability to impact others and be a great teammate or leader doesn't stop with youth or athletics. Those who believe have hope for the future, and those with hope have power in the present.

Mike Gentry's Coaching Bio

- 1982-1986 - East Carolina University, Director of Strength and Conditioning
- 1987-2000 - Virginia Tech, Director of Strength and Conditioning
- 2001-2009 - Virginia Tech, Assistant Athletic Director for Athletic Performance
- 2010-2016 - Virginia Tech, Associate Athletic Director for Athletic Performance

Achievements & Honors

- 2003 - Master Strength and Conditioning Coach, Collegiate Strength and Conditioning Coaches Association
- 2004 - National Collegiate Strength and Conditioning Coach of the Year, American Football Monthly
- 2011 - USA Collegiate Strength and Conditioning Hall of Fame

Professional Certifications

- 1986-Present - Certified Strength and Conditioning Specialist, National Strength and Conditioning Association
- 2002-Present - Collegiate Strength and Conditioning Coaching Certification, Collegiate Strength and Conditioning Coaches Association

Professional Services

- 2006-2012 - Collegiate Strength and Conditioning Coaches Association, Member of Board of Directors

Education

- 1979 - Western Carolina University, B.S. in Physical Education
- 1981 - The University of North Carolina at Chapel Hill, M.A.T. in Physical Education
- 1999 - Virginia Tech, Doctorate in Education - Curriculum and Instruction

CHAPTER 9

The Bert Hill Story

I was the middle child of a middle-class family, growing up in Montgomery, Alabama with my older sister, Lauren, and my younger brother, Brant. Larry Hill, my dad, was an electrical contractor with a degree in math from Texas A&M, and my mother, Mary Hill, was a registered nurse. I was taught at an early age that if you wanted something you had to work for it. I played football and baseball through high school and into junior college at Marion Military Institute. I went on to play football at Wichita State for a year before returning to Montgomery, where I started coaching football at Cloverdale Junior High with Coach Skip Wolf. I enrolled at Auburn University at Montgomery, and two years later I graduated with a Bachelor of Science in Physical Education.

As a young coach, my ambitions often exceeded my qualifications.

My first job out of college was at Nicholls State University—a small campus down in Thibodaux, Louisiana. Sonny Jackson, the head football coach, hired me as a graduate assistant. There my aspirations started to materialize.

While I assisted Coach Barrett Murphy—defensive line and strength coach— I gained hands-on experience training players in the weight room. When Barrett was out recruiting, I'd run the program for him, and I really began to enjoy the strength training side of things. I knew that's what I wanted to pursue, but I was lost as to how to go about it.

So, I made a phone call.

I called Dr. Bob Ward, the strength and conditioning coach for the Dallas Cowboys. I told him who I was, where I coached, and my desire to one day coach in professional football. When I asked him what I needed to do to get to that point, his answer was quick:

"You need to go to Auburn University and get your master's. It's the only university in the country that has a curriculum in strength physiology. It is led by Dr. Mike Stone."

"Well, Dr. Ward," I said. "I'm just a poor GA at Nicholls State. I don't know if I can afford to do that."

Again, his answer was quick.

"Well son," he said, "you're going to have to make sacrifices in your life at some point in time," and he hung up the phone.

A few months later, I took the GRE.

Principle of Training: Science, Experience and Best Practices

Before Coach Murphy arrived at Nicholls State, he'd been the head football and strength coach at Catholic High School in Baton Rouge, Louisiana. While there, Mike Stone contacted him.

Stone—who was at LSU working on his doctorate in strength physiology—had an idea for his thesis, and he needed Barrett's help to do it. When Barrett obliged, Mike set up his very first study on periodization. Stone divided the football team into two groups—one did periodization while the other did three sets of six, which stood as the best practice for training at the time. Then he took the girls softball team and did the same thing. They tested, trained for six weeks, then re-tested. This study became the basis for Mike's thesis on periodization. Several years later, Dr. Mike Stone was credited with bringing the concept of periodization—in a usable format that fits our system—to this country.

Working with Coach Murphy and implementing the periodization schedule during the summer and in-season programs at Nicholls State only increased my interest in learning how training affected the body. When the season was over—with the help of Coach Murphy—I applied for and was accepted for a GA position in the physical education department at Auburn University.

In Auburn's Strength Physiology Curriculum, I learned how training itself doesn't make you stronger, rather, training increases the body's ability to recover from stress. That's the main concept of periodization—manipulating the volume and intensity of your training to allow the body to recover and avoid overtraining. Overtraining, after all, leads to injuries, and injuries lead to training setbacks.

Dr. Stone wasn't my only mentor at Auburn. When I arrived on campus in 1982, I found Virgil Knight, the head strength coach. I gave him my background and told him I'd like to volunteer to help him and Paul White, the assistant strength coach. I'd do whatever he needed me to do. He handed me one t-shirt and one pair of shorts, and my work with Auburn football began.

At that time, Auburn's program was one of the most respected in the country. The players were as disciplined and hard-working as any group of football players I've ever seen. I adapted Virgil's organization and methodology of training: total body, three days a week. I still follow a version of this program in my training today.

When I design a program, I always ask myself these questions:

1. Where are we coming from? (i.e. "What did we just finish?")
2. Where are we going to be when the training is over? (i.e. "What's going to happen next?")

Those two questions help determine the appropriate starting point, taking into account your athletes' current level of fitness to avoid overtraining.

In my experience, I've learned that once you find things you really believe in, you'll keep bouncing back to them throughout your career. My principle has always been, "If it works, keep it; if it doesn't, throw it out and find something that does work."

Principle of People: Attack the Problem, Not the Person

When I was at Southern Methodist University, and with the Detroit Lions, I coached with a man named Frank Gansz. Frank passed away in 2009, but during our time together he gave me a phrase that's stuck with me to this day:

"Attack the problem, not the person."

Frank was in the high-performance business. He defined a problem as "anything that keeps you from playing at your highest level."

It resonated with me then, and it motivates me now. On multiple occasions, I've witnessed coaches take it personally when players don't respond to their direction. They then disrespect the player by getting personal. When that happens, the player loses respect for the coach, and, in turn, trust disappears. If you want to bring a group of people together, eliminate disrespect, attack the problem (not the person), and you will build trust and unity.

When I meet with a group of players for the first time, I tell them up-front: "If I have a problem with you, I'll pull you aside and talk to you about it. If you have a problem with me, I would expect you to do the same." I got this idea from my good friend, June Jones, who I coached with at SMU.

Principle of Mind: Understanding the Big Picture

While I did my undergraduate program at Auburn University at Montgomery, I had a professor by the name of Dr. Joe Elrod—who's been very influential in my life. On a regular basis, in class, Dr. Elrod would emphasize the importance of setting goals in our lives, so I shared my goals at the time—becoming a coach in college football.

Sure enough, shortly before graduation, he came to me with a job opportunity. His good friend and former baseball teammate, Sonny Jackson, had just been hired as the head football coach at Nicholls State in Thibodaux, Louisiana. He had a graduate assistant position available. After a six-hour car ride I got hired on the spot, based on Dr. Elrod's recommendation.

That goal-setting focus set my foundation moving forward. I now had my sights set on coaching professional football. If something happened along the way—good or bad—that's how it was supposed to be. I had a singular focus, and I was going to accomplish it. This focus started after that phone call with Dr. Bob Ward from the Dallas Cowboys when I took the GRE and applied to Auburn, North Texas, and LSU.

I stopped in at North Texas first—but they told me I fell 30 points short on my GRE to earn admission into their grad school, and suggested I reapply next year. A couple weeks later, I called Tim Jorgenson, the strength coach at LSU. He had a GA job available and wanted to know how soon I could be there. "I'll be there tomorrow!" I told him.

I had just about settled in at LSU, when I received a call from Dr. Mike Stone offering me a GA position at Auburn. If I stayed at LSU, it would take me two years to complete the master's program with an emphasis in cardiovascular physiology. If I left for Auburn, I could complete my master's in one year with an emphasis in strength physiology.

I took the position. I loaded the 76 Monte Carlo the next day and drove to Auburn. Between my GA spot in the P.E. department, volunteering with the football strength staff, and my class work, I was staying busy and loving life. I was on track to accomplish my goal.

About a year later, several strength programs were looking for Auburn master's graduates. Auburn offered to create a position for me, but I'd received two other phone calls around that same time. One came from Mississippi State, and one came from Dave Williams—the head strength coach at Texas A&M. He offered me another GA position, so I made the trip to College Station.

After about three weeks at A&M, I received a call from Coach Al Miller at Alabama. He was also looking for a GA. Kent Johnston had been Coach Miller's GA but had moved to assisting the defensive backs coach as a football GA. Coach Miller needed a number-one guy. It looked like the right move at the time, so I took it and the next day, I was headed for Tuscaloosa.

After about a month of living at Bryant Hall and working as Coach Miller's GA, I received a call from Dave Williams telling me he had just created a full-time position and wanted to know if I would be interested in coming back to A&M.

"By the way," he said. "The position pays $18,000."

About a year after returning to College Station, Coach Williams's father—who was living in Virginia—became ill, so Dave left for Liberty University. Jackie Sherrill, the head football coach, hired me into my first head strength coach job at 26 years old.

All of this movement—bouncing from one GA job to the next—happened within one or two years. At the time, I didn't think anything of it. I knew it all had to be part of a master plan and, eventually, everything was going to work out.

After I was hired (again) at A&M, I hired two other staff members—Istvan Jovarek as a full-time assistant, and Allen Kinley as a GA. The three of us worked with football while Coach Javorek and Coach Kinley also trained the other 12 sports.

The original weight room, in 1982, was about 4,000 square feet and, unfortunately, despite being in Southwest Texas, wasn't air-conditioned.

In 1985, our staff at A&M helped design the largest strength and conditioning facility in the country (at that time)—The Netum Steed Laboratory—at 23,000 square feet. It was large enough for two 40-yard dash lanes down the middle, and large enough to train the entire football team at one time. We felt we had the best program in the country, and now we had the weight room to prove it. We even had personalized weight plates—complete with the A&M logo.

Texas A&M weight room - 1985

All of our equipment in the new facility was designed and manufactured by Samson Equipment Company out of Las Cruses, New Mexico. I wanted to deal with just one company, and Dave Schroeder convinced me he was the guy. At the time, Samson had just completed equipping Arizona State's new strength training facility, and Virgil Knight knew the head strength coach at Arizona State, Ronnie Jones.

I called Ronnie and set up a trip to visit his facility. They happened to be in spring football at the time, so during my visit Ronnie introduced me to his head coach, John Cooper. Coach Cooper would later accept the head coaching position at Ohio State University, and Ronnie would move on to the Philadelphia Eagles as their strength coach.

In 1987, I was offered the head strength and conditioning job at Ohio State University. After six years and three Southwest Conference Championships at Texas A&M, my salary was up to $35,000, but Ohio State was offering $50,000. Having met Coach Cooper in 1985 on my Arizona State visit, and hearing all of the positive comments about Coach Cooper from Ronnie, I knew it was time for a change.

Moving to Columbus, Ohio was exciting for me. It was the first time I would live somewhere that had four seasons. Although, when you're in coaching, there's really only two seasons—in-season and offseason. Shortly after my arrival, we were in the middle of re-equipping the football weight room and I was trying to have it set up as a mini version of the facility in College Station. I called Samson Equipment Company again.

My staff working with football at Ohio State consisted of one GA, Rick Spielman and me. Rick's brother, Chris, had just completed his rookie season with the Detroit Lions and came back to Columbus to train for the offseason. He asked me to help him, and we developed a friendship during the next few months.

I really enjoyed my short time in Columbus. With Coach Cooper's backing, the great work ethic of the players, and the new facilities, it was one of the premier jobs in the country. Although the players worked hard, it did not equate to wins on the field. We lost to Michigan on the last play of the game and finished the season with a record of 4-6-1.

A couple of weeks after the season, I received a call from my old friend Tim Cassidy. Tim and I started as GAs at A&M and worked up to full-time positions. Tim was the football ops guy. He told me Coach Sherrill had departed, R.C. Slocum, the defensive coordinator, would be announced as the new head coach, and Coach Slocum wanted me to come back to A&M.

With all of the talk after having such a bad first year, I wasn't sure we would see season two in Columbus, so I was off to College Station for the third time.

Back at A&M in 1989, I got a call from Rick and Chris Spielman. Rick had just started scouting for the Detroit Lions. He told me the former strength coach was on his way out, and they wanted to know if I would be interested in coaching in Detroit. Two weeks later, I was headed to Pontiac, Michigan.

I coached for the Lions from 1990 to 2000—assisting with the defensive line coach (Lamar Leachman for five years and John Teerlinck for two years) when I wasn't doing my day job of training the players. Detroit gave me the opportunity to work with some of the best players in the game—guys like Barry Sanders, Dan Owens, Marc Spindler, Jerry Ball, Chris Spielman, Brett Perriman, Kelvin Pritchett, Bennie Blades, Sheldon White, and many others. I was truly in the best work situation of my life.

The Lions were a great organization, headed by Mr. William Clay Ford, the owner, Chuck Schmidt, the GM, and Head Coaches Wayne Fontes (1990-1996) and Bobby Ross (1997-2000). I did not have an assistant until Coach Ross created a position, and I hired Don Clemons.

I'd been in Detroit for 11 years, and possibly had the opportunity to stay longer, but I didn't see the big picture. When you get fired, everything stops. The world stops, and you stop along with it. You try to look back to see where you've been and look forward to see where you want to go, but you realize you're just somewhere in between those two places. It really makes you stop and think,

"Where have I been? Where am I going from here?"

In 1985, I had an interesting meeting with Mr. Billy Pickard—the head trainer at Texas A&M. He called me into his office one morning, and it went like this:

"Come in here young man," he said. "Have a seat right over here."

He pointed to a bucket on the ground.

"Do you see that bucket of water in front of you there? Put your hand in there."

I did as he'd instructed, then he told me to take it out.

"Do you see a hole in that water?" he asked.

"No sir," I said.

"That's what it's going to be like when your ass is out of here!"

Mr. Pickard's point? No one is irreplaceable.

———

I have been truly blessed with all of the great jobs I've had. It's really not the place, though, that makes or breaks your day—it's the people—and I have had the opportunity to work with so many great people, too many to mention in this short story.

When Coach Sherrill hired me back in 1983, he asked me how much I wanted to make.

"$30,000 and a car," I told him.

He agreed almost immediately.

"Dang," I thought. "I didn't ask for enough."

Times have definitely changed—and this industry along with it. Salaries have increased, staff sizes have grown and weight rooms have more square footage. Education has improved, career paths have diverted and the number of qualified strength coaches has risen significantly since the '80s.

In my opinion—and in my life—however, these three themes have remained true:

1. Have a principle you believe in.

2 Treat others how you want to be treated.

3. See the big picture.

In 2005 I was hired by Coach Nick Saban and the Miami Dolphins, but that's a story for another time...

Bert Hill's Coaching Bio

- 1979-1980 - Cloverdale Jr. High School, Assistant Football Coach
- 1981 - Nicholls State University, Graduate Assistant Defensive Line / Graduate Assistant Strength Coach
- 1982 - Louisiana State University, Graduate Assistant Strength Coach
- 1982-1983 - Auburn University, Graduate Assistant Strength Coach
- 1983 - Texas A&M, Graduate Assistant Strength Coach
- 1983 - University of Alabama, Graduate Assistant Strength Coach
- 1983-1987 - Texas A&M, Assistant Strength Coach / Head Strength Coach
- 1988 - Ohio State University, Head Strength Coach
- 1989 - Texas A&M, Head Strength Coach
- 1990-2000 - Detroit Lions, Head Strength Coach / Assistant Defensive Line Coach
- 2005-2006 - Miami Dolphins, Assistant Strength Coach
- 2008-2014 - Southern Methodist University, Defensive Line Coach
- 2015 - Lakeview Centennial High School, Defensive Line Coach
- 2016 - West Texas A&M, Defensive Line Coach
- 2017 - East Carolina University, Assistant Strength Coach
- 2017 - Southlake Middle School, Middle School Athletic Coordinator
- 2018 - Montreal Alouettes, Defensive Line Coach

CHAPTER 10

The Jeff Hurd Story

My story begins, even though I didn't realize it at the time, as an 8-year-old boy lifting weights with my dad in our garage. (see picture). Nothing heavy, and always two sets of 10 reps. My dad used to remind me of how I would wear him out, always asking, "When can I start lifting heavy weights like you?" His response was always the same: "Seventh or eighth grade. You have to be able to do your bodyweight number for pushups in two sets and 25 strict pull ups."

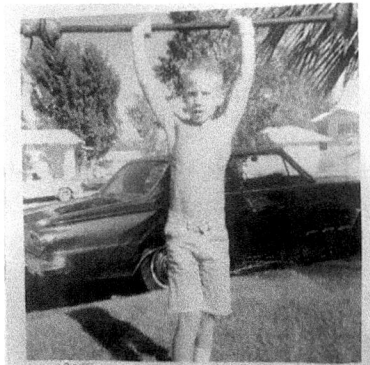

Me at age 8.

I look back and realize it was sound advice for youth training, even for the mid '60s. As a side note, the push up/chin up goal was accomplished, and it sure helped that I was a late bloomer and weighed only 80 pounds as an eighth grader.

As it turned out, I didn't have a significant growth spurt until after my freshman year in college. Strength and conditioning was a matter of survival for me in my sports participation. I was fortunate to have a high school coach, Greg Beauchman, who placed a high importance on weightlifting. We had limited equipment, a Universal machine (which are in museums now) and no free weights. Coach Beauchman would push and challenge us. The program was three sets of 10, and, if you completed all the reps, you added weight at the next workout. Simple, but effective. We also always tested for max pushups, dips, sit ups and chin-ups.

Although football and basketball were my favorite sports, recruiters were not knocking on the door of a 5'7", 138-pound senior in high school with average speed to play football or basketball at their schools.

My baseball coach in college didn't think weights and baseball were a good mix, other than using Nautilus machines. I used to sneak over to the football weight room to train, realizing the impact strength training could have on performance. I wished I had started the big three lifts (Clean, Squat, Deadlift) sooner. I knew I wanted to learn all I could and coach with a passion to help athletes achieve their goals.

After graduating from college, I took a job at my high school for a year. I coached baseball and helped Coach Beauchman with weight training in the new weight room he had established. Free weights and squat racks were included! It was a great learning experience.

I decided to continue my education at Fort Hays State University. As a graduate assistant, I helped with the Strength and Conditioning program for baseball while studying and I received my master's degree in Physical Education with an emphasis on Exercise Physiology.

Before I continue with my story, I must thank my wife Kathy. We have been happily married for 33 years. She has supported me every step of the way. My career choice has caused her to endure many moves, 10 different times across this country, while raising three wonderful children. I couldn't have done it without her. Above all, I thank God, who we have kept at the head of our household.

My first job was at Delta State University in Cleveland, Mississippi. Delta State is a Division II school in the delta of Mississippi. I am very grateful to Coach "Red" Parker, who was the head football coach, and Jim Holland, the defensive coordinator. They played competitive football while being facility challenged. Delta State had an excellent group of athletes and coaches who worked their butts off and loved football.

I learned so much about volume, intensity, cycling, and periodization from Coach Holland. We spent hours discussing strength training and watching football tape at night in the small, dark film room filled with his cigarette smoke, and occasionally, the smell of ancient, aged bourbon. He said it made him "creative."

The weight room at Delta State was somewhere between 1800 and 2000 square feet. All the benches, racks, and platforms were made by local tradesmen Coach Holland had befriended. They were actually very well built and of high qual-

Delta State weight room - 1985

ity. The bars and weights were purchased and donated. The room serviced all sports, with football having priority.

It was a lot of hours programming and coaching. I'm not sure young strength coaches realize how hard things were early on in our field. I also helped with film breakdown and film exchange, dorm monitoring, and even moved irrigation pipes daily to keep the fields watered. I had to transport three to four people on work release who were doing soft time at the county farm to get all the irrigation pipes moved on schedule. I never felt quite comfortable transporting them.

Compensation was three hot meals, a cot, and free work clothes. Seriously! My wife and I lived for free in married housing and I got a meal card to the cafeteria. I received a small stipend that I could either accept as payment or use toward post-graduate courses. I believe it was the huge amount of $2500 a semester. We wouldn't have survived if my wife hadn't found a job.

The married housing was an adventure in itself. It was old, with cement floors and gaps around most of the windows and doors. We would wake up in the mornings and there would be green tree frogs on the walls in our bedrooms. One night I was awakened by something crawling on my face. I slapped it off my face and it made a loud "smack" on the wall. I turned the lights on, and saw a giant cockroach lying on its back. I reached for a shoe to finish him off, but he scrambled back outside, through the gap under the front door.

It was an exciting day when I got a call from Gary Wade, the head strength and conditioning coach at Clemson University, to interview for an assistant job. We moved to Clemson in June of 1986. Clemson is a wonderful place and it was a great period in my career, my first exposure to big time football. Even back then, the weight room was outstanding. I had only seen weight rooms like that in pictures. I believe it was 8000 square feet, which was quite a change from Delta State.

My salary jumped to approximately $13,000, including summer camps, but we also had to pay for one class per semester to receive that stipend. The assistant strength staff included Joe Batson, Matt Munford, Brett Dalton, and myself. We spent many hours discussing our training principles.

We all put in a lot of long hours with the football team and all the sports we were assigned. We also spent a lot of daily and evening hours cleaning the weight room. And I mean military inspection style. We painted the front entrance of the weight room every recruiting weekend and before every home game.

Danny Ford was the head football coach. He christened me during my first summer camp. He shouted, "Hey Weight Boy, come here. The other assistants told me that you were kind of fast in college." He then asked me what my 40 time was. I said I wasn't that fast but could consistently run a 4.7. He said, "Well that's fast enough." He handed me cash and said, "Run down to Hardee's and get us all some burgers for lunch." Hook, line, and sinker. We had a really good football team. We went to the Gator Bowl that year and I received the first Bowl Game gifts of my career.

We obviously had very gifted and higher caliber athletes at Clemson. I can remember hearing Coach Ford bark with his bullhorn, from his tower, at practice, "Michael Dean Perry, take it in, son. We can't get anything done on offense today when you are on the field." Michael Dean is the younger brother of "Refrigerator" Perry, and he went on to also have a good NFL career of his own. Coach Wade was a big believer in the Overload Principle, which to him, meant we would max test every second week. Michael Dean would wait until everybody had maxed and then come in to do his test. He would ask me what was the most weight done by a defensive lineman. I would tell him the number, and he would put 5-10 more pounds on the bar and do it. And he did it every time. It was incredible.

Eventually, I wanted to be a head strength coach again and run my own program. I applied for the job at Western Michigan University (WMU) and got it. We spent six years at Western. My first son was born in Kalamazoo.

Funny thing, though, I did not get to see the weight room when I interviewed for the job at Western Michigan. They said the weight room and locker room were under the stadium, which was being repaired and were not safe to tour yet. I said the same thing for the first year I was there, every recruiting weekend, until we got the room to what I considered at least acceptable.

WMU weight room before 1987.

Even though I was the head strength coach at a Division I school, when I first saw the weight room I was really disappointed. So I rolled up my sleeves and went to work. Delta State University had prepared me for this. And what the heck, I was going to get paid $25,000, a year! Western Michigan University had 16 varsity sports and my graduate assistant and I were responsible for all of them.

The weight room was approximately 2000 square feet. We also had access to a Campus Rec weight room, when it was avail-

WMU weight room after 1987.

able. Our days started at 5:30 a.m. and finished late at night. It was long, long hours. We had one coach from the football coaching staff assigned to help us with just football, and eventually were given a couple volunteer student helpers. We were highly over-worked and grossly underpaid, but we loved what we were doing. We embraced the challenge and the workload. With the support of the football staff toward the strength program, the players bought in.

Back to the weight room transformation at WMU. It was a makeshift room in an auxiliary locker room. By selling the importance of strength and conditioning to the boosters and administration, we were able to turn it into a small but effective weight room. We convinced local vendors and boosters to help with donations and discounts. We got the room painted and carpeted. We built platforms and refurbished benches and squat racks with donated materials. The athletic department bought bars, bumper plates, and more weights. It became a place the players took pride in and it became a room we were not embarrassed to show recruits. The transformation of that room was a true labor of love.

In the off-season, we lifted three days per week, Mondays, Wednesdays, and Fridays, total body. The intensities were heavy, light, and medium. We used nine-week cycles which included two weeks of prep/muscular endurance (hypertrophy), three weeks of strength, and three weeks of strength/power with an unload week between the strength and power phases.

The 1988 football team won its first conference championship in the school's history and we went to the California Bowl. While at WMU, I was able to implement the program I truly believed in. And yes, it was the program I learned from Coach Holland at Delta State University.

After six years at Western Michigan, I felt it was time to take another step. It seemed like even though we were a successful football program, assistants from bigger conferences were getting bigger jobs, and I wasn't.

While at Western Michigan, during the time period before our two-a-days, I began working training camps for the Kansas City Chiefs with the head strength coach, Dave Redding and his assistant, Russ Ball. We developed a good relationship and I view them as mentors. Dave Redding, aka "Red Man," is a true pioneer in our profession. I watched how he handled players, things that go way beyond sets and reps. These are things that I think a lot of young strength coaches have lost sight of or don't think are important anymore. I truly believe you coach the person/man first, and the athlete second. Once the person believes and trusts that you truly care about them as a person and want to help them be better, you will be able to be demanding and coach the athlete in them. That's the stuff that doesn't show up on a computer, and it's something a GPS can't tell you. Although a GPS can be important, it can't gauge trust or a man's heart.

Red Man offered me a position as a paid intern for the Kansas City Chiefs, one of the first positions of its kind in the NFL. The offer was $900 a month with no benefits. I knew my goal was to coach in the NFL. I am sure my family, friends, and the people at Western Michigan thought I had lost my mind when I seriously considered leaving a full-time job for an internship.

We rolled the dice and accepted the internship. We made the decision to do whatever it would take to make it work. Besides working all day at the Chief's weight room, I ended up working at the airport during the late shift throwing bags for America West Airlines. I worked until midnight five nights a week. I also worked for Belger Moving Company on weekends.

I'm not sure how I survived. My goal, my love for our profession, my faith, and the need to feed my family kept me going. I did the internship for two years. I used up a lot of my TIAA Cref retirement fund. We had our second child during that time period with no insurance. Needless to say, the debt was piling up and I figured the internship had run its course. It was time to find a full-time job.

Even though it seemed like the internship was a dead end move after two years, it paid off later. It truly was a great experience, not just one of the hardest periods in our life. I feel it helped form us and prepare us for greater successes.

My next job was at The University of Tulsa. I had the opportunity to work for and become friends with one of my all-time favorite people, David Rader.

After a year at Tulsa, my friend Jerry Palmieri asked if I would be his assistant for the NFL expansion team, Jacksonville Jaguars. The salary was $35,000 in 1995. I accepted the job. The Kansas City internship had finally paid off.

Being part of an expansion team from its beginning is an unbelievable experience. We went to the playoffs in our second year at Jacksonville. The playoff money paid off most of the debt we incurred during the internship. Another bright spot in our time at Jacksonville was the birth of our daughter.

After our third year at Jacksonville, Coach Marty Schottenheimer offered me a position as his head strength and conditioning coach for the Kansas City Chiefs. The internship paid off again.

I was the head strength and conditioning coach for the Kansas City Chiefs for nine years. I was also the head strength and conditioning coach for the San Diego Chargers for Norv Turner for six years and the assistant strength coach for the Minnesota Vikings for three years. While with the Chiefs, I had the opportunity, twice, to work as a consultant for our Special Forces. It was very intense and rewarding. My good friend Shannon McKinney, a member of the Special Forces, orchestrated the opportunity.

I have worked for some excellent head coaches in the NFL. This included Tom Coughlin, Marty Schottenheimer, Gunther Cunningham, Dick Vermeil, Herman Edwards, Norv Turner and Mike Zimmer. All the coaches I worked for have had a huge impact on me as a coach and as a man.

There are a couple things I would like to express in closing. The more things seem to change, the more clearly you understand the important things that have stood the test of time. Sound, basic principles of strength and conditioning are tried and true. I am all for sport science, Omega waves, force plates, GPS, etc., but they should be used to

Pro Bowl - 2008

improve the essentials of strength and conditioning, not to disprove, nullify or dispose of the principles that are the pillars of strength, power, and speed. You can never go wrong if you keep the basis of your program simple and effective, and never put good strength on a bad movement pattern.

To all you young gurus, please keep improving our field with "good" science. Respect those who helped establish our profession. Don't ever hesitate to take advantage of an opportunity to visit with an old head.

Don't be too impatient. Pay your dues. Volunteer, intern, be a graduate assistant. Make your boss as successful as possible.

And lastly, coach what you know, not what you think, or hope, may work in your program. Work hard to improve, learn, and keep our profession moving forward. Never lose sight that we are coaching people, not computers or machines.

Stay strong, my brothers in iron.

Jeff Hurd's Coaching Bio
- B.S., MS, CSCS, RSCC*E
- 1982 - Parker High School, High School Coach
- 1983-1984 - Fort Hays State University, Graduate Assistant Coach
- 1985-1986 - Delta State University, Strength and Conditioning Coach
- 1986-1987 - Clemson University, Graduate Assistant Strength Coach
- 1987-1993 - Western Michigan University, Head Strength and Conditioning Coach
- 1990, 1991, 1992 - Kansas City Chiefs, Volunteer Coach (training camps)
- 1993-1994 - Kansas City Chiefs, Strength and Conditioning

Intern Coach
- 1995 - Tulsa University, Head Strength and Conditioning Coach
- 1995-1998 - Jacksonville Jaguars, Assistant Strength and Conditioning Coach
- 1998-2007 - Kansas City Chiefs, Head Strength and Conditioning Coach
- 2003, 2006 - U.S. Military Special Forces, Consultant
- 2007-2013 - San Diego Chargers, Head Strength and Conditioning Coach
- 2013 - Dallas Cowboys Training Camp, Volunteer Coach,
- 2013-2014 - US Olympic Training Center, Volunteer Coach
- 2014-2017 - Minnesota Vikings, Assistant Strength and Conditioning Coach
- Current CEO of Hurd Performance, hurdperformance@gmail.com

CHAPTER 11

The Allan Johnson Story

Early Beginnings

I grew up in Parkersburg, West Virginia, a city of 40,000 people located at the confluence of the Ohio and Little Kanawha rivers. I was the son of hard-working, blue-collar parents, Charles and Evelyn Johnson. My dad was an electrician who worked in a factory for 45 years, and my mother operated and ran a bar. As a young kid, growing up, I watched my dad work multiple shifts at the factory five to six days per week, and then he went to work at the bar that he, my mother, and my grandfather owned, until closing. It was normal for my mother to be on her feet 12 to 15 hours a day at the bar, seven days a week. For me, it was school, playing sports, being around my two sisters and two brothers, going to the Boys Club, and spending time with my parents and grandfather at the bar. After the Boys Club closed, I would go to the bar and stay until it closed, and many nights I fell asleep on empty beer boxes. From these early beginnings, I saw what work ethic was all about and watched how my parents and grandfather handled different people, personalities and attitudes. Little did I know that I was building the foundation of hard work and learning how to create and develop relationships with people from all walks of life.

During my high school years, in the mid to late '70s, I played for some coaches who helped shape my thought process about strength training and what it meant to work hard to compete. Keep in mind, during this time strength training was new, and there was not much information out there. My high school coaches, Head Football Coach Daniel "Buddy" James and assistants Tim Swarr and Bill Boggess at Parkersburg High School, put us through the early beginnings of "circuit training," a grueling combination of bar exercises, running, jump rope, handball, and wrestling (sometimes against our football coaches, who used it to assess our mental toughness). Players who were mentally weak were exposed, and definitely weeded out. During my freshmen year, while playing baseball I broke my ankle sliding into home plate. For the next two years, I went through winter conditioning and "circuit" training only to be unable to play football due to health issues. My coaches and teammates wondered and questioned why I continued to put in all the work when I would not be able to play. It was then, the first day of my senior year, when we were running sprints at the end of practice, that I became light-headed and passed out on the field. I would recover and compete and win a starting offensive line position. The value of hard work and fighting through adversity during this time proved an invaluable insight into what the human body is capable of doing.

During my high school years, I met a man who would have a great influence on me for a lifetime, Rev. Charles Williams, the minister of my church. Charles was a big, strong man who was very fit and was always lifting, running, and was a black belt in karate. Rev. Williams not only shaped my faith, but also my mental approach to taking care of my body. He would always tell me that a strong mind equals a strong body and would challenge me to push my limits to become a stronger person physically, mentally and spiritually. The people that shape our lives and help us develop are all around us, if we are willing to listen.

I played small college, Division II football as an offensive guard and center at WV Tech, and that was where I really began to realize the importance of strength training. I met a teammate my freshmen year who really trained hard in the weight room. Dana Buckley was a big, strong offensive lineman, and he encouraged me to do extra workouts with him. We would spend countless hours doing extra bench and squat on our own. Our strength program at that time was a 24-station circuit, utilizing a Universal gym, barbells, sandbags, dumbbells, and eight to 10 large trash cans (to puke in if you needed to) with 60 seconds of work and 60 seconds of rest. A circuit long on strength endurance and short on strength and power. The coach I played for, Roy Lucas (brother of former Ohio State and NY Knicks Basketball player, Jerry Lucas) was an intense, take-no-prisoner type of coach. Being in shape, working hard, and bringing your best everyday was expected at all times.

After three years, I transferred to a school closer to home, Glenville State College, due to my mother's illness. We did not have a structured weight program, so any workouts to be done were all on me. We had one bench, one squat rack, two weight bars, a Universal multi-station machine, and about 400 pounds of free weights. It is here where I begin to utilize the Big Three more consistently in my training, with bench press, squat and power cleans. During my college years, to stay in shape during holiday and summer breaks, I would earn extra money unloading boxes out of tractor-trailers. I would unload one to two trailers in the wee hours of the night and fight extreme heat or cold temperatures daily. It was physically demanding and hard work, but it helped keep me strong, flexible, and driven.

The Passion Begins

My first coaching job out of college was at Federal Hocking High School in a small country town in Southeastern Ohio. I coached high school football, middle school track, and ninth grade basketball. I taught kindergarten through sixth-grade physical education at Coolville Elementary, still one of my favorite jobs during my career. The people were genuine, grounded and very friendly. During my three-year stint there, I had a football player, Glenn Singer, who one day missed the activity bus to take him home after lifting. He needed a ride home so myself and another coach gave him a ride. As we approached his house, we noticed tree stumps and different size axels off to the side of the barn. There were four to five stumps and two of them had two-by-fours nailed between them. I asked him if I was looking at his weight equipment and he said yes. I was amazed, and, at that moment, I knew that you could get an overload with any weighted implement if you were creative enough. On the days that he and his brother could not stay after school and lift with our Universal multi-station machine, curl bar, and four dumbbells, they had it covered with their makeshift weight equipment.

It was during my time in Southeastern Ohio that I started competitive powerlifting. During this time, I was competitive in the 220-pound class and competed regionally. During a power lifting meet in Charlottesville, Virginia, I met renowned powerlifter, strongman, and Hall of Fame Coach John Gamble. I knew then, watching him compete, that he was a man among boys, even back in those days.

During my third year teaching and coaching, I decided that I needed to pursue a master's degree and try to obtain a graduate assistantship. I applied for 60 positions throughout the country, and either received no response or was rejected by 59 schools to become a GA football coach. I pressed on, applied for one strength GA position, and secured one at West Virginia University. I got married one month before I was to report for fall camp in 1982 at WVU. A few days later, I found out that the GA position was not coming open, so I had to decide whether to go to WVU as a volunteer with the strength program or to find a teaching and coaching job.

I went to WVU and met one of my first mentors, Dave Vanhalanger. Dave was a former All-American Tackle for the Mountaineers and the first Strength Coach in school history. Dave was a great coach to learn from, and was very instrumental in teaching me his strength program utilizing the bench, squat, power clean, and deadlift, and the importance of faith, family, and motivating athletes. After one year with Coach Van, he left to work for Bobby Bowden at Florida State. Dave had it set up before he left to have me named as the interim

S&C Coach at WVU. After three months, at the age of 27, I was named the Director of Strength and Conditioning for 21 sports and was making $17,000. I was rich! I was so thankful that Coach Van, Head Football Coach Don Nehlen, Men's Basketball Coach Gale Catlett, and AD Fred Schaus believed in me and gave me a chance. Coach Nehlen, a College Football Hall of Fame inductee, was great to work for, and always told me get them strong and keep them healthy!

I got my start at WVU as the Head Strength Coach working with one GA, 21 teams, and three weight rooms, with the main facility being 3,000 square feet. Utilizing a progressive overload with the Big Three and Manual Resistance, I began developing the total athlete. I also began to use alternative-functional

WVU weight room - 1980

strength modes with car pushes, pushing army transport carriers, and moving tons of rock and gravel across parking lots. The athletes were great and were eager to improve their performance levels. During these early days of my career I fully appreciated the importance of training athletes to "bend to win."

During my tenure at WVU, in the 1980s, I had the good fortune to meet two people who would affect my training philosophy on weight training and speed training—Walt Evans, the Strength and Conditioning Coach for the Pittsburgh Steelers, and Dr. George Dintiman from Virginia Commonwealth University. Visiting Walt, I learned the importance of using progressive overload and adjusting the loads and volume to each player on a daily basis, and also the importance of nutrition. I first met George at Lock Haven University one Saturday when he was hosting a speed camp for athletes. I was attending the camp to observe and learn new techniques of speed training, but on this day, George was shorthanded for staff and I volunteered to help. This was the beginning of a 30-plus year friendship and mentorship.

I stayed at WVU for seven years, then accepted a position to become the third Strength Coach in MLB history with the Baltimore Orioles. My last game at WVU we played for the National Championship against Notre Dame, and then four days later it was off to Baltimore to prep for spring training in Sarasota Florida. Two months before leaving for the O's, I hired a young guy to be a GA for me, Mickey Marotti, and he still is one of the top strength coaches in the country, now at Ohio State University. WVU let me choose two candidates to interview for my position, Tim Wilson of the Chicago White Sox and Chip Sigmon, Head Strength Coach at Appalachian State University. Both men are still great friends to this day. It's funny how life is; Tim was very influential in me going to the Baltimore Orioles in 1989, and he and Chip, now more than 30 years later, are still very close friends. Life is truly about relationships and how you treat people!

While with the Orioles, I was responsible for six minor league teams and the major league team. I would set up the strength and conditioning programs for all the teams, and then I would fly all over the country to each minor league city and implement it. Back then, the athletic trainer would run the day-to-day strength program. At the major league level, with a 25-man roster and players who had different levels of weight room experience, exposure, and thoughts on training, I had to custom design each program, whether it was manual resistance, cuff weights, bands, dumbbells, bars, or Iso-Lateral equipment. When I first arrived, manual resistance, body weight, shoulder cuff exercises, and calisthenics were what players were doing. My manager was Hall of Fame Frank Robinson; he was old school but was supportive of what I was trying to do. While in Baltimore, I met the Ironman of Baseball, Cal Ripken, Jr., who would influence my training philosophy for baseball players forever. When I first arrived at my first spring training with the O's, I realized that in order to be accepted I had to get him on board with strength training. Initially, it was not easy, but I think I gradually wore him down and he began to trust that I would do everything in my power to keep him healthy. Once the

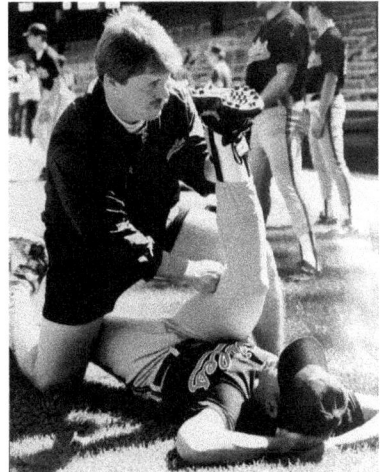

Baltimore Orioles - 1989

rest of the team saw that he bought in, the dam broke loose and players began to be more receptive to strength training and the idea that weights and baseball do mix. I loved my four years in baseball and the cast of characters I met and worked with. It was especially fun to have my son Adam around the clubhouse after home games and watch him learn baseball and interact with Oriole players at the age of three to six years old. From Frank Robinson, I learned humor. My only regret from being in baseball (and to this day still believe I was set up) was being the first strength and conditioning coach to ever be ejected from a game in my first season when we played the Royals in Kansas City. After four seasons of baseball, I returned to my roots of strength and conditioning at WVU.

Coming Home

Coming back to WVU to a 22,000 square foot weight room (at that time, the third biggest weight room in CFB) and to work for my old Head Football

Coach Don Nehlen was exciting. I loved WVU because the athletes were blue-collar and knew how to grind! When I left WVU the first time, we were working out of a shoebox of a weight room at 2,500 square feet, and now I was returning to a weight room the size of a barn. This time back, my staff now consisted of three assistants and three GAs to train 21 teams.

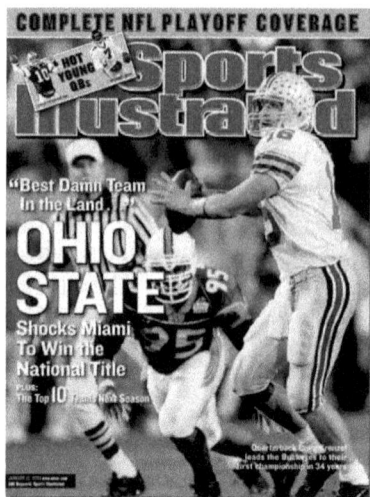

Ohio State - 2002 National Champions

After being back for eight years, I left and accepted a position with Coach Jim Tressel and the Ohio State Buckeyes and would go on to be part of a National Championship team that beat Miami in the 2002 Fiesta Bowl. The facility at Ohio State was 7,000 square feet and the equipment was older. People asked me the difference between the Buckeyes and the WVU Mountaineers athletically, and I tell them that the first day at OSU that I measured the vertical jump, I had four guys go over 40 inches, and 13 years at WVU I had only two guys over 40 inches. Unbelievable athletes to train and push!

After leaving Ohio State, I would go on to work in the private sector as a sports performance coach and a middle school athletic director for five years. I did not really enjoy being an AD, because I was disappointed in my coach's ability to lead, organize, communicate and motivate. I felt like I was an electrician trying to be a plumber, and really missed the college setting of the same colors, same mission, and being part of one unit.

In 2011, I accepted a position at Northwestern as an assistant strength coach under one of my former GAs at OSU, Jay Hooten. Along with Jay and Head Football Coach Pat Fitzgerald it was a memorable three years.

I accepted the position at East Tennessee State University, who were restarting football after dropping it 12-years earlier. Coach Lee Morrow, a great friend who was the former ETSU Strength Coach, recommended me for the job to Coach Carl Torbush, and I am forever indebted to both of them for the great opportunity I was provided. Coach Torbush was awesome to work for and he realized the importance of the strength and conditioning program. Coach Torbush retired in 2017, and ETSU hired former Tennessee, Kentucky, and Florida State Assistant Coach Randy Sanders. I am excited for the future and leadership Coach Sanders brings to the ETSU Football program. I have had the privilege to work with not only some great athletes but also great coaches: Don Nehlen, Jim Tressel, Pat Fitzgerald, Randy Sanders, Frank Robinson, Gale

Catlett, Tony Skole, and Greg VanZant. I've had some excellent assistants and GA's: Dave Lawson, Holly Cole, Mike Joseph, Mickey Marotti, Butch Reynolds, Bernardo Amerson, Jay Hooten, Karen Brannick, Bruce Hayhurst, Jim Hopkins, Brett Rice, Daniel Wedding, Ben Rabe, Dylan Leffingwell, Rob Kohlhaus, Marcus Kinney, Corey Benson, and Connor Myers. To everyone who has been a part of my career, I want to say thank you for all your effort and dedication to excellence. Also, I would like to give a special thanks to Chuck Stiggins, Executive Director of the Collegiate Strength and Conditioning Association, who had an unbelievable vision to create the CSCCa in 2000. There were so many, that affected my life and career and I hope in some small way I did the same for them.

My Principles
- I am a firm believer that you can't coach if you can't teach!
- Bring energy and be positive every day; the athletes feed off you!
- Challenge the athletes you work with every workout to see improvement.
- You have to keep the bar raised high every day and never lower your standards of excellence.
- Be the same person every day. If not, the athlete's wont trust you and give you their best.
- Coaching is not only a science, it is definitely an art; can you motivate the unmotivated, and can you motivate athletes to take their preparation to a championship level every workout?
- Successful coaching is about building relationships with your athletes.
- To be a successful in any chosen field or endeavor you must never stop learning!

In my 32-plus years of coaching, I have never had a *job*; it has always been a *passion*! Even today, I have never dreaded waking up at 4 a.m. for a 6 a.m. workout group. I have been so fortunate to be in this profession all these years, and not one day goes by that I take what I do for granted. We as strength coaches must always have an attitude of leaving the soil richer than we found it. We are one of the few professions left that can still impact and influence America's youth.

Bring it every day and change lives!

Allan Johnson's Coaching Bio
- 1982-1988, 1992-2001 - West Virginia University, Director of Strength and Conditioning (21 sports)

- 1989-1992 - Baltimore Orioles, Director of Sports Performance, (Six Minor League Teams and Major League Team)
- 2001-2005 - Ohio State University, Director of Football Strength and Conditioning
- 2012-2014 - Northwestern University, Assistant Director of Football Performance
- Currently Director of Football Strength & Conditioning at East Tennessee State University
- Currently in 32nd Year of Coaching at Collegiate Level

Professional Certifications

- Certified with CSCCa (SCCC), NSCA (CSCS), and NASE
- Original Member of CSCCa Board of Directors (2000)
- Member of CSCCa Board of Directors (2000-2005)
- Master Strength and Conditioning Coach (MSCC) with CSCCa (2002)

Achievements & Honors

- 2002 - National Strength Coach of the Year by the NFL Strength & Conditioning Coaches Association
- 2003 - Inducted into the USA Strength/Conditioning Coaches Hall of Fame
- 2006-Present - Training and Conditioning Magazine, Editorial Board
- 2010 - Elected into the Mid-Ohio Valley Sports Hall of Fame
- Six-Time Recipient of the Big East Conference Strength and Conditioning Coach of the Year
- Speaker at several national seminars, clinics and conferences

THANK YOU COACHES

CYTØSPORT®
BRAND

CHAPTER 12

CYTOSPORT™
The Mike Pickett Story,
Founder of CYTOSPORT™

My family has been deeply involved in the nutrition business since the '50s. We're nutritional guys, protein people, it's what we've always known and what we've always done. My grandfather was one of the original pioneers. He started working in the nutrition business in 1958, and my father got started working with his father in the mid-'60s, when he was 18. Together they created a variety of nutritional products as a family business. When they sold the business in the '70s, the company was producing seven out of 10 protein powders on retail shelves. After the sale, my father got involved in an early sport nutrition company called Champion Nutrition.

When I was in high school, getting ready to go to college, my dad came to me and said, "I'd like you to get involved in the family business. I'll teach you everything you need to know, and I think we can have a lot of fun together. It's a rewarding business; you're helping people do better things for their lives, be healthier, and achieve their dreams. I think you'll really enjoy it."

I took him up on it. I skipped going to college, and went to a "college of my father," who taught me all the ins and outs of the business. I started sweeping floors and working on the production line. Through this, my father taught me how to work hard, and I worked through the business from the ground floor. This experience was invaluable, and when I got the ability and the opportunity to run the business, I knew every aspect. And now my oldest son is doing the exact same thing. He's working with us, he's working in the lab, he's working in production. He's learning the way that I did.

My dad and his father taught me a few things that I use as my guard rails to this day.

1. **Make quality products:** Never sacrifice the quality of the product. Ever. People remember the quality of the product far longer than they remember the price, so make really great products and never violate the trust of your customer.

2. **Do what you say you are going to do:** Be fair and be straightforward.

3. **Take care of your customers:** At the end of the day, the person who really owns your brand is the consumer, so you have to take care of your customers.

4. **Make sure you deliver quality products to the end user:** always take care of your distribution partners to make sure your product gets to your customers.

Working alongside my dad, I admired his amazing ability to identify where he thinks markets are going and his ability to make terrific products that taste great, with high quality and functionality. He's been doing that since he was 18 years old. We discovered that I have a talent for building relationships, so I went out and ran the manufacturing and the sales end of our business. We developed into a family team—my dad designed great products, I manufactured and sold them, and my sister was in and control of the branding and the marketing—and we came together to build one heck of a brand. I think we did as well or better than anybody in this business, and I appreciate my dad for giving me the opportunity and teaching me.

Grabbing a Tiger by the Tail

In 1997, my father and I left Champion Nutrition to form CYTOSPORT™, with the idea that if we could make great nutritional products for people and create a $20 million business, we'd have a nice family business that we could enjoy. Our company took its name from our first product, CYTOMAX®, an exercise recovery drink that bikers, triathletes, and marathoners used to reduce lactic acid. CYTOMAX® gave us sales to start off with, and ways into retailers that helped us with our later products—Complete Whey, CytoGainer®, and of course the Muscle Milk® Brand.

We struggled along in the beginning, making private-label proteins for other companies until we created Complete Whey. You could actually drop it into water, and it mixed thoroughly with a blender. Now all proteins mix in, but my dad was among the first one to do that, in a big way.

After Complete Whey, we created a product called CytoGainer®, which became one of the popular products for football players and athletes trying to gain ten or fifteen pounds. CytoGainer® was a protein shake with 900 calories, low sugar, and low fat. It really took off with a lot of help from GNC, Vitamin

Shoppe, and of course Europa Sports.

My dad started wondering why infants on breast milk grew leaner and faster than infants on formula. What we found out is that mother's milk has a lot of really cool qualities, and a lot of fat and carbohydrates, which was different from anything that had been on the market. This inspired a product called Muscle Milk®. At the time, everything in the marketplace was low carbohydrate. And my dad just didn't believe that was the right way; we had to have everything in ratios. It was 32 grams of protein, 18 grams of fat, and 12 grams of carbohydrate.

Another interesting thing about Muscle Milk® was that Muscle Milk® could be used however you wanted to use it. Most proteins were, and are, for a specific use. Muscle Milk® was, and still is, used for weight loss, building muscle, a healthy snack, grab-and-go nutrition. It is a great product for different people's needs at different times. So, Muscle Milk® is a protein supplement, but doesn't necessarily fit in a specific category, which was very different then, and still is today.

Most people in the nutrition business said, "It will never sell." They felt that even though Muscle Milk® tasted unbelievable, it wouldn't sell because you had to have no or low carbohydrates. Boy, they couldn't have been more wrong. When we came out with Muscle Milk® it just started taking off, like something we had never imagined. And within two or three years of introducing Muscle Milk®, we got that little guy up to $60 million in sales.

My dad said that if we really wanted to make a difference in this business and we wanted more people to enjoy a quality product, we needed to make an RTD, which meant "ready to drink protein." It took us about two years, and we were able to make a really great tasting, quality protein shake that was ready to go in a tetra pack. Once again, when introduced, most people said, "Oh, people aren't going to do that. It's pretty expensive. They don't mind using their blenders, etc." Very quickly, we couldn't keep up with demand.

Up to that point, our products were being sold in the specialty channel—health food stores, gyms, GNCs, etc.—but we had never gone to broader market retailers—Safeway, Costco, 7-11. When distributors reached out to sell Muscle Milk® in mass channels, we couldn't believe it. I didn't think someone would walk into a 7-11 and pay five dollars for a protein shake. That seemed like an awful lot of money. Much to our surprise, Muscle Milk® took off.

When we got product into Safeway, my dad suggested we all get in the car and go see if our product was on the shelves yet. There it was. My dad started getting teary-eyed. We could not have dreamed that big. When we saw a guy in the aisle buying a four-pack, my dad actually chased him down and gave him the money for the purchase. Seeing a general consumer buy it was like a validation. It started to pop up everywhere. We never, ever, in a million years thought that we would see Muscle Milk® in airports. To this day, when I find myself in a Hudson News and I see Muscle Milk® in a cooler, I'll start adjusting them to make sure the Muscle Milk® is facing out. We were happy selling product in gyms. We never thought we would see the shelves of almost every retail location that sold drinks. I still can't believe it.

About this time, we decided to get into the beverage business. We started signing all sorts of beverage distributors across the country. Around the same time, we got inbound calls from Coke and Pepsi. They were looking to get healthier products on their trucks. We formed a partnership with Pepsi Bottling Group, and they distribute Muscle Milk® on Pepsi trucks across the country. Pepsi was an amazing partner, and this partnership changed our business, and really changed protein in this country forever. Every day, about 25,000 trucks went out on the streets, and everywhere you saw Pepsi you started seeing Muscle Milk®. That fundamentally changed the way people saw sports nutrition and protein in the retail market in this country.

Around the same time that we established this broader distribution channel, we got heavily involved in college sports. We loved colleges, there is so much loyalty. When you have brand signage all over these schools and athletes using your product, there's affinity and loyalty being built. We got a lot of distribution on and around campuses because we were part of the schools' athletic communities. We made special commemorative bottles with the school logo and sold them in the marketplace. The college program was really important to us and elevated the brand. We signed major colleges, USC being one of our first, and then Cal, Stanford, Ohio State, and others followed. Then came athletes. We had relationships with Steph Curry, Clay Matthews, Clayton Kershaw, and many others. We didn't pay them much in comparison to other beverage deals; they did it mostly for the product, because it's healthy for them and part of their training regimen.

Our business went from $0 with hopes of having a $20 million business to doing about $430 million in sales. We got a lot of cool accolades: Small Beverage Company of the Year, One of the 25 most innovative companies, Best Functional Beverage, and many more. We had this tiger by the tail, but we could barely hang on. It was really an amazing experience.

Four years ago, we sold our business to Hormel, one of the greatest CPG companies in the world. It was bittersweet, I'd say, for everybody involved. We were sad as a family; we had an amazing culture, 350 employees, everybody loved our business. But at the end of the day, we sold our business and did really well for our family. My sister and I stayed on for two years to transition the business. While we still check in, we're now making flavors at a company call Flavor Insights, enjoying ourselves, working as a family, and working will some old friends, trying to help them make great tasting products.

CYTOSPORT™ and Strength Coaches

We loved working with the colleges because we got to work with the strength coaches. One of the very first strength coaches that I got to work with was Garrett Giemont, who was with the Oakland Raiders. He was a terrific strength coach, one of the best in the business. Garrett was battling with young athletes that are very gifted and working out hard, but it's hard for them to get proper nutrition. A strength coach can tell them all that he wants them to do. You can work them out, you can train them, and then they go off, and what do they eat? What a lot of nutritional guys are doing is making sure they hand their athletes protein shakes the minute a practice is over, so at least they're getting proper nutrition in their bodies at the proper time of need.

Working with strength coaches was really powerful for us in that we really were aiding them and trying to make sure that they could do their job in a complete way. We were like the final cog. You've got a great athlete, you give them great training, and then at the end of the day you have to give them proper nutrition to finish. That's what Muscle Milk® and CYTOSPORT™ came to do, to help the strength coaches give their athletes the nutrition they needed. High protein. They don't need a lot of sugar. They don't need a lot of carbohydrates. What they needed was protein to recover, and that's what we provided, and that's what we were about. I really think we were there to aid and help them finish their job and give athletes the proper nutrients to recover and be ready to compete the next day, week, or hour.

We listened to the strength coaches. When we first did protein flavors, there was chocolate, vanilla, strawberry. It was a couple strength coaches that said their athletes would love having proteins without having to put them in a blender and add all the carbohydrates and sugars. They also asked for other flavors, and we created banana cream, root beer float, blueberry, piña colada.

We got into all sorts of areas due in part to our association with strength coaches. They told us their needs and goals, and we came up with solutions. They would say, "hey, I could use a gainer that is like this." We would listen and incorporate their feedback into products, and those products became very successful. We made a product called Fast Twitch, a caffeinated product that helped their athletes in the pre-workout area. We made glucosamine products for their joints to try to help them recover and have less joint pain. We used all that input from strength coaches to make amazing products that we took to market. The general public got to enjoy them because of the input from strength coaches all over the country, and they were a really valuable part of the relationships we developed at CYTOSPORT™.

We were trusted. The most common way most athletes will take your product is through the strength coach, because the athlete listens to the strength coach, and we worked really hard at those relationships to build trust. Any time someone hands an athlete something to put in their bodies it's a huge amount of trust. We took that very seriously. CYTOSPORT™ was one of the first companies to achieve NSF Sport Certification—which guaranteed there are no banned substances in the products—because we felt that the trust of the athlete was everything. When that happens, it's great for everybody—teams win games and athletes achieve their goals. We can help give them longevity and help prevent injuries. So, strength coaches were a critical part of what we did, and those relationships were everlasting and really important to us.

At the end of the day, the CYTOSPORT™ slogan was "Driven by science and inspired by performance." And we really enjoyed making efficacious, quality products that help people live healthier lives and help their dreams and aspirations come true. And CYTOSPORT™ made nutritional products for athletes and people all over the country and all over the world that helped them achieve their goals. CYTOSPORT™ brought protein, which everybody knew they needed, but made it taste good so that the average person would enjoy drinking it. It was cool, it was fun. We changed the marketplace, and the way people viewed drinks. Now you have functional beverages all over the place, products with amino acids, proteins, probiotics, fiber. Everything in the category has to have some kind of added function, and I think we were part of that. The protein part of that function, which I think is the most important. We were able to help change that landscape because we were able to help bring healthy, great tasting drinks to the masses through convenience and distribution. This functional beverage thing is for real. People read labels. They want to know what's in their products and they want more (or less) from their food and beverage choices. At the end of the day, that was what made our family and CYTOSPORT™ very successful.

Note: Mike Pickett is no longer employed by or associated with CYTOSPORT™

STRONG FEELS GOOD™

MUSCLE MILK®
BRAND

CHAPTER 13

The Kent Johnston Story

All of our lives are defined by the opportunities given to us. How we accept and take hold of the opportunities determine in large part our success or failure. Some of the greatest regrets, looking back over one's life, are the opportunities that were presented that we did not embrace because of ignorance or fear. Coaching is no different, in this regard, than any other profession.

Beginnings - High School

My coaching journey began in the summer of 1978 as a high school coach in Teague, Texas. It came down to two choices of vocational career for me—pastor or coach. I settled on coach. My desire was to be a positive influence in the lives of young men and do it through the platform of sports and athletics. In reflection, it was never a goal to reach the NFL or be a part of a major college program. There was always great contentment in coaching high school athletes. This is an important aspect of goal-oriented coaching. Always set your goals around your players and athletes. If you do a good job with them, then others will often notice your work. This will enhance your opportunities to reach secondary goals such as advancement in your career. Advancing to college and the pro ranks occurred in my journey simply by meeting the right people, working hard, remaining loyal, and most of all trusting the Lord to guide my path.

The late '70s and early '80s mark the genesis of the Strength and Conditioning coaching position. Initially, I coached football, basketball, and track. It was my responsibility to provide and oversee lifting and conditioning of the various sports. Weight training had been a love and hobby of mine for some time. As a young man in high school, I had been greatly influenced by a fellow member and mentor in my church named Sonny Bowden, who introduced me to weight lifting. Sonny was well built and hard working. He invited me to work out with him in his home gym and taught me how to squat, bench press, and perform a wide variety of body building exercises. These were new concepts to me since high school coaches in that day primarily presented us with two options for weight lifting: no lifting at all or The Universal Gym. The Universal Gym was a multi-station piece of equipment that took the country by storm in the 1970s. It was simply a series of selectorized plate exercise stations built into a single unit. This piece allowed coaches to provide strength training to their athletes with no coaching and little risk of injury. Universal also did a great job of marketing this piece of equipment to coaches across America. I always have been grateful to Sonny for actually teaching me how to perform exercises with correct technique.

In 1978, I took home a little over 600 dollars a month for coaching various sports, teaching five classes, and handling the duties of a strength and conditioning coach. I was not married at this time, so it was much easier to make ends meet financially.

The Small College Years

One of the turning points of my career occurred in 1979 when I met one of the greatest mentor figures in my life, Al Miller, a high school and college coach. In the late '70s, Al had taken a job at a training center in Waco Texas. He was hired by the owner to run and manage the center. I had moved and was coaching at a high school near Waco and was a member of the center Al ran. We immediately hit it off. Al recognized me as a hungry young coach who knew very little but was willing to work. I became his test subject for new programs he developed and wanted to implement. Little did I know that Al would soon become the Head Strength and Conditioning Coach for Paul "Bear" Bryant at the University of Alabama. As time passed, Al recommended that I consider taking a job at Northwestern State College in Louisiana. Al had coached there previously and had a connection with the head coach, A.L. Williams. Within a few months, I was in Louisiana coaching defensive ends as a graduate assistant and handling Northwestern Louisiana's strength and conditioning program. One of the players I coached there, Barry Rubin, would also come to play a profound role in my career in later years. Barry was my assistant at Green Bay in the mid 1990s.

We had a very talented football team at Northwestern Louisiana. This opened doors for assistant coaches. Our Linebacker coach, Ronnie Alexander, was hired as the defensive coordinator at University of Louisiana at Monroe. Ronnie invited me to go with him and assistant with the defensive backs and manage the strength and conditioning program at Monroe. This was still in the capacity of graduate assistant, but I was promised that I would be hired as the first full-time strength and conditioning coach at a future date. This was where my coaching compass had been shifting towards, so I was content to remain a graduate assistant coach for that time period of my life.

It is important to mention that in most cases it is vital to consider the reality of financial sacrifice when working towards your first full-time strength and conditioning or athletic performance job. There were two reasons that I was able to do this. First, my parents. I did my best to live frugally and on little, but my parents stood in the gap for me financially when I was broke. Second, was simply a willingness to live on very little.

I enjoyed the time spent at Monroe, however, I would soon experience one of the biggest disappointments of my young coaching career however. In late spring of 1980, Pat Collins, the head coach, called me in and revealed the news. Pat had decided to hire a more knowledgeable and more experienced head strength coach. His name was Al Miller. Reality hit me square in the face. What could I say? Everything that Pat said was true. My only disappointment was that he broke his word to me, but I did not dwell on it. We will all have to deal with disappointments. Put them behind you and continue to move forward. Coach Miller was hired at his alma mater, the University of Louisiana Monroe in 1980. He left Mississippi State in order to return home. I was happy for him.

A Short Stint in High School

In 1981, I returned to Teague High School as defensive coordinator and strength and conditioning coach. My expectations were to remain a high school coach for the remainder of my coaching career. There is a word that needs to be said about Texas High School coaches. I have known many that are better coaches than a number that I coached with in the NFL. They were simply never presented with the same opportunity that many in the NFL were. This idea that the "cream of the crop" coaches reside in the NFL and college is fictitious. I spent one year there before moving to the Houston area and taking a high school job at Willis High School. It was while coaching at Willis that my career was about to take a major turn.

Roll Tide

Al Miller called me in 1982 and asked if I would be interested in working as his graduate assistant at the University of Alabama. Al was the head strength and conditioning coach at the time. I jumped at the opportunity to become a part of the legendary Paul "Bear" Bryant's Crimson Tide. Coach Miller, for the second time, became the man that offered me opportunity in my coaching career. I will always be grateful to Al Miller for all he did for me. He was a man's man.

Shortly after I arrived in Tuscaloosa, Coach Bryant passed away. Alabama was devastated by the event. The new Alabama coach, whom Coach Bryant had selected to take over the program, was Ray Perkins. Ray left the New York

Giants to take over the Alabama program. Ray also played a major role in influencing my coaching career and we worked well together. I learned and grew in the strength and conditioning profession by watching and listening to Al.

As we approached the beginning of spring football in 1983, Al encouraged me to talk to Ray Perkins about working with football as well. I went to Coach Perkins and explained my coaching background, and he told me that

Coaching at the University of Alabama.

I would be the defensive staff's graduate assistant for football. In those days, there were only two graduate assistants in the football program – an offensive and defensive G.A. I continued to help Coach Miller until Ray gave him another graduate assistant spot and moved me full-time to football for the football seasons. My goal was to work as hard as I could for Ken Donahue, our defensive coordinator, and Coach Perkins. Money was hard to come by. My earnings amounted to just over $200 a month. It was hard to make ends meet from month to month. Coach Perkins found ways to help me though. He was good to me when he did not have to be.

It was at this point that I began to contemplate which direction I truly desired to go as a coach—football or strength and conditioning. My first love was the strength and conditioning field, but Coach Perkins had given me the responsibility of coaching the corner back position under Secondary Coach Louis Campbell. Coach Perkins felt I had a future in coaching football and I had been given favor with him. Over the course of time, it became very clear to me that strength and conditioning was the route I would go if given the opportunity.

In the spring of 1985, Al Miller was offered the strength and conditioning job with the Denver Broncos. I hated to see my mentor leave but was excited for him to have the opportunity to work in the NFL. Al encouraged me to talk to Coach Perkins about taking over the strength and conditioning program for him. I did just that and Ray told me I was in the mix for the job. The day soon came when he called me into his office and said, "Do you see that stack of papers on my desk?" I replied, "Yes sir." He went on to say, "Those are all resumes of the people who have applied for the job that I am going to give you." I do not remember what I replied but I do remember the feeling of thankfulness and amazement that it was actually happening. In 1985, I became the head strength and conditioning coach at Alabama. It was beyond my wildest dreams and expectations.

Going Pro

At the end of the 1986 football season, Ray Perkins left Alabama to become the head football coach for the Tampa Bay Buccaneers. Ray again became a major influence in my coaching career when he asked me to go with him as head strength and conditioning coach of the Bucs. I was 30 years old. He warned me that it would be a major challenge because of my age, but he thought I was up for the challenge. I loved every minute of my opportunity at Tampa. As I recall my salary was around $34,000 for the first two years I worked in Tampa. In those days, I had no assistant. I was responsible for nutrition, return to play, and the strength and conditioning of the team year around, and coaching tight ends.

We were not really successful over the five years I spent in Tampa, but I became friends with a number of players—Vinny Testaverde, Steve Deberg, Randy "Bubba" Grimes, and one of my closest friends to this day, Joe Ferguson. It was a great blessing to be in Tampa those five years. I made a lot of mistakes but also learned a lot of lessons from them. When my boss was replaced by Sam Wyche as head coach in 1992, I was not retained.

The Mike Holmgren Years

Mike Holmgren was named the head coach of the Green Bay Packers in 1992. He hired me as his strength and conditioning coach. Our first year together we just missed the playoffs, going 9-7. I learned a lot of lessons that first year in Green Bay. In those days we had a 14-week off-season program and one mini-camp for veterans. The first off-season we had eight players who participated in the voluntary off-season program. Green Bay was not a place that a lot of the players wanted to volunteer to spend the off-season. To try to change this lack of participation, we started an off-season traveling basketball team. I was in charge of the team and we scheduled about 40 games each off-season. Players could make anywhere from $500 to $1500 a week. In order to play in the games, they had to get in four days a week of off-season training at our facility

Back Row: (L to R) - Marty Mornhinweg, Tom Lovat, Harry Sydney, Mike Holmgren, Johnny Holland, Kent Johnston, Bob Valesente. Front Row: (L to R) - Andy Reid, Gil Haskell, Sherman Lewis, Nolan Cromwell, Fritz Shurmur, Jim Lind, Larry Brooks

Green Bay Packers coaching staff - 1996

Reggie White and I during our Packer days.

in Green Bay. I would estimate that our attendance tripled once word spread.

Mike Holmgren was great to work for, and working for him made me a better coach. Mike called me up to his office after our first season together and did something for me that changed my career. He told me that he wanted me to seek out the best of the best in regard to performance training or rehabilitation. He told me to set up meetings with the expert individual and the Packers would pay them for their time. I did this for the next 12 years that I worked for Coach Holmgren. I visited performance specialists, nutritionists, return to play experts, and soft tissue professionals. This made me a better coach, and also allowed new concepts to be introduced to the teams that Mike and I coached over the years. We coached together at Green Bay and Seattle for 12 years. I also worked for him for three years in Cleveland, where he was the President. All performance specialists know that having the right head football coach is crucial to having any success. Mike Holmgren was a great blessing to me as both a man and coach.

Winding Down

I have always wanted to be a man that did not retire, but simply shifted gears. We do not really have the luxury to make such decisions for much of our lives, but the good Lord has been merciful and gracious to me. I spent the final four years of my NFL career with the San Diego Chargers. They were great years.

Our work is really about the people we work with. Mike McCoy, Philip Rivers, Mike Windt, and my fellow strength and conditioning coach Rick Lyle, among others, made it fun to go to work. Always look to surround yourself with good people as much as it is in your hand to do so. In 2016, my boss was fired from his position as head coach. I followed him out the door within a week. If you stay in the business of coaching long enough, you will probably see times in which you will be fired and times in which you will sit at the top of the heap. Hold both times loosely. Your vocational life should never be defined by the W-L column, but by the people you have the opportunity to work with.

Lessons learned along the way

- How you treat people is *always* more important than plans, methods, and victories.
- Be thankful for every opportunity but proceed with caution.
- Keep learning.
- Be content where you are—put your hand to the plow you have—trust the Lord for outcomes.
- Submit to authority. Until you learn to do this, you will not be able to exert authority or even understand it.
- The green grass on the other side of the fence is not always what it

seems to be.
- Establish your principles but don't consider them to be absolute truth. Opinions, at best, are experiential or educated guessing, or both.
- Realize that time is your most valuable and costly commodity.
- Always honor your fellow coaches and co-workers.
- Don't waste your time on the fellow that has it all figured out.

Kent Johnston's Coaching Bio
- 1983- 1987 - University of Alabama, Assistant Football and Head Strength and Conditioning Coach
- 1987- 1992 - Tampa Bay Buccaneers, Head Strength and Conditioning Coach
- 1992-1999 - Green Bay Packers, Head Strength and Conditioning Coach
- 1999-2003 - Seattle Seahawks, Head Strength and Conditioning Coach
- 2004-2006 - University of Alabama, Coordinator of Strength and Conditioning Department
- 2006-2010 - Young Champions Academy, Owner of Childhood Development Center
- 2010-2013 - Cleveland Browns, Head Strength and Conditioning Coach
- 2013-2017 - San Diego Chargers, Head Strength and Conditioning Coach

Achievements & Honors
- 1995 - NFL President's Award
- 1996 - NFL Strength and Conditioning Coach of the Year
- 2005 - Strength and Conditioning National Hall of Fame

Personal
- Married wife Pam in 1987
- We have 4 sons: Kody, Kole, Clay, Cade
- Reside in Central Texas near Waco

CHAPTER 14

The Dana LeDuc Story

I was born March 22, 1953 in Tacoma, Washington, attended Marymount Military Academy, graduated from Washington High School in 1971 and took a track scholarship to the University of Kansas. After one year I transferred to UTEP and then on to the University of Texas where I would stay for the next 20 years. During my college years I was surrounded by some of the greatest athletes and weight room technicians in the history of track and field—Karl Salb (6 time NCAA shot put champion and Pan American Games champion), Bruce Wilhelm (great Kansas shot putter), Jim McGoldrick (NCAA discus champion and Highland Games world champion), and Bishop Dolegiewicz (Canadian Olympian in the shot put and competitor in the World's Strongest Man Contest). Prior to my senior year, I took a semester off to train at Spoon Barbell Club in Dallas with founder Tom Witherspoon, Sammy Walker (1976 Olympian) and Jim Napier (Pan American Games champion). In 1973, during my red shirt year at Texas, I represented the USA at the World University Games which were held in the Soviet Union and finished fifth place in the shot put. We were there for roughly 18 days, during which I had a chance to weight train with some of the greatest young throwers and Olympic lifters in the world and learn techniques and philosophies on training from athletes of many different countries. I continued to throw the shot put and discus throughout my years at Texas and in my senior year, 1976, I won the NCAA shot put championship.

Up to this time, football players at UT were for the most part discouraged from lifting weights for fear that they would become too tight and lose their speed and agility. The only athletes using the small weight room (located in a non-air-conditioned room on the second floor of the stadium) were about five of us throwers. A few of the football players could hear us lifting and dropping weights from the second floor, became curious about what we were doing, and

UT weight room - early 1970s

began to come into the weight room. Some of these players were interested in learning how to power clean and do the explosive lifts that we were doing. After a period of time, these players gained functional weight and became much more powerful. You could see their confidence growing. When I was about to graduate, Charlie Craven—who worked in the PE department and was in charge of the Texas athletics rehabilitation program (a pioneer in strength and conditioning)—knew that a few of these players were training with us and spoke with Head Football Coach Darrell Royal about hiring me to be their first strength coach. Coach Royal called me in and told me that he was the first to hire a brain coach (academic counselor Lan Hewlett) back in 1956 so he may as well be one of the first to hire a weight coach, "whatever that is." This job changed my life forever and for this I can never thank Charlie Craven, Darrell Royal and The University of Texas enough.

My starting pay was the same as a first-year school teacher: $10,000 a year. I was hired to be the strength coach for football, but one by one most of the men's head coaches came to the weight room to visit me about training their teams. Not long thereafter, the new women's athletic director came to me and offered me one month's salary ($834) to train the women's athletes for the year. A year or so later I was asked to run the physical training class for the UT system police academy. This would be two 12-week courses, one fall and one spring. They ran from 5 a.m. to 6 a.m. and the pay was to be $750 for each course. My weekday hours at UT in those early days would start at 5 a.m. and normally finish at 7 p.m., Saturday was a five-hour day and Sunday was a day of rest. It was a lot of work for little pay compared with today's salaries, but I loved every minute of it.

In 1981 I hired my first grad-assistant, Robbie Robinson, and by the time I left in 1993 I had two full-time assistants and five grad assistants to help train all sports plus a part-time secretary. One of the benefits of being involved in the shot-put at a high level was that I was always around athletes who were the best in the business and, as an athlete, that kept me hungry. When I became a coach, I surrounded myself with high-quality coaches who knew as much if not more than I did about weight training for all sports. I felt that being surrounded by these knowledgeable coaches would only help to make our program better. Among the assistants that I hired were Oskar Jakobsson, an Icelandic Olympic shot putter and excellent weight room technician, and Angel Spassov, a world-class strength coach from Bulgaria who had coached all throughout Europe including the eastern block countries. I was never threatened by their vast levels of knowledge, only intrigued, and wanted to bring together the best coaching staff that I could for our athletes at UT. All decisions that were made in the weight room were made together as a staff.

As I stated earlier, the weight room at UT was very small, not air-conditioned, and had very little equipment. In the fall of 1976, Coach Royal asked me, the head trainer Frank Medina, and Dr. Craven to visit the Nautilus weightlifting equipment plant in Deland, Florida to see about purchasing some equipment. It seemed as though every football powerhouse in the country was purchasing this new weightlifting equipment and Coach Royal decided that UT football would be a part of this also. This was the first step towards a new strength and conditioning program for all sports at UT.

We now had brand new nautilus equipment but were still very archaic with other equipment. There were two wooden 4x4 power racks, 1 wooden 2x12 standup, 45-degree incline press, and two wooden benches that we would slide into the power racks to do our pressing. All 3 Olympic bars that we had were bent and all of the plates were metal (some chipped), and we had no bumper plates. My first move was to convince our assistant athletic director, Coach Bill Ellington, that we needed six benches and six inclines (which I was able to get built in downtown Austin for $75 each thanks to Mike Graham at the Texas Athletics Club). I was going to need a total of $900 for this purchase. Coach pulled out his bottom right drawer, looked at his ledger and said "Dana, I think we can afford that." I said, "Coach, I have a few more things on my wish list like weightlifting belts, a chalk tray with chalk, 14 new power bars, and three new Olympic weightlifting bars with

Myself and Mac Wilkens - late 1970s

bumper plates. And by the way, we will need to add on to our platform so that we will have room for three athletes to power clean at the same time." Coach looked at me and said "Dana, let's do it."

Eight years later there was talk of a new football complex and weight room to be built at the south end of the stadium. I began to research the best equipment we could purchase anywhere in the world. In 1985, my assistant Oskar Jacobson and I flew to Europe to visit weight lifting equipment companies and were in roughly 15 countries in 30 days throughout Scandinavia and Europe. We visited Eleiko and Uddeholm in Sweden, Leoko and David in Finland, Berg and Schnell in Germany, Pignatti in Italy, and then Eagle Cybex, Sampson and Universal in the USA. We were able to negotiate with a few these companies and bought directly from them while the American dollar was strong against their currency. I thank Doyle Wilson, a local home builder, for taking us in his private jet and making this a once-in-a-lifetime trip. Today UT continues to have a state-of-the-art weight room in the Nassar Al-Rashid weight room with all the best equipment any athlete could ever want.

In 1993, I had an opportunity to coach at the University of Miami and just as it was at UT, my assistant and I were responsible for all sports. I left a beautiful, brand-new facility at Texas to go to Miami where the facilities needed some help. It just goes to show you that in some cases facilities aren't everything because UM had been and still was one of the greatest college football programs and we had some of the greatest college athletes that I had ever been around (Ray Lewis and Warren Sapp to name a few).

In 1995, I got to head home to the Seattle Seahawks only 30 miles from where I grew up. The NFL was a whole new experience but one that I loved just as much as college. I was now coaching only one sport and was able to hire an assistant after two years. Just like at Miami, the weight room in Seattle was very small. We had to run the rookies and first-year players early in the morning to make room for the veterans during the prime time. I stayed in Seattle for four years. In 1998, after 22 years in the business, I got fired along with the rest of our coaching staff in Seattle. Dick Vermeil gave me an opportunity to come to the St. Louis Rams, and my first season we won the World Championship. What a thrill! During those 10 years I went to two Super Bowls, playoff games and had the privilege of training "the greatest show on turf" along with many eventual Hall of Fame players. I lasted through five head coaches, three full-time and two interim. In 2009 I retired after 32 years of working as a strength and conditioning coach. Since then, I have volunteered with young athletes in St. Charles, Missouri, Austin, Texas, and in Hoquiam, Washington, where I co-founded a non-profit organization and fundraiser for youth athletics in Grays Harbor County.

My early association with athletes and coaches from around the world exposed me to the concept of periodization, a year-long training plan rather than a day-to-day plan. Periodization plans have to be tweaked from time to time based upon the condition of your athlete. My philosophy of training athletes is the same philosophy that I had as a shot putter; train explosively using Olympic lifts like cleans, snatches, and jerks. This training is essential in the development of total body power and must be taught correctly. The priority of the movement is not the amount of weight lifted but the acceleration, speed, technique, and synergism of the movement. Additional weight can be added after these four are mastered. Early on I emphasized the pressing movements too much, in particular the bench press, which has always been a universal measure of strength. Using the bench press as a primary exercise develops pectoral and triceps muscles which when working together are, in my opinion, best suited to help the player get off the ground (and hopefully our players would not be spending too much time on the ground). Whenever our football players would go out in public, people would inevitably say, "you have got to be a football player, how much do you bench press?" Would they ever ask them, "how much do you power clean?" No. As a result, changing this mentality of what the important lifts were took a great deal of work. The incline press became more important in our routine and the bench press was used only as a supplement to our upper body routine. The incline press hit a better angle for the development of the muscles that our players would be using on the field, and the only time we did the bench press was for the development of our triceps strength, primarily using a close grip.

I also preferred front squatting over back squatting, because otherwise much of the time the players would end up overworking their low back. The beauty of the front squat is that it forces you to stay upright, putting more of a workload on your quads and your core. If an athlete begins to fail in the front squat, he could simply dump the weight forward. The back squat, on the other hand, puts the lifter and spotter in harms way if the athlete loses control of the weights.

At the end of the day, my primary focus of training was using the Olympic movements and specific exercises for each sport at high rates of speed. Medicine ball work, plyometrics, and one-legged bounding were incorporated into our program as the improvement of overall body speed and movement was paramount for my athletes. My feelings were that if you trained like a plow horse, slow and heavy all the time, you will be a plow horse. I wanted every athlete on the field to be as fast, explosive, and lean as they could be. Never have my strongest players been the best players, it is always those who knew how to use their strength on the field who were the best. So, do not think that as your players continue to get stronger and stronger that they will get better and better at their sport. You and their coaches must help them learn to bridge the gap between the weight room and the field of play so that they know how to use that strength.

One of the big issues, as time went on from the '70s to the '80s to the '90s, was that the incoming freshmen were getting bigger and bigger. This was not necessarily beneficial to them, and in some cases, it actually hampered them. Our goal became first and foremost to get them to a weight where they could be most productive. Functional body weight became much more important than taking a big high school player and trying to make him bigger and stronger; get him lean first, and then begin to improve his functional levels of strength.

When I first got the job at UT, my motivational skills for team sports were untested, having come from the world of track and field where it was one-on-

one and where you must be self-motivated or fall by the wayside. I only knew that, when training our athletes, I wanted to get the most that I could out of each player. I wanted to push each athlete individually to the edge of the cliff but never let them fall off. I wanted our players to realize the importance of training for their position and sport, to understand that as a result of becoming a self-starter in their training program they could become a much better athlete on the field of play. I also wanted them to understand the vital importance of nutrition in sports, and to this end the Biochemistry and Nutrition Departments at UT became an integral part of educating our athletes. Over the years, many personalities have come through the doors of my weight rooms. Some you would have to show much love to, and others would be the total opposite. In time, I recognized that all these athletes had different buttons and my job was to push the hot button on each individual athlete to help make him/her the best that he/she could be. I eventually realized that the science of periodization and the teaching of the techniques of the exercises were only as good as the art of pushing the hot button. Being a strength and conditioning coach is as much, or more, an art than a science. Don't get me wrong, you also have to be a salesman and a psychologist as well. Once your athletes start to see improvements on the field as a result of their training, it will be easier to get the younger athletes to buy in to your program. You will get out of your athletes what you expect, and no more.

There have been ups and downs in my 32-year career (including a Super Bowl win and championship-game losses) but one thing is for sure, I do not feel like I have ever gone to work a day in my life! And if you were to ask me what I miss most about being a strength and conditioning coach I would tell you from the bottom of my heart that I miss my athletes, interacting with them and watching them grow both mentally and physically. I have had the opportunity to work with excellent male and female collegiate athletes from all sports, two first-overall NFL draft picks (Earl Campbell and Kenneth Sims), numerous All Americans, Pro Bowl players, Hall of Fame football players, and Olympic athletes but I must say that some of my happiest moments were watching young athletes start out as walk-ons in college, then earn a full scholarship or join the team as an NFL free agent, then become a Hall of Famer (Kurt Warner). Even though we are hired as "Head" strength and conditioning coaches, it is important to remember that we are still support personnel for each of the head coaches we work for. At some time in your career, your head coach may not want his/her athletes to do certain exercises, it is up to you to heed their advice and devise alternative exercises to meet their goals. Always realize that you work for the head coach, he does not work for you. My late, dear friend, former player, and NFL Hall of Fame inductee Cortez Kennedy had a personal chef and he used to always say to me "Dana, why are these chefs always hating on other chef's food?" He was right, I had seen that myself. There are many different recipes in the world of food and in the world of strength and conditioning. So, don't worry about the other guys recipe, worry about how good you can make yours because the proof will always be in the pudding.

Dana LeDuc's Coaching Bio

- 1977-1992 - University of Texas, Strength and Conditioning Coach
- 1977-1992 - Summer Strength and Conditioning Camp for Jr. & Sr. High Athletes
- 1993-1994 - University of Miami, Strength and Conditioning Coach
- 1995-1998 - Seattle Seahawks, Strength and Conditioning Coach
- 1999-2008 - St. Louis Rams, Strength and Conditioning Coach
- 2009-Present - Volunteer High School Strength & Conditioning Coach
- 2012 - Co-founder Grays Harbor Youth Athletics Charitable Organization

Achievements & Honors

- 1970-1971 - All-State, All-Northwest & All-American Tenor Sax
- 1971 - Shot Put Champion, Washington State
- 1974-1976 - 5 Time All-American Shot Put (Indoor & Outdoor), University of Texas
- 1974-1976 - 6 Time Southwest Conference Shot Put Champion (3 Indoor, 3 Outdoor)
- 1976 - NCAA Shot-Put Champion, University of Texas
- 1997 - University of Texas Hall of Honor Inductee
- 2000 - Super Bowl XXXIV World Champs
- 2002 - Super Bowl XXXVI
- 2006 - USA Strength & Conditioning Coaches Hall of Fame Inductee

Education

- 1977 - University of Texas, B.S. in Physical Education
- 1987 - Studied Strength and Conditioning in East Germany & The Soviet Union

CHAPTER 15

The Jeff Madden Story

What a great opportunity it is to be a leader amongst men and women. What a tremendous blessing it has been to live a life full of helping others go above and beyond themselves. We help people find their inner spirit and truly give them more belief in their inner power than they ever dreamed existed.

I grew up the 1960s, a tumultuous time in our nation with the civil rights struggle and women's rights. The question adults asked was always "What do you want to be when you grow up?" and my answer was always a policeman, fireman, secret service, or someone who protected the less fortunate.

I was a WWF fan at an early age, and loved Johnny Powers, Bobo Brazil, George "The Animal "Steel, and the outlaw Dusty Rhodes, to name a few. These guys were big, strong, mean, and athletic.

My dad was a Marine, and I woke up daily to push-ups, pull-ups, sit-ups and dips. These basic exercises became a mainstay to my fitness programming for the last 35 years and made a good strength foundation, coupled with martial arts training and flexibility, before I ever entered a sports arena. We also used to have gym class daily in school which helped us work on general conditioning, rope climbing, pegboard climbing, jump rope, balance beams, coordination, and rings, all great exercises for general preparation.

I also watched and mimicked the Jack La Lane Fitness show weekly to get stronger at lifting my bed and dressers, anything heavy I could find. I worked cutting grass and shoveling snow in Cleveland Ohio to raise money to buy the Joe Weider 110 pound cement plastic weight set, a multi-purpose with leg extension, leg curl, and dip station, an E-Z curl bar and triceps bar, leg weights, and power twister. I would do exercises on the Joe Weider program for 100 repetitions with 110 pounds on every exercise as I got stronger. I started off with three sets of 10 repetitions like the program stated, but if you wanted to build up to Hulk status, you have to lift more! So I found manhole covers at the junkyard and purchased them. They were about 50 pounds each, and I used the same rep scheme, but now I was really growing.

I started looking at muscle, fitness, and muscular development magazines at the bookstore to get more ideas from Mike Menzter, Sergio Olivia, Ronnie Robinson, and many other great bodybuilders. I prayed one day to meet some of these gentlemen. My prayers came true when I met Joe Weider, Arnold Schwarzenegger and Lou Ferrigno and Ronnie Coleman.

I played all sports and excelled at St. John's Lutheran Middle School. I was the Center on the basketball team, fullback and defensive tackle on the football team, played on the volleyball team, and set records in the shot put. This brought the attention of the local parochial schools, and I ended up attending Cleveland St. Joseph High School.

It was there that I met Coach Storey, who was six feet, three inches tall, with a military haircut an iron jaw, and a big, muscular man that many guys feared. He was the lineman coach in football, head wrestling coach, and a former state champion wrestler who could easily toss our national champion, Notre Dame Superstar wrestler Bob Golic around the mat in practice. He received a tremendous amount of respect wherever he would go, and I wanted to be just like him.

I was in gym class, playing basketball, when I was approached by a man who would become a dominating force in my life, Coach John Storey. He said, "Madden, get over here. I need to talk to you," and the other players all backed away. I saw a little smile on Coach Storey's face as he described the moves I had just made on the basketball court while winning the two-on-two championship trophy. His smile put me at ease as he tried to talk me into playing football. He convinced me, but I told him he would have to speak to my mother, because she had already made me promise that I would focus on academics and basketball, and no other sports.

My mother was the Head Nurse at a major hospital in Cleveland and she had seen a lot of football-related injuries. It took about a week of Coach calling, talking to her and working with my grandmothers to convince her to let me play football. I say with great appreciation that Coach John Storey helped me become an All City, All State, All Scholastic, and All American football player recruited by over 100 Schools. He was a great coach and I am blessed. Coach Storey and I have kept in touch for all of my 35 years of coaching and we have always helped each other.

In our high school weight room we had a universal machine, running machine, neck machine, a random selection of dumbbells, and curl bar. Weight Training was just beginning in the 1970s and the general thought was, if you lifted weights, you would become slower and inflexible, and the muscle would turn to fat when you stopped lifting. These are terrible rumors that we spent a couple of generations disproving.

During high school, I worked out daily at the Cleveland Clinic and trained with Calvin Robinson, Reginald Marzetti, Tyrone White, and Robert Stonewall Jackson from the Cleveland Browns and Texas A&M University. We had great workouts for years and pushed each other to greatness all the time. I also trained at Shubert's Olympic training facility on the Cleveland Westside. I went there to learn the Olympic movements and prepare for college. The Shubert family had three generations of Olympic lifting champions in different weight classes. John Schubert was very nice to me and allowed me to train in his private facility! They were all commenting on how much stronger I was than most grown men at only 17. That early foundation helped me to achieve some great lifts: Bench Press 602, Incline Press 550, Squat 800, Power Clean and Press 350 at 3 repetitions! I am always thankful for those years of training.

Black's weightlifting gym was the big-time powerlifting gym in Cleveland, Ohio. John Black, the powerlifting champion, allowed me to train in his gym. When I was a senior in high school and headed to college, he let me into his special lifting sanctuary. Within that sanctuary, I met the great Lyle Alzado, defensive tackle extraordinaire. He was one of the all-time best, and I was fortunate enough to work out with him on several occasions. Those guys all had kind souls and allowed me to train with them during difficult times and a heightened racial climate. They would stand outside with me to wait for my bus and make sure no groups of people bothered me during those tough times! We practiced love, not hate, in the Iron Brotherhood. I remember, when it got dark and I had to go stand in front of the bar to wait on the bus to take me back to the east side, they told me, "We got you, brother," and they meant it!

During my official college visits, in 1978, I met Mike Gittleson at the University of Michigan. He had several rooms full of Nautilus equipment, game helmets, practice helmets, game shoes, and practice shoes, overall an extremely impressive setup. He spoke about high-intensity training, making the guys their best selves, and winning games in front 105,000 people. This college stuff was really big time! When the Michigan football team arrived, they all dressed in blue blazers. Bo Schembechler, the famous head coach, came over and shook my hand. I had seen him on television many times and was very impressed that he knew who I was. For an inner-city kid out of Cleveland Ohio, it meant a lot that he knew who I was, and I wanted to play for him. Milan Vooletich recruited me, and became a *tremendous* support in my career even though I did not go to Michigan. Many years later, I coached his son.

My mother wanted me to go to Vanderbilt. They stressed academics the most and had more Rhodes Scholars than any other program in the Nation at that time. On my visit there, I met Strength Coach Martin Poe. He was buffed up like Coach Storey, just not as tall. The Vanderbilt weight room was between

2500 and 3000 square feet and had free weights, some machines, dumbbells, and rubber weights. It was my first true indoctrination to strengthen conditioning at the collegiate level and Coach Poe's Power Explosion Program.

Power Explosion was working in a small room with the heat thermostat blazing and position coaches smoking cigars while we lifted. Coach Poe taught us complex combination movements such as high pulls, power cleans, front squats, push press, high reps, and multiple sets. We also were sprinting stadium steps and six 220-yard sprints! Day two was snatch combo, complex failure, sprint one mile, walk one lap, Sprint one mile, then ten 100-yard sprints. Hard work pays off!

Coach Poe retired and went back to his sporting goods store, and in walked E.J. Doc Kreis.

Doc Kreis was six feet, two inches and 300-plus pounds, a super-heavyweight powerlifter and a guard from the Georgia State Penitentiary. Doc came in with his posse and lifting buddies, all who used our maximum lifts for their warm-ups. They were: Dennis Arnold, big time bench presser; Johnny Langston, big time squatter; and Chuck the truck Braxton, a world-class lifter who allowed semi-trucks to run over his body and also held airplanes from taking off, a tremendous strength athlete. In addition to visits from former lifting champions, the who's who in Nashville trained with us daily. From the mayor, the police chief, and police officers to country music stars and McConnell's catering crew, the Vanderbilt weight room was the place to be.

They gave Doc a free car to drive, an apartment, he wore shorts to work every day, everyone in the city knew who he was, and they always brought him gifts. He was a role model who would stand beside you and cared about you as a human being, not just a football player. He taught us how to fight adversity when no one thought you had a chance, a life lesson that all strength coaches should know. Doc held a yearly Music City Invitational lifting Championship meet and he invited the best strong man in the world. I always assisted with this production, and I remember I wanted to be that guy! We had the Hawaiian Champs, Gabe Aio and Dwayne File, and Dr. Squat Fred Hatfield, the 1014 pound world record holder, who also played a major role in my successful career. I learned a lot from all of the different strongmen and lifters that I came in contact with. I was also fortunate enough that, while in college, Doc brought in the Canadian national team and coaches every year for two weeks to train with us.

In 1983, I coached defensive line and strength and conditioning for the University of Cincinnati. Our facility was half the size of the Vanderbilt weight room, but we adapted it using calisthenics, burpees, up downs, mountain climbers, lunges, partner bodyweight lifts, and whatever else we could find to lift. We were also one of the first teams to try out John Cox's strength shoe for speed!

I was instructed by Doc Kreis to go find and talk to some of the best coaches at that time: Dana LeDuc at Texas; Bruno Pauletto, University of Tennessee; Boyd Epley, Nebraska; LeBaron Caruthers, University of Alabama; Louie Simmons, a strongman & world champion trainer in Ohio; Al Miller, Denver Broncos; Dr. Bob Ward, Dallas Cowboys; Johnny Parker, New England Patriots; Dr. Terry Todd, Wide World of Sports, and many more. These gentlemen we're ahead of their time, trying various techniques, and they all gave me some good advice for my career. I also sought out great track and field coaches: Victor Lopez from Rice University, Curtis Frye from University of North Carolina, and Beverly Kearney from Florida, all of them at championships in track and field. Dr. Michael Yessis and James Radcliffe were always on hand when I wanted to discuss plyometric training. There are many others that played key roles to develop all the explosive power training systems, such as the National Association for Speed and Explosion, which gave us the explosive power pyramid and the foundations of training, along with the National Strength and Conditioning Association, the Collegiate Strength and Conditioning Coaching Association, International Sports Science Association, and National Association Sports Medicine.

Old school strength and conditioning coaches' duties were vast. Most of us worked alone, and although some of the bigger schools had graduate assistants or full-time assistants, we all worked with all sports. My roles consisted of dorm duties, assignments, nutritionist, analytics, and psychologist. I would tape wrists and ankles if needed, ice players down, make sure meals were prepared properly, ensure the buses were on time, sometimes even hotel scheduling, whatever it took. We had to know all different types of training, and keep abreast of everything that the winning team in the country was doing. Strength coaches have been big brothers and even dads, and in some cases we handled all discipline for all sports in addition to speed training multi-directional movement and whatever else coaches needed.

I would suggest all strength professionals should develop a performance team that consists of all the people athletes see daily. This includes the strength coach, training staff, team physician, academic personnel, the nutritionist, psychologist, equipment manager, and anyone else that can meet at least bi-weekly to help your team. Research and read about everything you don't know. Hire people that are smart and talented, that can help you have a great staff. I trained all of my assistants to be able to take over at the drop of a dime. And listen to people; your opinion is not the only opinion, sometimes others know a more efficient way. One Program does not fit All athletes. Give them the instruction; they need don't just rely on a computer program. Be respectful and flexible with coaches and training staff to get what is best for each individual athlete. Be humble and confident, educated and certified in strength and conditioning as well as CPR, AED, and First Aid.

I have had the privilege to work with great head coaches: Watson Brown, Mack Brown, Bill McCartney, Jerry Berndt, and Fred Goldsmith. I've had excellent assistants: Donnie Maib, Ken Shepard, George Smith, Dave Plettl, Tim Cross, Chuck Faucette, Jesse Ackerman, Kelly Justice, Sandy Abney, Quadrian Banks, Angel Spassov, Lance Sewel, Nate Moe, Trey Zepeda, Meleah Matthews, Lee McCormick, Derrick Lewis, Johnny Olgin, Linda Lipscomb, Bruce Johnson, and Ed, as well as the 10 volunteer assistants, the Graduate School of Kinesiology, Health and Physics students we had every semester for the past 16 years at Texas, and many others!

Jeff "Maddog" Madden's Coaching Bio

- 1983 - University of Cincinnati, Offensive & Defensive Line GA/ Head Football Strength Coach
- 1983-1984 - United States Football League, Memphis Showboats Offensive Guard
- 1984-1989 - Rice University, Associate Strength & Conditioning Coach
- 1989-1992 - University of Colorado, Assistant Athletics Director Human Athletics Performance, Head Strength Coach
- 1989-Present - Owner Operator Mobile Fitness Training
- 1992-1998 - University of North Carolina, Associate Athletics Director for Human Athletic Performance, Head Strength & Conditioning Coach
- 1998-2014 - University of Texas, Associate Athletics Director for Human Athletic Performance, Head Strength & Conditioning Coach
- 2014-Present - Chief Operating Officer of Velo Energy Management
- 2014-Present - Owner of Maddog Explosive Power Training

Achievements & Honors

- 1984-2012 - National Strength and Conditioning Association Member
- 1985 - National Association of Speed & Explosion, Expert Certified
- 1988 - International Sports Science Association (ISSA) Master Certified
- 1990-1991 - AP College Football National Champions, Colorado Buffalos

- 1995 - Stan Jones Award, Master Coach of the Year
- 1996 - National Strength & Conditioning Specialist of the Year
- 2001 - Admiral Ulysses Grant Sharp Award
- 2001 - Master Strength & Conditioning Coach CSCCa
- 2001 - Master Strength & Conditioning Coach NASE
- 2001-2009 - Vice President Collegiate Strength & Conditioning Association
- 2003 - USA Strength & Conditioning Hall of Fame Inductee
- 2004 - Professional Football Strength & Conditioning Coaches Society, National Collegiate Strength & Conditioning Coach of the Year
- 2005 - Collegiate Strength Coach of the Year, Samson Equipment
- 2005-2006 - BCS National Champions, Texas Longhorns
- 2009-2016 - President of the Collegiate Strength & Conditioning Association

CHAPTER 16

The Ken Mannie Story

"Just as iron sharpens iron, so must we sharpen each other."
- Proverbs 27:17

Origins

To fully appreciate the path that I took to arrive at this point in my career as a strength and conditioning coach, we need to go back to Steubenville, Ohio, in the mid '60s. Steubenville embodies the grit and hard hat mentality of a classic steel city environment. With Pittsburgh, PA, only a forty-minute drive to the east and the rolling hills of West Virginia forming a natural skyline along the opposite side of the river, the 'Ville—as it is respectfully known—is a diverse dichotomy of tough people with an assertive work ethic.

It was in this setting that I learned that respect was not a given—it was a hard-earned privilege. Every day you proved who you were, what you stood for, and where you wanted to go. There were no shortcuts in Steubenville, comprised of an aggregate of people who were built with a calloused hands, bloody knuckles, and a fire in the heart mindset. You were constantly challenged in Steubenville—mentally and physically. If you weren't up to it, you were sure to get your ego bruised and your nose disjointed.

My brother Steve and I were raised by my mom, Antoinette, and Grandpa, Gabriel, in a cockroach infested apartment building on 422 Logan Street. My father was out of the picture by the time I was three years old, so Grandpa was the father figure in our family. Our apartment building was directly across the alley from our church, St. Peter's, along with the elementary school of the same name that Steve and I attended.

It was the training sessions in the cellars, garages, and well-worn gyms of the 'Ville that proved to be the genesis and nurturing of my passion for the iron game.

I was first inclined to strength train after reading a sports magazine article on then Minnesota Viking's fullback, Bill Brown. Those longer in the tooth will remember Bill as a large, well-put-together, unrelenting runner and blocker. In the article, Bill attributed his power and durability to his weight training regimen. As a young, impressionable, wannabe fullback, I took notice. I soon proceeded to purchase a set of the plastic-coated Ted Williams weight sets from Sears and Roebuck's, and I was officially on the first phase of the journey.

When I showed up for football physicals—going into my sixth-grade year, in 1964—one of the coaches looked me up and down, told me to wait for a minute, and returned with a tool kit full of hardware for repairing equipment. He thought I was there to sign-up for equipment manager. I looked at him tersely and replied, "I am here to play football, not to be the water boy!" And I felt that I was physically ready to do so; I'd been working out!

The basic lifting that I performed at home in my bedroom from sixth through eighth grades at St. Peter's Elementary served me well while playing both full-back and nose tackle. I remember feeling strong and solid with every ounce of the 115 pounds filling my uniform. My fullback dream was squashed, however, when I soon realized that it would have to be traded for undersized offensive guard and linebacker in high school.

At Steubenville Catholic Central High School, I arduously grew into a 185-pound guard and linebacker, and developed the necessary demeanor for those positions. Doing even the rudimentary amount of strength training I did was a tremendous help in both my performance and durability. I started my junior year at guard, and during senior year, from the opening kick-off onward, I never came out of the game.

Since there wasn't a high demand for 185-pound guards or linebackers at the collegiate level, I resigned myself to the strong possibility that I was going to be working at Wheeling-Pittsburgh Steel after graduation. Money for college was non-existent, and I wasn't going to receive an academic scholarship, that was for sure.

A close friend and high school teammate of mine, Paul Coppa, had decided to walk-on the football team at the University of Akron. Thanks to Paul, I took a look at the University of Akron. There were some grants and loans available that would help me with my first year's tuition, at least, but I still had to make some money for living expenses, books, and food. With some coaxing from his father, I decided it was worth considering, so I stepped away for a short while to give it serious thought.

The Awakening

Immediately after graduation I began work as a cinder snapper in the blast furnace of Wheeling-Pittsburgh Steel. A cinder snapper has the dangerous, filthy job of removing remnants of molten steel from the runners (i.e., canals). There were two runners for each of the two furnaces we worked, and the release time for each furnace was staggered so that one furnace was producing the molten steel while the other opened its doors to let it flow. After a fire hose cooled the molten steel, I would step into the runner, shovel the cinder into a wheelbarrow, and cart it off and dump it into a cinder pile. On several occasions, I emerged from a canal with smoking boots that I furiously hosed-off, and at the end of a shift, I would head to the locker room to shower and clean the thick soot from not only my body, but also my nose, ears, and mouth. It wasn't uncommon to be spitting-up black phlegm several hours after a shift. A couple of months of that experience were all I needed. I wanted to go to college, play football if I could, and become a coach. My decision was made; I was going to give the University of Akron an earnest try.

My workouts that summer consisted of lifting in my friend Bernie Battistel's garage. Nothing fancy, mind you, just bench presses, squats, dead lifts, overhead presses, and some various pulling movements I had learned by hanging out with a group of amateur power lifters at our YMCA. But they were blood-letting workouts, as all of us trained with passion and purpose.

Our equipment was archaic, and some of it was actually made clandestinely in the steel mill. We had a vast assortment of plates that were not labeled, so we had no idea how much they weighed. If they looked similar in size, we matched them up. That proved to be a mistake on occasion, with near disasters when unevenly loaded bars got away from us. There was the occasional rickety pulley system bolted or nailed to the ceiling and wall, mostly of the plate-loading variety. We never heard the principle of "function dictates design." Our battle cry was "keep using it until it breaks."

My running program consisted of two to three days per week of 100, 200, or 400-meter intervals on the Catholic Central track, along with repeats up a dirt hill that was on a near-vertical 30-yard incline. Our family did not own a car, so that routine was complimented with my nightly two-mile run along the berm of Route 7 to the mill's graveyard shift in those heavy, steel-tip boots.

In the summer of 1970, I was in the best shape of my young life. By the August reporting date at Akron U, I was ready to go. My first season was spent on the scout squad, and my goal was to at least be noticed as a hustler and a hitter.

That approach finally paid dividends in the spring of 1971, as I came out of spring football practice with a starting position and a full scholarship as a 210-pound offensive guard. I was the smallest player on the O-line, but my penchant for lifting proved to be a major asset.

There was a small contingent of Zip players who enjoyed lifting, so we set up a small training area in a back room of the Buchtel Fieldhouse with whatever equipment we could muster up. Several of us brought implements from home to stock the room, and we put together a fairly decent training lair. There was no mandatory strength training, but our little "band of lifting brothers" gradually grew.

Giving Back

After a mediocre college football career I went into high school teaching and coaching. Reno Saccoccia, who would be my future brother-in-law, was instrumental in me landing a position at United Local in Hanoverton, OH, where I worked for one year. United Local was my "first shot," as I told the principal in the interview when he asked if I thought I was experienced enough for the position. I taught health and physical education classes, coached football, track and field, and trained athletes in the weight room.

A position opened that spring at my alma mater, Steubenville Catholic Central, and I was blessed to move back to my hometown and give back to a very special place. For the next nine years, my duties included coaching football, wrestling, track and field, and running a strength and conditioning program for most of the school's athletes. Those were great years for me, in a lot of different ways. I married the love of my life, Marianne, in '81, and she has been my beacon and true source of strength ever since.

Teaching and coaching at the high school level is extremely rewarding, and I wouldn't trade those years for anything. Times have changed, of course, and it would be difficult—if not impossible—for young, aspiring strength and conditioning coaches to start at the high school level and elevate to the collegiate ranks in the current landscape. In my case, though, those years proved to be the underpinnings of what would follow.

A New Direction

I attended various clinics on a year-round basis. The big one each spring was the trip to State College, PA, and the Penn State Football Clinic. It was there that I met Dan Riley, Penn State's Head Strength and Conditioning Coach. Dan had a unique way of training his players, which diverted from most mainstream systems, but no one could argue with his results.

What most impressed me about Dan was the way he worked with his players; much of it was one-on-one, or one-on-two. It was very personalized, individualized, and demanded a high level of coaching expertise, grit, and energy. And, it was around the clock, physically draining work from a coaching perspective. Very few coaches were training a full team of over 100 football players in that fashion, with minimal assistance. Dan was a coaching machine!

Since I already had an affinity for training athletes, when I saw how Dan approached his work, how the players responded to him, and the relationships he built, I was inspired to change my coaching career path in my late 20s and become a full-time collegiate strength and conditioning coach.

In the early spring of '84, I was made aware of a strength and conditioning graduate program at Ohio State University. Steve Bliss, OSU's Head of Strength and Conditioning, directed the program and Earle Bruce was the head football coach. I applied, interviewed, and got one of the several coveted spots available. It was truly a unique graduate program, especially for that era. We had several GA's, both male and female, from diverse backgrounds and with different ideas and training styles.

It was also a pivotal time for me in the sense that it was where I first met Mark Dantonio, who served as a GA on the football side at the same time. We would both later work under Nick Saban as assistants at MSU, and of course, Mark is the current head football coach for the Spartans.

Marianne worked as a bank teller to supplement my modest GA stipend. I put in the long days of classwork, worked with Buckeye football players, and spent a few hours each evening and Saturday morning at Dublin High School training their athletes. Dublin, along with several other Columbus area high schools, helped subsidize the graduate strength and conditioning program, so each of us had a high school assigned to us.

The OSU graduate program went for one full calendar year—June to June. We had to accumulate 54 quarter-hours of academic work, and then take a combination of a written and oral graduate exam. It was a true grind, and a great learning experience. I was fortunate to take several classes from two stalwarts in exercise physiology, Dr. Robert Bartels, and Dr. Donald K. Mathews. I would also meet Ted Lambrinides, a doctoral student at OSU at the time, and we've developed a close, lifelong friendship. He has since been an invaluable source of information and guidance throughout the years.

The Buckeyes had a great football team in '84, loaded with talent in all classes. We were the Big Ten Champs that year and lost a close Rose Bowl battle to USC, 20-17.

Upon receiving my master's degree in June of '85, there was a dead period as far as job opportunities were concerned, so Marianne and I moved back to Steubenville where I volunteer-coached at Catholic Central and substitute taught at various high schools in the Ohio Valley. We knew we were going to have to be patient, so we gutted it out for a few more months and prayed something good would happen.

Rocket Fuel

In late November of '85, I caught word that The University of Toledo posted an opening for a full-time strength and conditioning coach, the first position in the Mid-American Conference (MAC). I applied, interviewed with Head

Football Coach Dan Simrell, his staff, and administration, and was offered the position.

The first four years of the nine I worked at Toledo were spent in one of the small towers in The Glass Bowl Stadium. The Glass Bowl is an architectural icon built in 1937 through the Works Progress Administration (WPA) project for a little over $300,000. Most of its original, unique stone wall construction and projections are still intact. It has since gone through several renovations to make it one of the classic football facilities in the MAC.

Those years in the tower, which was very small (maybe a few hundred square feet) and sparsely equipped, were challenging. We got it done with smoke and mirrors, a few benches, two squat racks, two hip sleds, and a mish-mash of different styles of dumbbells, plates, and bars.

Dan Simrell was let go after the 1989 season when we went 6-5, a record that was deemed inadequate by the administration. Dan was a good football coach, a great person, and I will always be indebted to him for giving me my first collegiate position.

Enter Nick Saban, defensive backs coach with the Houston Oilers, and former defensive coordinator for Michigan State. Nick had recruited in the Steubenville area when he was an assistant with West Virginia and Ohio State in the late '70s and early 80s, and he stopped to visit Catholic Central on a couple of occasions during my tenure there. It was an informal relationship at the time, but enough for him to retain me as strength coach. We would soon grow to be great friends.

The Glass Bowl underwent a major renovation leading into 1990, complete with a new football building, the Larimer Complex. It housed a 6,000 square foot weight room that was best in the MAC for many years. It has since been expanded, and I look forward to visiting UT soon to check it out.

In Nick's one and only season with the Rockets in 1990, we went 9-2 and won a share of the MAC with Central Michigan, a game we lost 13-12 in what would prove to be the de facto championship game. Our only other loss that year was to Navy, 14-10.

Nick decided to head to the Cleveland Brown's in February of 1991 as Bill Belichick's defensive coordinator. Gary Pinkel came in from The University of Washington, and we would continue to have several very successful seasons under his tenure. He would eventually leave Toledo—several years after I had left—after a long, superlative run for an outstanding tenure at The University of Missouri.

Without question, the highlight of the Toledo years centered on Marianne and I adopting our daughter, Alaina, in 1988. That entire process of bringing a little angel into our lives will always be our most cherished memory of those years.

Heart of a Spartan

After four years on Gary's staff, I got a call from Nick and he told me that he was being considered for the Michigan State (MSU) head football position. Since the Browns were still involved in the playoffs, he couldn't discuss specifics. He left me to "think about it."

Soon after the Browns were eliminated from the playoffs, I received a 2 a.m. call from Nick.

"Ken, it's Nick. Did I wake you?"

"No, I was just getting in my last set of push-ups before going to bed," I replied.

A moment of dead silence on the other end.

"I've just been named head football coach at Michigan State. You coming, or what?"

"Absolutely!"

"OK, I'm heading up there to meet the team on Sunday. I'll pick you up."

My career at MSU began with that very short, to the point discussion.

Nick warned me before our arrival on campus that the weight room "needed some improvements," but not to worry, because plans were on the table for an upgrade. Upon first sight, I learned that his comment was severely understated. The weight room was barely 4,000 square feet, with racks that looked like they were made in a high school welding shop, and the equipment choices went downhill from there. The one saving grace was a very nice set of Eleiko dumb-bells, which we used for much of our training routines.

Thankfully, we got to work on those upgrade plans immediately. The result in the spring of 1997 was a 9,000 square foot room adjacent to the indoor practice field with high ceilings, an open floor plan, windows on two walls, indirect ballast lighting, and top notch equipment from stem to stern. Over the 20-plus years that have followed, it has undergone two additional renovations. We added 7,000 square feet in 2006, and just recently put down a new floor with built-in platforms and installed a new Rogers Athletic rack system.

After the 1999 season, Nick left MSU for LSU. Everyone knows of his extraordinary success since then. Today, he is widely considered to be one of the best – if not *the* best – football coaches of all time.

At this writing, I am in my 24th year here at Michigan State. It has been a true rollercoaster of events, with some very trying, difficult stretches, as well as great successes along the way. I've worked with four head coaches during that span, and I'm fortunate to be currently reunited with my great friend, Mark Dantonio. There have been other opportunities along the way—LSU, Ohio State, and Alabama to name a few. I guess you could say that part of my legacy will be that I've turned down more national championship opportunities than just about anyone in the world. But Michigan State has been good to my family. We bleed green, feel truly blessed, and are proud to be Spartans.

Alaina, who was in first grade when we came here, is a 2010 graduate of MSU, and works on campus in Bio-Medical Sciences. She and her husband Bill Burghardt, one of my assistants, have a beautiful three-year-old daughter, Annabelle, who makes all of our hearts smile.

When asked about my longevity in the profession, my first suggestion is to surround yourself with good people. I've surrounded myself with *great* people on the S&C staff here at MSU: Mike Vorkapich, Tim Wakeham, Tommy Hoke, Bill Burghardt, Lorenzo Guess, Molli Munz, Marshall Repp, Emmanuel Hibbler, and Zach Smith.

To all young strength and conditioning coaches, I offer this advice:

- Love what you're doing, where you're doing it. Opportunities will come if you're cut from the right cloth.
- Put the safety of your student-athletes first. Remember, they are someone's children.
- Learn something new every day.
- Be persistent and ready to face adversity, as it will come.
- Give back to the profession by conducting yourself as a professional in every sense of the word.
- Develop strong, steadfast, meaningful relationships with everyone around you.

I urge you to stay strong, stay in the fight, and make a positive impact on young people!

Ken Mannie's Coaching Bio

- Taught and coached at high school level for ten years.
- Currently in 34th year of coaching at the collegiate level.
- Currently Head Strength/Conditioning Coach for football at Michigan State University, and oversee strength and conditioning programs for all men's and women's sports.
- Longest tenured football strength/conditioning coach in the Big Ten Conference.

Achievements & Honors

- 2014 - Inducted into the USA Strength/Conditioning Coaches Hall of Fame
- 2015 - Football Scoop National Strength/Conditioning Coach of the Year
- 2017 - Recipient of the U.S. Grant Sharp Trophy at Holiday Bowl

- 2018-Present - Member of CSCCa Board of Directors
- 2018 - Named to Board of Directors for the USA Strength/ Conditioning Hall of Fame
- Columnist for *Coach and Athletic Director Magazine*, the nations' oldest and most prestigious coaching publication, since 2000. Written over 300 articles and several book chapters on various aspects of training, motivation, nutrition, anabolic drug abuse, and athletics.
- Keynote speaker at several national seminars and conferences.
- Coached numerous All-Americans and a host of players who have gone on to have highly successful NFL careers.
- Coaching tree is far-reaching, with former full-time staff, GA's, and interns working in the NFL, Big Ten, SEC, ACC, Big 12, MAC, and American Athletic Conferences.

Professional Certifications

- Certified with CSCCa (SCCC) and NSCA (CSCS)
- 2002 - Master Strength and Conditioning Coach (MSCC) with CSCCa

Education

- 1974 - Bachelor's degree in Physical Education and Health Education from The University of Akron
- 1985 - Master's degree in Exercise Science from Ohio State University

Personal

- Married to former Marianne Saccoccia, daughter Alaina Burghardt, and granddaughter Annabelle (3).

CHAPTER 17

The Mike Marks Story

In the summer of 1977 I received a phone call from Coach Sam Bailey, the Associate Athletic Director at the University of Alabama that unexpectedly began my strength training and conditioning career. Coach Bryant wanted me back in Tuscaloosa in two days for the beginning of fall practice. I was working at Kanakuk Camp in southwest Missouri and needed to drive back almost 600 miles. Apparently, over the summer, several members of Coach Bryant's Football Staff had felt we needed a strength and conditioning coach and approached Coach Bryant with the idea. At that point, I was an assistant track coach in charge of the throwers and had experienced success with a national champion in the shotput (Gary England) and six All Americans in the throws. These athletes were incredibly hard workers and worked year-round to achieve their success. Since I had played two years of football and four years of track at Oklahoma State University, our staff felt I could do the job. The next morning, I began the drive to Tuscaloosa for my new career.

I reported to the football staff meeting, and Coach Bryant asked me to briefly describe my plan regarding warmups, flexibility, and in-season weight training. Prior to 1977, the strength program was primarily circuit related, and although good for local muscle endurance, was not particularly advantageous for strength gains. As I concluded my thoughts, I said to the staff, "What do you all think?" Coach Bryant quickly corrected me and said, "It doesn't matter what they think, it matters what I think." I did not make that mistake again. It is funny now, but it was not so funny back then. I was very fortunate; the entire coaching staff and Coach Bryant were very receptive to the changes and new ideas. We balanced the program so that our players would be fit, powerful, and flexible. We went on to win two national championships in 1978 and 1979. In 1977, we were voted number two in the nation.

Regarding weight training, we incorporated more of a power development program (not power lifting) and less local muscle endurance. The warm up, flexibility program, and testing procedures were also modified. Our conditioning test still utilized the mile run, as Coach Bryant understood the times I assigned each player and he wanted to see which players would "gut it out." We also introduced the 300-yard shuttle run. Each player was assigned a time to complete two sets of six 50-yard shuttle runs. Between each shuttle, there was a five-minute rest period. Players were required to complete both runs in the assigned time. It was possible to make the first time if you were slightly out of shape, but not both. Each player had to meet his mile run time, 300-yard shuttle time, and assigned body weight. Failure to complete these standards was not taken lightly by Coach Bryant and the staff, and certainly influenced the players' standings on the depth chart, as well as additional training sessions.

At the 25-year reunion of our 1978 National Championship team, several former players were kidding me, in a good way, about the body weights I assigned for reporting to camp. Players were not as big back then as now, and our emphasis was on quickness and power. In the late '70s, many players were not exposed to year-round weight training in the high schools.

As the 1977 season progressed, the athletic trainer at Alabama, Jim Goosetree, stated about midway through the 1977 Season that he felt injuries were down from previous years due to the new program. Coach Goosetree had been with Coach Bryant since 1958, so his opinion was highly respected.

I had many friendly discussions with Ken Donahue, our defensive coordinator, and a coach long involved in personal fitness himself. I presented ideas regarding when to condition intensely and when to utilize "active rest." He always felt one day of rest was enough recovery before games, and I countered with some tapering concepts, particularly after two weeks of intense two-a-day football workouts. As mid-season came along, conditioning drills were reduced to reduce fatigue.

The weight room at Alabama, from 1977 until my departure in 1982, was vastly different than the facilities of today. We had one room, roughly 2,500 square feet, with four bench press racks, four squat racks, four power clean platforms, and a full Nautilus circuit installed the year prior to my arrival. Our squat racks were welded together by our facilities manager. Also included was a Universal Gym. My last year, we were able to add another room across the hall for other sports to begin using. Off season running drills were sometimes conducted on the concourse of Memorial Coliseum, as there were no indoor facilities like the ones there are now.

In the fall of 1981, the Alabama basketball coaches asked if I could implement a pre-season strength and conditioning program. In the past, there had been conditioning drills but no structured weight training. After completing the warm up drills for football, I would begin the basketball team's weight training, flexibility, and conditioning. In addition to the workouts done on campus, I would drive the basketball players to the university's golf course and conduct uphill and downhill runs, and sometimes a little bit of cross country. I would then return in time for the football conditioning drills and in-season weight training. The basketball players and coaches felt they were coming into the official start of basketball practice very well prepared.

After the Sugar Bowl in January, we soon began the off-season program, which allowed a significant period of time for substantial improvements in all areas of fitness. We handled spring training like the in-season, then led into summer training, which allowed for more improvement time. There was a time during spring training where I was trying to squeeze in another weight session when the football players had a day off from practice. I brought the idea up in the staff meeting, and Coach Bryant said, "I want those boys to have a day off to fish." In the '70s and '80s, spring training for football was much longer than it is now, so I obviously agreed with Coach Bryant.

In the fall of 1981, Dave Williams came on board at Alabama as a graduate student and as a volunteer strength coach. He was looking to gain

Cotton Bowl practice with Coach Bryant (left) - 1981

experience at a major college program, and moved his family to Tuscaloosa. Dave was well-versed in all areas of fitness, and I really enjoyed his time at Alabama, as we could share information and bounce ideas off each other. There were no paid assistant positions back then, so Dave really had to sacrifice. He moved on from Alabama to obtain his first full time job at Texas A & M as Head Strength Coach, then to Liberty University, and had an outstanding career.

During my time at Alabama, and for others in this new profession, the transition really began for the strength coach to be hands on and develop athletes year-round. This included all phases of training, even psychological and nutritional. Training techniques and principles evolved, and continue to do so. I was very fortunate to be in the right place at the right time.

I was privileged to train many great athletes during this time. Several who had great work ethic and playing ability were E.J. Junior, Barry Krauss, Tommy Wilcox, Dwight Stephenson, Jim Bunch, and Marty Lyons to name a few. All of them were All Americans and moved on to professional careers.

My starting salary at Alabama was $18,000. We were provided a car, health insurance, four-season football tickets, and access to the athletic training table. When I left Alabama, I was paid $22,000. These figures were not far removed from the assistant coaches' salaries at that point.

Before Alabama and UNC

In my eighth-grade year in Richardson, Texas (1965), I began to take an interest in "lifting weights," as it was called back then. I felt if I was stronger, I would be a better athlete. Some of the best athletes in the United States were in Texas—including Randy Matson, the world's first 70-foot shot-putter, and the Dallas Cowboys—and I was highly motivated when observing their success. Weight training was not widely accepted at that time; some coaches felt if you lifted weights, you would become "muscle bound." This was before structured weight training workouts were put into place and included flexibility, specific conditioning, and skill work.

The next year, Richardson High School hired a new football coach, Joe Simpson. He was the first coach in the Dallas area (I am aware of) who put into place a structured, year-round training program. All of our football and track athletes benefitted from these sessions. Two years later, our football team advanced to the Texas State Semi-Finals in the highest football classification with two of our games played in the Cotton Bowl in front of 45,000 fans. Since I competed in track as well as football, the coaches made certain we were in shape. Each day, before throwing drills, Coach Jack Huffman required us to complete sprints, agilities, rope jumping, and stadium steps. Twice a week we also worked on the trampoline as a form of plyometrics, as we know the term now. The concentration on quickness and explosion was critical to my success as a state and national-class shot-putter. Coach Huffman pushed us hard, and I am grateful to this day. Strength training facilities were very limited. Our high school, like all schools back then, did not have a weight or fitness room. Coach Simpson had our booster club make weights out of concrete blocks and bars. It was crude, but effective. Some of us joined a small local health club, which had some bench press and squat racks, but was mostly machines. The bottom line was, we got stronger.

As an athlete, strength training made a huge difference for me. I was ranked number five in the US in 1969 as a high school shot-putter, and finished number six in the NCAA 1974 at Oklahoma State. From a football standpoint, it provided me an opportunity to increase my size and compete in my position on the offensive and defensive lines.

UNC 1982-1987

In the summer of 1982, I left Alabama and took the Head Strength and Conditioning position at the University of North Carolina Chapel Hill. Coach

Bryant was nearing retirement, and I had a close association with Associate Athletic Director and former Strength Coach Paul Hoolahan, with whom I had served with on the NSCA Board of Directors. At that point, UNC had a nationally recognized sports medicine program, including nationally certified trainers for all sports. I would work closely over the years with Skip Hunter, head football trainer, a very knowledgeable and compassionate individual. My primary responsibility was football, and Skip and I were a good team.

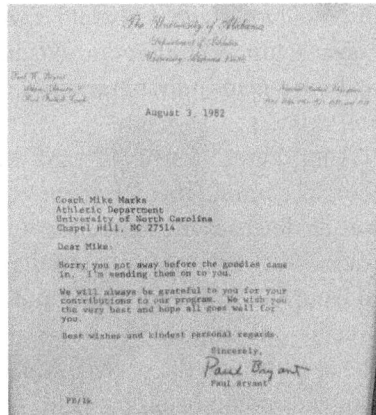

Letter from Coach Bryant - 1982

I was fortunate to have a part-time staff for basketball and other sports, which trained at the Woolen Gym weight room in Carmichael. Included in this basketball group were Michael Jordan and James Worthy. In the fall of 1982, I was visited by Basketball Assistant Coaches Roy Williams and Coach Eddie Fogler. They already had a good program in place. We had a great discussion regarding pre-season basketball training, and they were eager and receptive to ideas I brought from my work with Alabama's basketball players. Eventually, Coach Williams went on to Kansas University and returned to UNC as Head Basketball Coach. During this time, Coach Williams has won three NCAA National Basketball Championships. As the profession was growing, UNC allowed us to hire several part-time strength assistants. Chip Sigmon, Jerry Palmieri, Harley Dartt, and Bunn Rhames were invaluable, and allowed us to give more personal attention to not only football, but other UNC Sports programs as well. Chip and Jerry moved on to outstanding careers in their own right. All were incredibly eager to learn, and it was great to exchange new ideas.

The initial football weight room at UNC was roughly 2,000 square feet. There were five bench press racks, four clean platforms, dumbbells, incline benches, and a small set of Nautilus machines.

Due to size limitations in our weight room, we had to rotate two groups of players during the in-season workouts. Group A would train Monday/Wednesday and Group B trained Tuesday/Thursday. Similarly, during the off-season, we ran three workout sessions every day.

Head Football Coach Dick Crum was always open to new ideas. Upon my arrival in 1982, the tradition was in place for players to weight train outside under a tent to become more acclimated to the heat. We did this for three summers until the new weight room was built in 1985. Our off-season workouts sometimes utilized aerobics to music and karate movements to supplement the program, as we only had a small room to exercise in, the "Rams Club" a booster club meeting room. We did conditioning drills in the "Tin Can," which had a wooden indoor track and an AstroTurf infield that we used for sprints and agilities.

I introduced a new 40-yard drill which I felt was specific to the pace of a football contest. There were three groups: group one was all linemen; group two was the linebackers, tight ends, and fullbacks; and group three was the running backs, receivers, secondary, and quarterbacks. Each group was assigned a time to complete a 40-yard sprint and was given 30 seconds before the next sprint. Usually we completed 12 to 16 sprints, but I would not announce that number ahead of time to the players. Much like a regular game, you did not know how long you would be on the field.

In 1985, we began construction on the new weight room which, when completed, measured 10,000 square feet and included a Lifecycle room. In this facility, we were able to train not only football, but most other sports as well. We installed 10 platforms/rack stations, a full line of Nautilus machines for single joint exercise, two hip press machines, multiple dumbbell racks, and a great stereo system that the athletes loved.

I was allowed input regarding the meal planning on the athletic training table. We were able to offer a more balanced menu for all sports.

My salary upon arrival in 1982 was $25,000 plus a car, training table access, and health insurance. My last year at UNC, I was paid $35,000.

There were several outstanding football athletes we trained at UNC, including David Drechsler, William Fuller, Harris Barton, Ethan Horton, Brian Blados, Carlton Bailey (All Americans), Tim Goad, and Brian Johnston, all of who provided great leadership on the field as well as in all phases of the strength and conditioning program.

In the early years of this profession, there was really no set budget for equipment and supplies. Since there was no way for administrators to compare previous expenditures, we had to be very careful in our requests.

Within the initial group of strength coaches in the late 1970s an early 1980s, there was great excitement. We were sharing information, conducting clinics, beginning national certification exams, and keeping each other motivated, since not everyone understood what we were trying to accomplish. There were always lively discussions regarding types of equipment, conditioning, free weights versus machines or a combination of both, power lifting versus Olympic, etc. Other considerations were the testing and evaluation of tools. Many of the new strength coaches came from different backgrounds; Some were football players, others were track and field athletes, power lifters and Olympic lifers, or from private clubs. This early group of strength coaches paved the way for the profession. As of 2018, schools now have large and fully equipped strength rooms, indoor conditioning facilities, full staffing, and outstanding salaries. Administrators are eager to provide funding for facilities not only for a practical use, but also for recruiting.

During this time, in the fall of 1977, I met my future wife, Lee Marks. She was an outstanding volleyball player at the University of South Carolina and was the first athletic scholarship recipient at USC in 1975. We met when she arrived in Tuscaloosa to obtain her master's degree in physical education. We were married July 1978. During this wonderful marriage, we have shared a common interest in the positive role of athletics and have raised two outstanding children, Whitney and Brandon.

Mike Marks's Coaching Bio
- 1977-1981 - University of Alabama, Football Strength and Conditioning Coach
- 1978 - Olympic Training Center, Colorado Springs, Strength Training for Throwers
- 1982-1987 - The University of North Carolina at Chapel Hill, Director of Athletic Fitness
- 1988-1994 - Spa Health Club Manager
- 1994-2014 - Riverside High School, Assistant Football and Head Track Coach, Athletic Director (1997-2009), Physical Conditioning classes
- Retired June 2014

Achievements & Honors
- NSCA Journal publication "The Off-Season Program at Alabama" (1981)
- NSCA Nationally Certified Strength and Conditioning Specialist
- NSCA Board of Directors
- Two-time Runner-up NSCA National Strength Coach of the Year
- Two-time NSCA National Convention Speaker
- Organized and Directed Strength and Conditioning Clinics in Tuscaloosa, Birmingham, and UNC at Chapel Hill.

CHAPTER 18

The Pete Martinelli Story

I was working as an assistant manager in an Italian restaurant, Mama Mia's, in Albuquerque, New Mexico when I met Bill Mondt. I had completed my master's degree in physical education from the University of New Mexico (UNM) in June 1973 and couldn't find any coaching jobs that interested me, so I worked as a restaurant manager. In January 1975, a coach named Bill Mondt came into Mama Mia's to have lunch. I happened to be working and decided I would congratulate him on being hired as head football coach at UNM. In doing so, I mentioned I'd like to talk to him about a program I wanted to put together to train the football players. He decided to meet with me and we met at UNM to discuss the possibility of a strength coach for the football team.

At the meeting, I explained to Coach Mondt why I thought a strength coach or strength program for his players would be very beneficial: it would reduce the risk of injury to athletes and allow them to perform at an optimal level. During the meeting, Coach Mondt seemed to be very interested and decided to talk to AD about the position. A couple of weeks passed and Coach Mondt called me and asked me to come down and meet with him. In that meeting, he told me he didn't have any money budgeted for such a position through June 1975 but that he would pay me $500 a month to start a part-time strength program for the football team. I was completely caught by surprise. I hadn't thought I'd ever have a chance to do such a thing. But I accepted the job and on February 1, 1975 I began to train players on a Monday/Wednesday/Friday schedule. On July 1, I received a full-time job offer from Coach Mondt to be the first football strength coach at UNM.

I started in a facility of approximately 1,000 square feet. We had two bench presses, two squat racks, a leg curl machine, a leg extension machine and a couple of extra seven-foot Olympic bars. At the time, I had been competing and continued to compete as a power lifter at the national level, and so I had access to the Russian and Bulgarian strength manuals that had been translated into English. I had been using those manuals to train myself and a couple of my workout partners. I decided the manuals would be my guiding light to develop and organize my strength programs for the UNM football players. I began to adapt the training cycles to fit the needs and schedules of practice and in-season game schedules. As a result of using these cycles, I began to have consistent improvement in all areas of strength that I thought were appropriate for my players. My basic philosophy was to train the athlete as a complete entity, making sure that all the major muscle groups were trained on an equal basis, therefore developing a total workout for each athlete. As I began the training, I noticed the athletes were eager to learn and that by teaching them the proper techniques for the lifts I was using, they began feeling comfortable and understand how important it was to develop proper technique.

In July 1975, I was competing in the U.S. Junior National Power Lifting Championships in Lincoln, Nebraska, where I met Boyd Epley, who at that time was the strength coach at the University of Nebraska. We discussed our comparable positions and decided that we would continue to be in contact with each other as we went back and started working on our programs.

This is basically the way that the strength training communications started among various coaches—simply meeting each other and talking over the phone about what we were doing, discussing any problems and finding solutions to those problems.

While coaching at UNM, I had the good fortune of working with a bunch of young athletes who were very eager to improve. One was a young man named Robin Cole. Robin was a sophomore defensive end from Compton, California, and at that time was probably the best player on our team. During the three years I worked with Robin, he was a very dedicated athlete who became very interested in developing his body with strength training so that he could play at an optimal level. He was the first linebacker the Pittsburgh Steelers ever drafted in the first round and he went on to play for several seasons with the Steelers and won two Super Bowl Championships.

Between 1975 and 1981, I got my weight room expanded from 1,000 square feet to 2,500 square feet and began to train not only the UNM football players, but also the basketball and baseball players. I was able to customize the workouts to each sport. My philosophy was to train each athlete as a complete entity emphasizing areas I thought would be more susceptible to injury in the sport.

I learned how to adapt my cycling schedules as they related to each sport. These schedules consisted of an off-season program and an in-season program, and each program had a separate set of goals to accomplish for the athlete's particular situation. The off-season program was designed to enhance strength and flexibility, while the in-season program was designed to maintain strength compatible to the seasonal demands of the sport.

In 1981, I was lucky enough to move to the University of Oklahoma (OU) and become their first strength coach. Coach Barry Switzer provided me with a brand new 5,000 square foot weight room and I was able to design and build my own strength training equipment.

When I came to OU, they had just come off beating Florida State in the Orange Bowl and winning the Big 8 Championship. I was presented with the challenge of working as a strength coach in a program that was highly successful. My biggest test was to earn the respect of these athletes and teach them the value of being a stronger, fitter athlete. To my surprise, I found that these athletes were very aggressive and very interested in improving their athletic ability along with their strength.

OU obviously provided me with much greater assets than what I had worked with at UNM. In 1981, OU had a dining hall that was primarily used for athletes, but mostly for football. The athletes were allowed to eat all the food they wanted whenever they wanted it. As I began to train them, I began to expand my philosophy as to what I needed to do to meet the needs of a football program.

The OU football team had great speed but wasn't necessarily a strong physical team. One of the immediate challenges Coach Switzer presented to me was that he wanted a more physical, stronger team without losing the speed. As I developed the strength program, I had to develop a running program that would meet these needs. I determined that interval speed work on a track would be the best way to condition these athletes while reinforcing their strength training program. The program got the athlete to the position of being well-conditioned enough to handle the demands of two-a-day practices and the conditioning programs we used after practice.

As the years progressed to 1985, we began to recruit tremendous athletes—athletes who were great football players but also very skilled in other athletic endeavors like basketball, track and field, and baseball. The majority of them had very little experience in strength programs because their time outside football was spent pursuing these other physical pursuits. We had to teach them how to work out. They began to adapt to the program, learned very fast and were dedicated in their consistency of training.

As I worked on my program over the years, I wanted to try to enhance it and make sure I was doing everything I could to reduce the chance of injury to athletes. One day I met Tommy Kono, who at the time was working with Olympic lifting athletes and was at OU for a summer festival program. I asked Tommy what the single most important thing about strength training was as far as he was concerned. Without hesitation, he said recovery. It wasn't about how hard you trained, but how well you recovered. Taking that conversation to heart, I began to reemphasize the nutrition aspect of our program and asked Coach Switzer if I could take over the dining hall. I explained that it would make a significant difference in athletes' performance and improvements. In 1983, I became in charge of the dining hall, as well as all meals on the road and during bowl games.

I had a meeting with the entire football team and explained to them what I was doing and why. It was important that they follow what was being fed to them and understood why and when we were feeding them. The players immediately accepted it and within a short time began to see even more improvements in strength, speed and endurance. The combination of the strength training program, nutritional meal planning, and the quality of athletes we were recruiting led to a very successful football program. We began to win and win big. We won four consecutive Big 8 championships (1984-1987) and won a national championship and played for two others.

My athletes began to realize the value of a strength training and conditioning program and how important it was to their wellbeing. I wanted them to understand that if they trained hard and recovered well, they would have an optimal chance of completing their college career without injury. We were very fortunate in that we had very few injuries that caused our athletes to miss games or the season. As we worked through these training programs, we began to see vast improvements in all our athletes and as a result, the program took off. I remained as strength coach at OU until 1993, when I resigned to take a position as sports medicine director at St. Anthony's Hospital in Oklahoma City.

Pete Martinelli's Coaching Bio

- 1974-1981 - University of New Mexico, Head Strength and Conditioning Coach
- 1981-1993 - University of Oklahoma, Head Strength and Conditioning Coach

Achievements & Honors

- 1977-1980 - Founding Member and Board Member, National Strength and Conditioning Association
- 1981-1986 - Final Five National Strength Coach of the Year
- 1982, 1983 - Region Three Strength Coach of the Year
- 1984, 1986, 1987 - University of Oklahoma, Big Eight Football Champions
- 1985 - University of Oklahoma, National Football Champions
- 1987 - Publications: "The Role of Strength Coach in the

Rehabilitation of the Knee After Anterior Cruciate Ligament Surgery", NSCA Journal
- 1991 - University of Oklahoma, NCAA Final Four, Men's Basketball
- 1992 - Strength Coach of the Year Award, Performance Nutrition
- 1996-2017 - Norman Regional Hospital, Norman Oklahoma, Program Coordinator Specialized Conditioning Programs
- 1997 - Panelist, Application of the Strength and Conditioning to All Men's and Women's Athletics, National Strength and Conditioning Association
- Presenter, "The Application of Staggered Volume Training in the Rehabilitation of Collegiate Athletics", Sports Medicine Symposium, Tyler Texas

Education
- 1971 - University of New Mexico, Bachelor of Science in Physical Education
- 1973 - University of New Mexico, Master of Science in Biomechanics

CHAPTER 19

The Buddy Morris Story

I was hired by University of Pittsburgh Head Football Coach Jackie Sherrill two weeks after graduating from the university in April of 1980. I had talked to Coach Sherrill about being a Graduate Assistant and running the strength program shortly before I graduated from Pitt, but after graduation I didn't hear anything from him and started interviewing for jobs whenever I could. I had just come home from interviewing at European Health Spas and accepted a position as a trainer with them when I received a phone call from Head Pitt Trainer Kip Smith. I'll always remember that conversation. Kip Smith said, "Jackie wants to see you in his office tomorrow morning at 8 a.m." I responded, "I'll be there!" and immediately called European Health Spa to say thanks but no thanks.

I wanted to be part of Pitt Football ever since my good friend from high school, Bob Jury, accepted a scholarship to play football there in 1974. (Bobby still holds the school record for career interceptions.) It was actually Bob Jury who asked me to train with him as he entered his freshmen year. He introduced me to "lifting weights" with the program the Head Trainer at Pitt (Kip Smith) had sent him.

After I graduated from high school, I accepted a scholarship to Indiana State University for Track and Field as a short sprinter. I transferred to Pitt after my freshmen year at ISU and was once again training with Bobby and a few of the Pitt players. I started helping athletes prepare for the forty-yard dash, as there was no combine at the time and athletes would get calls from scouts to time them and "work" them out. Since everyone showed great improvements, Sal Sunseri's older brother, Gus, a senior at Carnegie Mellon University, asked me if I would train him in preparation for the NFL draft. I now had a training partner and total access to the Pitt Football Weight Room. Coach Sherrill found out about the help I was giving his athletes and decided to offer me a GA position.

The day after Kip Smith's phone call, I woke up earlier than early to catch a streetcar and bus to the Pitt campus in Oakland section of Pittsburgh. To this day, I can remember how intimidated I was just sitting across from Coach Sherrill. He started the conversation off by asking me what I thought of his football team. My response was, "All the talent in the world *but* weak as water," to which he then said, "Can you do the job?" I answered "Yes," end of conversation. He reached into his desk, threw me the keys to the weight room, and said, "You're hired!"

Now here's the kicker, noticed I said in the beginning I was hired by Head Coach Jackie Sherrill, *not* the University of Pittsburgh! Jackie went out on a limb because he had the vision to see where college football was headed and understood the importance of having a "strength coach." He would give me money out of his own pocket until I was officially approved by the University in July of 1980. I worked for practically nothing the first 3 months and didn't receive a paycheck from Pitt until August of that year. My starting salary was $12,800.00 dollars and for the first ten years of my career I had no assistants. I always tell everyone that if it wasn't for Coach Sherrill (whom I respect, love and will always be grateful to) and his vision I don't know where I would be. The man taught me "college football" and took care of me. When he accepted the Texas A&M job a year later I was the first person he called into his office and he asked me to go with him, offering me $36,000 salary, but I turned him down to stay home. (Dumb mistake, I know!)

The "football" weight room was located at the back of the locker room accessible by only one door. It was roughly 2,000 square feet and had the equipment room on one side and the band room on the other side. I say this because when athletes were training at the end of the day the band was also practicing and it became a war between the band's music and the radio that we put in the weight room at the time. It gave me a headache every day! The room had subpar lighting, no windows, and no air conditioning. There was a home-built platform to the left of the door as you entered, with a full circuit of Nautilus machines (the new cutting-edge crazy) and three old-fashioned York power racks where the only thing that could fit in between the racks was a bar and bent pins for hooks/safety catches. Back in the "L" shape of the room sat three quarter-inch plywood benches with wide uprights that shook violently if you had over 275 pounds on the bar. There was a set of cast iron dumbbells on the floor with missing '40s, '50s, and only one of each 25-30 & 35 pound dumbbell. The matching pairs were located in the rooms of various players who wanted an "arm pump" before going out on the weekends!

My first order of business was to paint the weight room white so that it would appear larger and have the lighting replaced to bring brightness into a lifeless room. The second thing I did was get out a letter to all players announcing the new position that I would occupy. Since many of them knew me already and I had been writing programs for some of them and training in the facility with Gus Sunseri it was an easy transition.

Every day, my day began with asking the grounds crew to clean the weight room, which was like pulling teeth. Eventually, the university purchased me a vacuum cleaner and I spent the first hour and a half of my day running the vacuum and cleaning machines and mirrors. My weight room was spotless, and made athletes want to come in and train. I would lift and lean machines to clean the varnished floors and dust every machine daily with no help from assistants! In those first ten years I took one vacation, my honeymoon my first year of coaching, and that was it.

When I was allowed to start purchasing equipment, it was up to me and whomever I could talk into it to unload and place the equipment or assemble it. I'll never forget the day a long, flat-bed eighteen-wheeler showed up at the stadium on a wet snow, overcast day in December with two large wooden crates. The truck driver was not permitted to help so I climbed up on to the flat bed and opened the top crate. I unloaded one dumbbell at a time out of the crate to the flat bed, which I then loaded onto a large flat four-wheel dolly. When I could not fit another dumbbell on the dolly I pushed it all the way to the weight room and unloaded the dumbbells onto the racks that I had carried in first. From 5-120 pound dumbbells, the entire process took me four hours. That would be unheard of today, especially with strength staffs having multiple assistants and equipment companies doing the work themselves.

University of Pittsburgh weight room, 1990 - When I was in that area, I had step squat racks (from AMF), power racks and bench/incline stations. The weight room was actually two separate rooms.

During my first ten years, the weight room was expanded on two separate occasions, taking over the equipment and band rooms and making the total square footage to be around four thousand. During one of the expansions over the summer months (in those days most athletes went home for the summer) we had no lights and Jim Sweeney, Bill Fralic and a host of other guys went and got flash lights and candles so we wouldn't miss a training session!

I stayed at Pitt for the first ten years of my career even after a few other job offers. I worked for four different head coaches and countless assistants/GA's, including Jackie Sherrill, Foge Fazio, Mike Gottfried, and Paul Hackett. Some notable GA's were Kurt Ferentz, Bob Davie, Mike Sherman, and Joe Morehead. Along with great coaches came great athletes like Dan Marino, Bill Fralic, Jumbo Covert, Mark May, Hugh Green, Mark Stepnoski, Ricky Jackson, Chris Doleman, Curtis Martin, LeSean McCoy, and so many more who did or didn't make to the NFL. I always tell every strength coach and any clinic I speak at that the hardest thing I had to do my first ten years was open the door and turn the lights on! Which brings me to a very important point, NO strength coach ever won a football game!

I am blessed with two outstanding daughters, Kara and Claire. In 1989 my oldest daughter, Kara, was diagnosed with autoimmune chronic active hepatitis, a progressive liver disease that leads to cirrhosis and transplantation. She is now 32 and by the grace of God is stable (though a few prayers wouldn't hurt) and non-active on the transplant list. With Kara's diagnosis, I decided to step away from coaching and be a father. The Head Coach at Pitt at that time was Paul Hackett, who went to administration and I was granted a one-year sabbatical. After the year was up I decided not to return so I could be a parent and we moved to my then-wife's hometown of Hermitage, Pa, a small town in northeast Pennsylvania, 20 minutes to the east of Youngstown, Ohio. I accepted a position at Shenango Valley Osteopathic Hospital (my first exposure to DO's, which I much prefer for their alternative beliefs in treatment) and worked in what was then a "Work Hardening Program," a program began nationally to return injured workers to active employment. I also developed a program the hospital called "Pro Performance Plus," which trained local high school athletes for sporting activity (again one of the first attempts at a performance center for high school athletes). This in turn served as a "feeder" system to our physical therapy program. I also started working for Sports Agent Neil Schwartz, training athletes for the NFL combine as one of the first combine prep training programs. I had the opportunity to prepare athletes such as Rueban Brown, Darrell Gardner, Curtis Martin (thru Gus Sunseri), Sean Gilbert (Gus Sunseri), and Cornell Brown (Rueban's younger brother) to name a few.

In 1997 I got a call from two former Pitt players (both who were playing or had played in the NFL, Emil Boures and Jerry Olsavsky) asking me if I wanted to return to Pitt. They were about to make a change and a lot of alumni wanted me back. Next thing I know, I'm driving to Pittsburgh (my hometown) and accepting the Head Strength and Conditioning Coach position under new Head Coach Walt Harris. Along with this title came my first assistant! Under the guidance of a new athletic director, the program had expanded the weight room to 7200 square feet inside a separate part of the stadium with air conditioning. I wanted new equipment but was told there was no money in the budget that year, so I asked permission from the assistant director to raise money from former players. I raised over $100,000 dollars in donations from former players (Mark Stepnoski sent me a *blank* check) and re-outfitted the weight room. Two years after returning, they tore down "old Pitt Stadium," and in 2000 we played our home games at Three Rivers Stadium, home of the Pittsburgh Steelers. The University also partnered with University of Pittsburgh Medical Center and the Pittsburgh Steelers to build Heinz Field and a training facility on the Southside of Pittsburgh, which is now home to the Panthers and Steelers.

In 2001, I get a call from Butch Davis and the Cleveland Browns to interview for their open position. Foge Fazio, former Pitt Head Coach, was the DC, and Kevin Elko, well known sports psychologist, both gave Butch my name as a candidate. I was offered the job a week later, doubling my salary from $75,000 to $150,000. You can't refuse when someone offers you double your salary, and Pitt was telling me they had no more money to offer me, so I left for Cleveland. After three years and the "Browns" first playoff appearance in decades as a wildcard against the Steelers, we were "let go" and I sat around for a year under contract and searching for a job.

My contract ended in February of 2005 and I went on "unemployment" until May of 2006 when Turner Gill called me and asked me to interview at the University of Buffalo. I accepted the head job the next day and was back to making $60,000 a year, going from the penthouse to the outhouse. At the time, there were 119 teams in D1 football and Buffalo was 119, but I had a great Head Coach and Athletic Director in Warde Manuel. (More importantly, I was back coaching.)

After six months, I got a call from Chris LaSalla, Director of Football Operations for Pitt, who told me that Coach Dave Wannstedt wanted to speak with me. I returned to Pitt, again, for the third time, with my close friend Tom Myslinski (one of my assistants at Cleveland and someone I had trained during his NFL career) as my assistant and started at $95,000. Tommy returned to the Cleveland Browns a few months later and I brought in James Smith (a true genius who is now a close friend also). During my last tour at Pitt, I interviewed with Mike Shannahan for the Washington Redskins but turned down the job since Coach got me a three-year contract with Pitt and my youngest daughter, Claire, was in Pitt's nursing school and was granted tuition wavier since I was an employee at the time. During my second year, the original Athletic Director that hired me in 1997 returned and I remember going into Coach Wannstdedt's office and saying "we are not safe." One year into my new contract we were let go under some of the most bizzare circumstances ever in college football!

I stayed in Pittsburgh for the next two years collecting a contract trying to find a job but with no luck. Recently remarried, my wife wanted to return to Buffalo (her hometown) and we opened a Performance Center there. This left me flat broke and a struggling business to get off the ground with no business sense amongst three people! Before we even opened the doors, Bruce Arians called me and wanted to take me to Arizona with him in 2013. I accepted, only to be called a few days later and told he couldn't bring me in and to sit tight. I worked at the Performance center for one year, popping Welbutrin (an anti-depressant) like M&M's. I'm not going to express my feelings towards Buffalo, but I have only been back there once for a game where all week BA was telling

me, "you better have your [butt] on that plane!" I had accumulated so much debt, I was a step away from the streets. Without a doubt the worst year of my career and my life!

When we were let go at Pitt I was making $150,000. In Buffalo I was back to unemployment struggling to make ends meet. I went back to UB making $100,000 and spent six weeks

Coaching for the Arizona Cardinals.

there before BA calls and asked me to come to Arizona starting at $275,000, more that I had ever seen before in my life! It took the first three and a half years to pay off debt from that mistake of going to Buffalo and putting money aside to buy a house.

On Sunday August 26th, 2018 I stood at midfield of AT&T Stadium in Dallas, Texas and embraced an old friend, Mike Woicik. Mike is now 62 and I am now 61. He was the University of Syracuse's first Strength Coach and I was the University of Pittsburgh's first Strength Coach and we have known each other for close to forty years. As Mike spoke, it really dawned on me how long we have been doing this and the love we still have for this profession. The years have gone by quickly and the days now go faster. I don't plan on retiring; when you lose everything late in life you're really out of time to recover, and I really wouldn't know what to do with myself. So as long as someone gives me a chance, like the Arizona Cardinals have, and realizes I do move a little slower now a days, I will continue to be a Strength Coach.

Every day I read and study so I can become a better coach, even at 61, because I believe "we expect our athletes to get better, why shouldn't we expect the same of ourselves?" I don't have a philosophy, they are for philosophers, I have a "system, that is a living breathing organism adapting and changing/growing/evolving as I learn more." You can't get better unless you constantly pursue knowledge and over time you will gain true "wisdom", which is separate from knowledge, but the sign of a battle worn experience. In closing, it is a privilege to be a "strength coach," or as my close friend James Smith has always said,

Physical Preparation Coach. I am grateful for having been asked to write this chapter and blessed for having the opportunity to train and guide great athletes and work with great coaches!

Buddy Morris's Coaching Bio
- 1980-1990 - University of Pittsburgh, Head Strength and Conditioning Coach (first Strength Coach hired at the University)
- 1990-1997 - Shenango Valley Osteopathic Hospital, Head of Wellness and Pro Performance Plus for High School Athletes
- 1997-2001 - University of Pittsburgh, Head Strength and Conditioning Coach
- 2001-2004 - Cleveland Browns, Head Strength and Conditioning Coach
- 2006 - University of Buffalo, Head Performance Coach
- 2007-2011 - University of Pittsburgh, Head Physical Preparation Coach
- 2013-2014 - New York Performance Center
- 2014-Present - Arizona Cardinals, Head Physical Preparation Coach

CHAPTER 20

The Rob Oviatt Story

I was born and raised in Wooster, Ohio. When I graduated in 1972, I really had no idea what I wanted to do. My parents' goal was for me to go to college. They were both college graduates. My father was a lawyer and had also served in the Marines. He was strict, and he believed in hard work. There was no sitting around in the summer in our home. I started caddying at the local country club in sixth grade, and in ninth grade got a job washing dishes in a local restaurant. The pay: $1.10 an hour. I ended up bouncing around local factory jobs until after high school. That is, until the last job I had finally had an impact on me. My dad got me a job at a local plant that manufactured Bookmobiles. My job was to pick up bookmobile bumpers from a pallet and hang them on assembly line hooks—one after another, eight hours a day. That did it. I went home one day and told my parents I was applying to college.

In the fall of 1974, I was accepted to the University of Alabama. When I arrived in Tuscaloosa, I knew no one in the entire state. I had never been away from home, and it was time to start growing up. But I loved football, and I was at a great place for it. I majored in Physical Education (PE), and soon befriended several fellow PE majors who played on the football team. Ozzie Newsome, Richard Todd, David Hannah and I were often in the same classes and study groups. Ozzie and I even ended up student teaching together.

One day, I was reading the student newspaper and saw an ad for the Intramural Powerlifting Club. I knew nothing about lifting, but went to their meeting, liked what I heard, and decided to try it. I was green, but fell in love with working out. I got bigger, stronger, and I gained confidence that carried over to everything else. Power lifting gave me a sense of purpose and accomplishment that I had never felt. It forced discipline on me, and I needed all the discipline I could find. Within a year, I went from 160 pounds to 195 pounds. I was sold.

When my youngest brother was tragically killed in a house fire my junior year, it was my commitment to my powerlifting team that got me back to school afterwards. Otherwise, I almost certain I would have withdrawn from it completely. Joining that powerlifting team changed my life.

I graduated from Alabama in 1980 and headed to Midland, Texas with a high school friend, Jim Sparr. I found a job teaching elementary school PE, and started volunteering in the weight room at Midland High School. I found out I also loved teaching and coaching athletes, and west Texas had some of the best high school football in the country. I attended the Midland vs. Odessa Permian game, and had never seen an atmosphere like it. This is the same Odessa Permian school that the movie "Friday Night Lights" was based on. The thought of actually getting paid to work in a weight room still hadn't hit me yet. But, again, I loved lifting. And even more so, I loved seeing athletes train and physically improve. I had found a true passion.

At the end of the school year, in 1981, I enrolled at Ole Miss to pursue my master's degree in Education. On my first night in town, I met my current wife, Kathleen. That was a great omen of things to come, because I loved my time there. I taught four undergraduate weight training classes and used these same students as subjects for my master's thesis on strength training. However, the most impactful decision I made professionally was volunteering under Ole Miss Head Strength Coach Johnny Parker. I had just attended my first football game at Ole Miss against Georgia and Herschel Walker. I decided I wanted to get involved in helping train the Rebel athletes. Johnny didn't know a thing about me, but when I asked if he needed any help, he gave me an opportunity. He was straightforward, and said, "I can't pay you. Be on time, and I will put you to work." I was helping train college athletes, and, as I soon found out, working for one of the very best coaches and people in the entire country. Every day I learned something from Coach Parker. The Ole Miss weight room was no bigger than 2000 square feet, but none of us cared. Johnny commanded respect, but never had to raise his voice or use profanity to do it. He also taught me the value of discipline, integrity, and accountability. He was demanding, but didn't play favorites. He treated everyone the same, regardless of their ability or stature. To this day, 37 years later, we are still the best of friends and talk weekly.

At Johnny's suggestion, I also took a trip to the communist Soviet Union in 1988. JP had been there a year earlier. I went with a group of about 20 other American strength coaches. We spent a week touring Moscow, attending sport lectures, and also watched members of their Olympic weightlifting team train. The Russian athletes and coaches couldn't have been more hospitable, and they were ahead of the rest of the world in strength training. But when we landed back in the USA, I vowed to never complain about living here again. And I haven't. Our outgoing mail was being read and our rooms and luggage were searched while we were gone. We didn't have ice, fruits, or vegetables, and were served warm, bottled Coke at every meal. I was never sure what we were eating, and I didn't ask. I lost almost 10 pounds that week. We also went to the world's largest shopping "mall." I purchased a t-shirt, and watched the sales lady use an abacus to exchange my money–they didn't have cash registers. We had freedom, but those people didn't. Our Russian interpreter tried to defect when we were getting ready to leave the country. This trip was a life-changing experience. When people say God Bless America, they are right!

I graduated from Ole Miss with my ME degree in 1983, and immediately headed to Texas A&M University to work on my doctorate and continue my path towards a career as a strength coach. By then, I was up to 210 pounds. I also reunited with Aggie HSC, Dave Williams. Dave and I shared a Kinesiology class at Alabama together, and he had worked with the football team there himself. I called Dave "the mad scientist" since he was never afraid to try new ideas. I admired that. He was a great coach and person as well. We had another assistant working in the weight room named Bert Hill. You could tell he had a bright future ahead of him, and Bert went on to an illustrious career in our profession. He spent many years in the NFL, as well as coaching at Ohio State.

In 1984, I was reading the sports section of the Houston Post when I saw an article on the hiring of a new HSC at the University of Houston. His name was Mark Reiman. I had known a Mark Reiman growing up in my hometown. We had lived on the same street, and his father was our family doctor. Could it be the same person? It didn't seem possible, but I called down there, and unbelievably, it was him! What were the odds of that? I had lost track of Mark and didn't even know he was in coaching. Mark ended up hiring me as his first graduate assistant. For the first time in my life, I was getting paid to work with college athletes. I was only with Mark a year, but what a year it was! Bill Yeoman and our football team won the SWC Championship and played Doug Flutie and Boston College in the Cotton Bowl. Phi Slama Jama with Akeem Olajuwon went to the Final Four, and our men's golf team won the national championship. I learned a lot from Mark and owe him more than I can say. He is another tremendous coach and person. What are the odds of two guys from Wooster, Ohio, who grew up six houses apart, ending up coaching together in Houston, Texas! Mark, thanks for everything!

In 1985, I accepted my first HSC job at Oregon State. I replaced a gentleman named Reid Elam. Reid was a great coach and exceptionally smart. My time around Reid convinced me of one thing. If I was going to survive in coaching, I was going to have to outwork people. There were others that were a lot smarter than me. I inherited 14 sports and one assistant at Oregon State. My starting salary was $22,000, but I would have taken the job for free. As a matter of fact, I accepted the job without being told the salary. Again, it didn't matter. I loved living in Oregon. In 1985, we were the largest point spread underdogs in NCAA football history when we upset Washington up in Seattle. We also had a basketball player, Gary Payton, who ended up being pretty decent.

Our weight room was about 3,000 square feet, and our dumbbell room was a converted shower. They carpeted over the tile, but the room still sloped downward like a cone towards the spot where the drain had been covered. I got right to work trying to improve our windowless dungeon of a weight room. My assistant, Tom Emmons, and I ended up painting it and building lifting platforms. But that was not all. Money was extremely tight back then in the department. I became a volunteer fundraiser, not just a coach. In 1991 we were hosting a Garth Brooks concert at OSU. In a passing conversation with our AD, Dutch Baughman, he mentioned they were paying a crew $10,000 to clean up after the concert. I asked if they were contracted yet, and offered to have myself and the rest of the strength coaching staff clean up in exchange for the $10,000. I would then put the money in my budget to use for new weight room equipment. Well, he agreed! Little did I know what I had gotten into. I won't go into detail, but the refuse from a concert of 12,000 people is a gross mess. And it included cleaning the bathrooms. It took four of us working all night until mid-morning the next day to finish, but it was worth it. We used the money to buy brand new benches and squat racks. We eventually moved out of our dungeon weight room into a brand-new end zone facility.

As if things weren't challenging enough, in 1991, my assistant, Tom, got called up to serve in Operation Desert Storm. He was a Marine Reservist. He walked up to me in the middle of the spring semester and told me his unit was going overseas. I asked when he was leaving and he said in three days. Wow! For the rest of the term, I wrote the workouts for every sport, and the Head Sport Coaches helped supervise. We didn't have computers, so all workouts were on a legal pad. We got through it. And most importantly, Tom made it home safe.

As much as I loved Oregon, the pull of getting closer to my parents in Ohio was a strong one. So, when an opportunity at the University of Kentucky came open, I jumped at it. It was the SEC and it was a five-hour drive from home. Working for Bill Curry and Hal Mumme was like night and day, but they are two very special coaches and people. During my last year at UK, our quarterback, Tim Couch, was picked number one in the entire NFL Draft. We also beat Alabama, and LSU, and ended up in the Outback Bowl on New Years Day to play Penn State. That was the first New Years Day bowl game for UK in 75 years. I was happy there and had no thought of leaving.

After our 1998 season, I was surprised to get a call from a coaching friend asking if I was interested in the HSC job at LSU. The current HSC there was Vernon Banks, who was a close friend. I initially said "no" because of it. They called back a week later and asked again. This time I said I would be interested, but only if I could talk to Vern first and get his blessing. I called Vern, and he was very gracious and had no issue. When he told me what it paid, I was obligated *for* my family to pursue it. It was double my UK salary of $35,000. Somehow, I got that job, and even though it only lasted a year, I have no regrets. The athletic talent at that school was unbelievable, and working for people like Gerry Dinardo, Jack Marucci, and Joe Dean was unique and special. There is no place like LSU. I'll never forget it, or the heat. Our summer workouts and fall camp were like coaching in a pizza oven.

When Gerry Dinardo was let go and Nick Saban didn't retain me, I was out of work. My meeting with coach Saban was unique. After he informed me I was being replaced, I cut through my disappointment and asked him if he could recommend some off-season defensive back drills. At that point, what did I have to lose? I knew he had renowned expertise as a secondary coach. To my surprise, he took off his sport coat and dress shoes, and right in his office, spent 30 minutes demonstrating drills for me. Afterwards, we shook hands and I thanked him.

There were very few jobs open, but I applied for every single one. I interviewed at Washington State, and accepted the HSC job there in 2000. We had one of the best weight rooms in the country. I worked for two head football coaches, Mike Price and Bill Doba, and we won big. From 2001 to 2003, we had three straight 10-win football seasons, three straight top-10 national rankings, and a Rose Bowl, Holiday Bowl, and the Sun Bowl. Nobody ever had more success with their given resources than Mike Price and Bill Doba. That's how you truly measure any coach. I also had a great weight room staff. My number one assistant, David Lang, tragically passed away this past winter. As much as I miss him, I will always appreciate all he did to help our Cougar athletes and me. He impacted me and countless others as a coach and person. Any and all athletic success we had at WSU was a direct result of David's efforts.

In 2010, I accepted a job with Robin Pflugrad at Montana. We had coached together at WSU. Montana is an FCS school, with an FBS mentality. There was as much pressure to win there in football as any school in the country, and in 2011, we made it to the NCAA FCS Playoff Semi-Finals. Montana also leads the FCS in attendance every year. We had arguably the best FCS football stadium in the country, with 25,000 spectators at every game. The athletes there are tough, and I loved working there. The Montana Griz are one of the best FCS programs in the country. Thanks also to former Griz HFB Coach, Mick Delaney, who succeeded Robin.

Currently, I am at Massillon Washington High School in Ohio. While at Montana, I wrote to one school, Massillon, and their Head Football Coach, Nate Moore, gave me an opportunity. I am very grateful to him. Paul Brown coached here. Earle Bruce coached here. This is, arguably, not only the most tradition-laden high school football program in America, so is our annual rivalry with Canton McKinley. I am 20 miles from where I grew up, working at a great place, with great people. No matter how old I get, there is nothing like being part of a team and working with kids. Coaching is more than anything, managing people. That has never changed and never will change. Being a Strength Coach is a labor of love for me. It is a lot of hours, but I have never considered it a job.

I am a living example of a career that is the direct result of being raised by, and working for and around, the best of people. A special heartfelt thanks to the following people. I wouldn't have accomplished anything without all of you.

My family: my wife, Kathleen; my kids, Allison, Lindsay, April, and William; my parents, Lincoln and Cynthia Oviatt; my uncle, Hank Critchfield; my brother, Randy; and my late brother, Rich.

My former weight room assistants: David Lang, Nick Bucholtz, Katie O'Shea, Jennifer Williamson, Cori Metzgar, Tom Emmons, Mike Stryffeler, Jackson Coots, Aaron Shelley, Jeff Mori, Marco Candido, Brett Brungardt, Curtis Tsuruda, Matt Ludwig, Frank Previch, and Steve Yen.

Head Strength Coaches: Johnny Parker, Dave Williams, Mark Reiman, Charlie Woida, Reid Elam, and Terrance Roddy.

My mentor and great friend, Johnny Parker. I can never thank you enough for all you have done for me. You are a role model for our entire profession. As both a person and Coach.

Executive Director, CSCCA, Chuck Stiggins. The "Father" of the Collegiate Strength and Conditioning Coaches Association. There is no better person.

United States Marines, Jackson Coots and Tom Emmons. Thanks for bravely serving our country.

Gary Oden. You are the best friend anyone could have. Thanks for everything. You've always had my back.

And last but not least, to all my former athletes. Your hard work, commitment, and sacrifice means more to me than words can ever express. Thanks for believing in me, and allowing me the great honor and privilege to coach each one of you.

Rob Oviatt's Coaching Bio
- 1981-1983 - University of Mississippi, Volunteer Assistant Strength & Conditioning Intern
- 1983-1984 - University of Houston, Graduate Assistant Strength Coach
- 1985-1994 - Oregon State University, Director of Strength & Conditioning & Head Football Strength Coach

- 1988 - Lenin Institute of Sport in Moscow, Soviet Union, Professional Internship
- 1995-1998 - University of Kentucky, Head Football Strength Coach
- 1999-2000 - Louisiana State University, Director of Strength & Conditioning & Head Football Strength Coach
- 2000-2008 - Washington State University, Assistant Athletic Director & Head Football Strength Coach
- 2009-2014 - University of Montana, Head Football Strength Coach
- 2017-Present - Massillon Washington High School, Football Strength & Conditioning Coach

Achievements & Honors

- 1997, 1998 - Southeastern Conference (SEC) Football Strength Coach of the Year
- 2001 - Master Strength & Conditioning Coach Award Recipient
- 2001- Present - Member of the Collegiate Strength & Conditioning Coaches Association's Board of Directors
- 2003 - Holiday Bowl, Admiral Ulysses Grant Sharp Award Recipient
- 2003 - USA Strength & Conditioning Hall of Fame Inductee
- 2004-2008 - President of the Collegiate Strength & Conditioning Coaches Association
- 2009 - SAQ Strength Training & Speed Symposium, Featured Speaker, Omiya, Japan

CHAPTER 21

The Jerry Palmieri Story

My story is unlike most of the other coaches in this book. Many strength and conditioning coaches grew up lifting weights or fell in love with resistance training as an athlete. During my high school years, I played football and baseball, but my primary sport was boxing. I was fortunate enough to experience success on the state and national levels, while also having the opportunity to compete internationally representing the USA. I competed during the '70s, when weight training for boxers was off limits, so I had no experience in strength training throughout my high school and college years.

Upon graduating from Montclair State College in 1980, I taught and coached in my home state of New Jersey. Following football season, a friend of mine invited me to work with him at this new Nautilus club for some extra money. This job was my first exposure to resistance training. Throughout the ten months I worked at this facility, my mind began to question why the Nautilus system promoted one set to failure, why bodybuilders were doing multiple sets of high repetitions, and why power lifters were pushing heavy weights for low repetitions? My desire to learn more about how the body responds to resistance training heightened, so I began looking into graduate school programs offering degrees in Exercise Physiology. I was a little late in the game to apply for acceptance that year, so I taught and coached High School athletics for another year, while I applied for graduate school.

I was accepted into several programs, but the University of North Carolina at Chapel Hill not only offered me a teaching assistantship, but Mr. Paul Hoolahan, Associate Athletic Director and former Strength and Conditioning Coach at Carolina, assured me that I could volunteer as a strength and conditioning coach. In the summer of 1982, my wife, Ellen, and I packed up our New Jersey apartment and headed to Chapel Hill.

Since my conversation with Mr. Hoolahan, Mike Marks had been hired as the school's new Strength and Conditioning Coach. Coach Marks was unaware of the promise that I could volunteer, so he was reluctant to let me assist; I came to summer workouts and just watched. Coach must have felt sorry for me, because as the start of the fall semester neared, he informed me that I will be able to volunteer on his staff.

That initial strength staff at Carolina included Coach Marks, Bunn Rhames, Harley Dart, Chip Sigmon, and me. Coach Marks was the only full-time coach. I remember our first staff meeting taking place in the 2,000-square-foot weight room below the football offices at Kenan Stadium. Coach Marks asked me to demonstrate a power clean to the group. That was probably the first power clean I had ever done in my life. I only had an idea how to do it from watching the football players train in their summer workouts. Since Coach didn't run me off, I guess I wasn't terrible. At the conclusion of that meeting, Coach Marks assigned Harley, Chip, and me to the Woollen Gymnasium weight room, where we would train all sports, except football. Periodically, we would be asked to assist with the football team.

There was truly a large learning curve for me as a strength and conditioning coach. I listened a lot, learned from Chip and Harley, and applied everything I was taught in my exercise physiology program to strength and conditioning, but as a coach in the profession, I was very inexperienced. For the most part, my prescribed workouts were based on the research of Dr. Richard Berger: endurance athletes trained with 10 repetitions and strength athletes trained with sets of 6. Despite my lack of knowledge, our teams were successful in the ACC as well as nationally. A couple of highlights at Woollen Gym were leading the basketball team in ab exercises, while assistant coaches Roy Williams and Eddie Fogler watched, and coaching Michael Jordan on his cleans. It was only by the grace of God that I didn't get him hurt.

After some time, I found an article in the NSCA Journal written by Drs. Stone, O'Bryant, and Garhammer, introducing the concepts of periodization. This article not only impacted my training philosophy as a young coach, but also laid down the foundational principles of how I cycled and progressed every training variable for my athletes during the remainder of my career. With hands on experience, education, and reading the NSCA Journal, I began to progress as a strength and conditioning coach.

Upon completing my master's program at Carolina in the Spring of 1984, John Stucky asked me to join him as he took the Head Strength and Conditioning position at Oklahoma State. Coach Stucky became my "professional daddy." He built on the progress I made at Carolina and took me to another level. John was a firm believer in accountability and hard work. I recall him telling me shortly after I arrived in Stillwater, Oklahoma, "People do what you inspect, not what you expect. Jerry, if you expect your boys to be squatting 80% of their max for 5, you better be there making sure they are squatting 80% of their max for 5." In one of my first training sessions with the nationally ranked OSU wrestling team, I stood in the room and supervised the team as they flowed through their workout. Following the training session, Coach Stucky ripped my butt challenging me to coach the athletes, set the intensity tempo, and hold them accountable to fulfill the requirements of the workout. The next time the wrestlers came in to lift, I was prepared. I designed the workout into 6 stations with enough work in each station to last about 10 minutes. The athletes were put into training groups with each group assigned to a station. On the whistle, everyone had 10 minutes to finish the prescribed work at their station while I hustled from station to station coaching my team. When the 10 minutes were up, each group rotated to the next station. The workout was organized, intensity was high, and everyone was coached and held accountable. This "station training" was how I organized most of the Olympic sports training programs as we had to keep them on a strict schedule to train them in a small weight room.

Our weight room at Oklahoma State was only 1700 square feet located in the basement of Gallagher Hall. When we trained the lower body of the football team, we pushed all the benches to one side of the room, placed bars on the floor for cleans, squatted along the other wall, and did lunges out in the hallway. We eventually built a new "state of the art" 5,000-square-foot room overlooking the football stadium. Our training philosophy was pretty simple: get them strong and run them. Coach Stucky used to always say, "You can never be too strong." While it may have been a simple philosophy, our athletes gained strength and increased their speed. We did not do all the speed develop-

OSU weight room - 1984

ment and running technique training that we later advanced to, but increasing the athlete's ability to put force into the ground made them faster both linearly and laterally. Unfortunately, as our profession has progressed to put a greater emphasis upon movement, some coaches have minimized the value of strength in the overall development of the athlete. We must never forget, we are *Strength* and Conditioning Coaches.

When I arrived at OSU, our staff was Coach Stucky, a graduate assistant, and me. Technically, I was not even a full-time strength coach. In the morning, I had to teach nine semester hours of theory and weight training classes in

Myself at OSU.

the Department of Health, Physical Education, and Leisure Services, and then coach the athletes in the afternoon. My salary was $17,500. Even in 1984, it was tough to provide for a family with that income, but I was doing what I loved. I had the privilege to train some great athletes: Wrestler John Smith, Baseball Players Pete Incaviglia and Robin Ventura, Football greats Thurman Thomas and Barry Sanders.

In 1987, I received my first head position at Kansas State, making $25,000. When I began, it was a football graduate assistant and me in an old 2,000-square-foot weight room. The GA moved on by summer, and then there was me, conducting summer workouts. The players had to work and go to school, so, with the exception of an hour or so to grab some lunch, I worked 7:00 a.m. to 8:00 p.m. Monday through Friday, conducting lifting and running sessions.

KSU weight room - 1988

Prior to my arrival at KSU, only the football and men's basketball teams had organized strength training programs. I was committed to having a complete testing and resistance program for every sport in the athletic department. Naturally, there would be some hesitancy from coaches who did not understand the value of strength training for sports like women's basketball, baseball, and tennis, so educating them was critical. By August I hired my first assistant, Jim Peal, whom we paid $5,000. Jim, who went on to have a long career of his own, helped me accomplish my goal of developing a complete strength program for all the Kansas State athletes.

I loved all my kids at Kansas State, but one in particular helped me to realize why I grinded every day for such little pay. Russ Campbell was a "yes sir, no sir" tight end who was part of my first freshman class. Russ loved the weight room and wanted to red shirt his freshman year so that he could get bigger and stronger. All of my redshirts trained on a modified off-season program during the season, but Russ attacked it. He carried a jug of milk around with him all day long so he could be sure he was getting enough protein. In that first season, Russ grew from 225 to 250 pounds and went on to have an outstanding career at K-State.

Russ was more than a football player. He was a committed Christian who became part of my family. My son and daughter knew Russ as their older brother. It's pretty special when you can have a close relationship and impact the life of one of your athletes. Following the 2015 NFL season, the NY Giants fired Coach Tom Coughlin and tran-

Russ Campbell with my daughter, Annamarie, and my son, Tony.

sitioned me out of the weight room. Several of my athletes reached out to me, but Russ said something very special. He said, "Coach, the ideals you taught me 25 years ago, I now use to lead my business team." Coaching extends beyond the walls of the weight room.

My coaching philosophy was twofold. Intangibly, it centered around a scriptural verse from Ecclesiastes 9:10 "Whatever your hand finds to do, do it with all your might..." I challenged my athletes to be the best they could be, whether they were lifting weights, conditioning, doing agility and speed development, or meeting with their coach in the classroom. Whatever they did, they needed to give their best effort and do it as well as they could. Tangibly, I wanted to help them become the best sports player they could be, not an Olympic lifter, power lifter or body builder. My approach to accomplishing these two objectives with my athletes was to love and care for them while holding them accountable, with respect. I never felt the need to belittle others, yell and scream, or to motivate out of fear. I wanted to create an atmosphere in my program where my athletes knew I had their best interest at heart, so that they wanted to come in to train rather than they had to come in to work out.

In 1993, Coach Tom Coughlin hired me at Boston College to be his strength and conditioning coach, which would be my first of 21 seasons serving him in this role. BC had a hierarchy of their sports and they were labeled Level 1, 2, and 3 based on their value to the athletic department. I was told by my administration to train the level 1 sports, give a program to the level 2 sports, and not to worry about the level 3 sports. I told my assistant, Mark Wateska, that he and I, along with whatever intern we could get from Springfield College to help us, were going to train every athlete, because each one mattered. By the end of my first year, we were training all the sports in the 5,000-square-foot weight room in Conte Forum. In 1994, I was able to add Greg Finnegan to my staff as shown in the staff photo. Both Mark and Greg went on to have successful careers in the profession. It is encouraging to see that our profession has evolved over

Boston College staff: myself (center), Mark Wateska (left), and Greg Finnegan (right) - 1994

Strength Coach Jerry Palmieri praying with Hakeem Nicks of the NY Giants, prior to playing the San Francisco 49'ers. We pride ourselves on how well our athletes are prepared for competition, physically and mentally....here Jerry helps Hakeem spiritually prepare.

the years to where, currently, some schools have five full-time coaches training the football team, while another director and staff of assistants train the Olympic sport teams.

At all the universities I coached—Carolina, OSU, KSU, and BC—I was involved in leading the Fellowship of Christian Athletes on campus. Jesus Christ is my Lord and Savior and I wanted to create an opportunity for college athletes to come to know Him in this relationship as well. Through this ministry I watched young men and women develop the third dimension of their life, the spirit, and mature into outstanding leaders; then there were those who I had no idea that I made a difference in their life. Such is the case with Sarah Egnaczyk, who will later become the wife of NFL quarterback Matt Hasselbeck. Sarah was an outstanding field hockey player at Boston College who attended our FCA Huddles as Matt's college sweetheart. In 2014, I was at the NFL Hall of Fame induction of Michael Strahan in Canton, Ohio. Following the ceremony, I noticed Matt Hasselbeck, who was present to see his former teammate, Walter Jones, get inducted. We talked briefly, since Coach Coughlin was in a hurry to leave. When Coach is ready to go, the bus is leaving regardless of who is missing. As I was walking away, I heard a woman calling out, "Coach Palmieri, Coach Palmieri." As I turned, it was Sarah Egnaczyk Hasselbeck running toward me and she said, "Coach, I just wanted to tell you that those FCA meetings at BC changed my life, and I want to thank you." At that moment, I was overwhelmed with emotion and hugged Sarah as we said goodbye. It's unbelievable to think that this strength coach helped to significantly impact the life of a young woman.

Whether you were coaching in the '80s or are currently fulfilling your professional dreams in the 2000s, strength and conditioning coaches have the opportunity to develop better athletes and better people. If you want to know just how well you impacted the lives of your athletes, see where they are 20 years later. Never underestimate the awesome influence you will have on your athletes. Positively or negatively, you are going to influence them. The choice is up to you.

In 1995, Coach Coughlin asked me to be the first strength and conditioning coach for the Jacksonville Jaguars, a new NFL franchise team. I went to Jacksonville with a two-year contract paying me $75,000 and then $80,000. Coach did not want to give me an assistant, because he figured if Johnny Parker didn't have one during the years they worked together with the NY Giants, there was no reason I would need one. Somehow, I was able to convince Coach of the necessity of this position, so I hired Jeff Hurd, paying him $35,000. Jeff was an excellent coach who went on to have an outstanding NFL career.

It was ironic that I spent 21 years as a strength and conditioning coach in the NFL. Just three years prior to me leaving college athletics, while I was at Kansas State, one of our position coaches and I were talking on the field, and he said, "Jerry, wouldn't you love to coach in the NFL, the finest athletes in football?" I responded, "I have no desire to coach in the NFL. I love training college athletes and impacting the lives of young men and women." God has a way of changing a man's plans in life. I went from desiring to be a high school teacher and coach, to a collegiate strength and conditioning coach who never wanted to leave that level of coaching, and then to spending most of my career in the NFL. Proverbs 16:9 says, "In his heart a man plans his course, but the Lord determines his steps." The Lord knew His plans for me, and He blessed me more than I could ever imagine. To Him I am very thankful.

My family and me with the Lombardi Trophy for Super Bowl XLII.

I also want to extend my deepest appreciation to my wife, Ellen, who has loved and supported me through all the good and the bad over the years. God could not have blessed me with a finer woman. My two children, Tony and Annamarie, have willingly left schools and friends because of my profession. I love them dearly and am honored to call them my son and daughter.

Jerry Palmieri's Coaching Bio

- 1982-1984 - University of North Carolina at Chapel Hill, Volunteer/Part Time Assistant Strength and Conditioning Coach
- 1984-1987 - Oklahoma State University, Head Assistant Strength and Conditioning Coach
- 1984-1987- Oklahoma State University, Instructor of Health, Physical Education, and Leisure Services
- 1987-1993 - Kansas State University, Strength and Conditioning Coordinator
- 1993-1994 - Boston College, Director of Strength and Conditioning
- 1995-2002 - Jacksonville Jaguars, Head Strength and Conditioning Coach
- 2003 - New Orleans Saints, Assistant Strength and Conditioning Coach
- 2004-2015 - New York Giants, Head Strength and Conditioning Coach
- 2016-2017 - New York Giants, Football Operations

Achievements & Honors

- 1995 - National Strength and Conditioning Association Professional of the Year, Big East Conference
- 2000 - Professional Football Strength and Conditioning Association NFL Strength and Conditioning Coach of the Year
- 2007 - Contribution to Amateur Football Award presented by The National Football Foundation and College Hall of Fame
- 2007 - Samson's NFL Strength and Conditioning Coach of the Year
- 2008 - Super Bowl XLII Champion, New York Giants
- 2010 - YMCA of Greater Bergen County Professional of the Year
- 2012- Super Bowl XLVI Champion, New York Giants
- 2018 - Professional Football Strength and Conditioning Association NFL Lifetime Achievement Award

CHAPTER 22

The Johnny Parker Story

It was the weekend after Thanksgiving. All the other teams at Indianola Academy were having practice, so I figured my seventh and eighth grade girls' basketball team better have one too—considering we were the worst team in school.

When we got to the gym that chilly and windy Mississippi morning, I realized I didn't have a key, so I sent the girls on a scavenger hunt. In the end, they found an undersized, underinflated basketball on the playground and a net-less hoop over by the tennis court. I don't think we made a shot that morning—and it wasn't the fault of the breeze.

During the practice, one of the girls—Cindy Courtney—came up to me with a little devilish grin on her face.

"Coach Parker, can I have a ride home?"

"Sure, Cindy," I said.

"And Coach Parker," Cindy added. "Take me home last."

So, after practice mercifully ended, we started stuffing girls into my Volkswagen Beetle. By the time we got on the road, we couldn't even roll up the windows because of all the arms and legs hanging out. It was like a Guinness World Record or something.

Eventually, after we dropped off all the other girls, we got to Cindy's home. Her house was set back from the road a bit, so Cindy told me to pull up in the yard. As we were pulling up, Cindy pointed to her backyard and said, "Coach Parker, look! See?" It was obvious what she was talking about because of the fresh dirt—there was a new basketball goal set up in the backyard.

Little did I know, my life as I knew it was going to end in about three minutes.

—

Early Life: 1957-1969

I was born in Greenville, South Carolina, but I grew up in the small town of Shaw, Mississippi. I went to Shaw High School, where I graduated with 27 other students.

I ran track and played football in high school, and in ninth grade, one of our coaches, Richard Hamberlin, happened to have a weight set in his backyard. He opened his backyard up to us athletes, so I'd head over to his house and lift weights. At that time, I was five feet, 11 and a half inches, and 100 pounds on the dot, so there were several exercises where I couldn't lift the bar.

Thankfully, for Christmas that year, Mom and Daddy got me a set of weights, so I kept working. Coach Hamberlin only stayed for the one year, but he had got me started. I was never an above-average athlete, but lifting weights helped me become a real contributor in both football and track.

After graduating from Shaw High School in 1964, I went to Ole Miss to study history. I planned on becoming a teacher, so when I finished my time at Ole Miss in 1968, I took the first teaching job I could find—teaching ninth grade history at a small private school in Indianola, Mississippi.

A few years prior, in 1963—unbeknownst to me at the time—a man by the name of Alvin Roy became the first strength coach in professional football.

For Mr. Roy, it had all started in Baton Rouge, Louisiana. He owned a health club there, but he'd previously been manager for the U.S. Olympic Weightlifting teams. So, at his club in Baton Rouge, he'd use the same principles he'd learned with the U.S. teams to train athletes. Mr. Roy helped revolutionize sports performance during the 1950s and '60s.

While managing his club, Mr. Roy eventually convinced the coach of a local football team—Istrouma High School—to start lifting weights with his team. Istrouma had been losing—which is why the coach eventually gave in to Mr. Roy—but after Roy implemented his program, the team began to see success. For a number of reasons—Roy's program being one of them—Istrouma won 10 state championships in 11 years.

During that period, Coach Paul Dietzel at LSU had been recruiting and coaching several Istrouma players—one of whom was Billy Cannon, the 1959 Heisman Trophy winner. Coach Dietzel began to notice how much more physically advanced the Istrouma players were, so he called Coach Roy.

After talking with Mr. Roy, Coach Dietzel started a lifting program at LSU. The Tigers won the National Championship.

In the late 1940s, Coach Dietzel had coached for Sid Gillman, who had gone on to coach the San Diego Chargers. In their conversations, Coach Dietzel told Coach Gillman about how much lifting weights had helped them at LSU, so Coach Gillman then hired Mr. Roy to become the first strength coach in pro football. The Chargers won the AFL Championship in Roy's second year.

In the period of a few years, Mr. Roy had become the father of strength and conditioning in high school, college, and in pro football. Although I didn't know it at the time, every one of us future strength coaches—including myself—would eventually owe our careers to Alvin Roy.

Back in Indianola, I wasn't focused on strength and conditioning or Alvin Roy. I was concentrating on teaching ninth grade history. However, teaching salaries were so low in Mississippi at that time that if I wanted to teach, I also had to coach. I was assigned to assist the head junior high football coach, and coach the seventh and eighth grade girls' basketball team.

I'd played football in high school, but I didn't know enough to contribute anything to the team at the time. My biggest contribution that year was standing as the finish line for sprints. Basketball wasn't much different. I'd never played, and I didn't try to learn. We didn't have an offense or defense, and I didn't know any drills for practice.

We were so poorly coached that, when I substituted a girl in during free throws, she walked in front of the free throw shooter and put her hands up. In our first game, we got nudged out, 51-9. That season dragged on, and I hated it. None of the girls got better because I didn't get better—and I didn't try.

We were the worst team in school, and I sure wasn't helping our case.

———

"Coach Parker," Cindy Courtney said as she pointed toward the basketball goal in her backyard. "I got Mom and Daddy to get it for me as an early Christmas present. I come home, and I practice every night until dark."

That was the last minute of the life I'd lived for the first 22 years.

All of a sudden, Cindy burst into tears—as only a seventh-grade girl can. Her nose started running, she was shaking and sobbing, tears were running down her cheeks. I didn't know what to say or do, so we just sat there. I have no idea how long we sat—for a minute, maybe two—but it seemed like forever.

Finally, Cindy calmed down enough to—through the tears and sobs—explain herself.

"Coach Parker," she said quietly. "I want to be good so bad, *but you never work with me.*"

That saying about "a knife in your heart," that's accurate. That's what it felt like when Cindy said those words to me.

At that moment, I realized I had just been coasting. For 22 years, I hadn't had any real motivation; I was just getting by, living today and having fun today. I was just breathing air that other people were putting to better use. A citizen of this world.

It wasn't that second. It might not have even been the day or that week, but pretty soon after that Saturday in late November, I made a vow. For the rest of my life, no one who ever depended on me for anything would ever be able to say what Cindy said to me. Without knowing it, little Cindy Courtney changed the entire direction of my life.

Indianola: 1969-1974

After dropping Cindy off that Saturday afternoon, I made some changes—both on the field and in the classroom.

I started reading books on football—on whatever I could get my hands. I started reaching out to people to learn about lifting and weight training. I figured if weights had helped me so much in high school, it might help other students get a college education or become better athletes.

I found colleges and pro teams I could drive to that were doing something well, and I'd go and pester the heck out of those coaches. These were the pioneers of strength and conditioning—Alvin Roy, Louis Ricke, Clyde Emrich. Throughout my years coaching, I'd visit them and asked them endless amounts of questions—some of which I know, in retrospect, were terribly dumb. But that's how I learned. Since the school I was coaching at couldn't help me financially on my trips, saving money was imperative. I would always drive back overnight, and I would stay in the cheapest hotel I could find. Often, I slept in my car and coaches would let me shower in the athletic dorms.

In my second year of coaching, I moved to assistant high school football coach under Head Coach Bill McGuire—one of the best in Mississippi. Every practice, I was reminded of how much he knew and how little I did. I was embarrassed to go out there every day, so I started accelerating my football learning trips—to the Universities of Alabama, Tennessee, Oklahoma, Houston, Arkansas—wherever I needed to go to keep learning. I knew I had a long way to go to even be a contributing member of Coach McGuire's staff.

I never stopped learning, and I tried to apply that same attitude in my classroom.

My first year of teaching was a disaster. I tried to be everybody's friend—what a calamity that was. My second year—boy, that was also a rough go. On the first day of class, I stood outside the classroom and waited for the second bell to ring. When it did, I walked into a classroom of chattering students, and addressed them harshly:

"Everybody, shut up!" I yelled. "Get up, go back in the hall, turn around, come back in, sit down, open your notebooks and don't say a word!"

Luckily, I was able to dispel that "everybody's friend" deal from the first year, but still, that second year was rough. Stories of the "monster" ninth grade history teacher began to spread around Indianola—one of which was heard by the mother of an eighth-grade girl named Clara Allison.

Now, Clara wasn't the most popular girl when she got to my classroom the next year, but because of what I'd learned on the football field, I tried to shine an extra spotlight and make the kids in my class feel important whenever I could. After that trip in my Beetle to Cindy Courtney's house after Thanksgiving, I knew what I owed my students—all of my students. I needed to find out what each of them was capable of and demand that every day.

For Clara—since she was a bit shy and withdrawn—that process started with bragging about her whenever I had the opportunity. Clara wouldn't say a word at first, so I started by just getting her to smile. When she'd do well on a test, I'd let the whole class know, and when she didn't, I wouldn't say much. Before I really pushed her, I wanted her to feel secure. I wanted her to know Coach Parker cared about her and felt she was special.

After I built that trust with Clara, I knew I could get after her when she didn't do her best because I also knew that she now had a feeling within herself of "I can do well." If she did less, I called her out on it, and she would respond. She knew I believed in her and cared about her, and now she also believed in herself. At least in my class, Clara became more outgoing, she spoke with confidence, and she looked me in the eye when I asked her a question.

Sometime during that year, Clara's mother reached out to me.

"Coach Parker," she told me. "From all we heard, you were just a monster. I didn't know how Clara was going to do in your class, but Coach Parker, *Clara loves you.* That's her favorite class, and you're her favorite teacher."

Back on the field, our football team was continuing to see success. In my fourth year, we made the state championship, but we got beat, 21-14. I felt like it was my fault.

Now, I'd started getting offers to coach in college at that time, and before that state championship game, I'd accepted one to coach at the University of Tennessee. After we lost, though, and I saw all of those kids start lifting weights again the following Monday, I knew I had to stay. I called Tennessee and told them I wasn't coming.

The next year, we *won* the state championship—33-0—against the same team we'd played the year before. It was time to move to college.

College and NFL: 1974-2008

A year after I left Indianola, I was sitting in my office at the University of South Carolina when the phone rang. It was the sophomore English teacher at Indianola, Mrs. Holloway.

We'd know each other back at Indianola, but we weren't very close, so I was wondering why she'd called. She explained that she'd had her five sections of sophomore English write an essay on the person who'd impacted their lives the greatest. She'd told them it could be anyone—a parent, a character from history, anyone who'd significantly influenced their lives.

"Coach, out of 94 kids," she said. "56 wrote on Coach Parker."

I was just stunned. I was shocked. I didn't know what to say, and I don't think I could say anything.

Finally, I managed to get out a question.

"Well Mrs. Holloway, what did they say?"

"If I had to condense it," she said, "it would be, 'Coach Parker cared enough about me to make me do my best.'"

That idea, in itself, shaped a lot of my thoughts about coaching—in high school, college, and professional football. After Cindy Courtney, I'd already felt it was my job to find an athlete's capability and demand that every day, but this call reinforced it. My goal was to help every athlete I coached reach a point of believing in himself or herself.

This was a big reason why I moved from coaching on the field to coaching in the weight room. As I coached football at South Carolina, I began to notice something about the relationships between the position coaches and the players. The starters were treated differently than the down-the-line players, and I didn't like that.

To me, the third-teamers' dreams were just as important as the first-teamers. I couldn't—either by my actions or lack thereof—tell a kid they weren't important. I needed to make *every one* of them feel special and important. When a young person knows you believe in them, then you can really coach them hard. You're no longer just someone that hollers at them; you're someone who cares about them. When they know *you* believe in them, they can begin to believe in *themselves*.

For me, that took a four-step process.

First, every relationship—teacher-student, coach-player, employer-employee—had to, at its onset have an element of fear that can't ever go away. Over time, it becomes less and less the main motivator, but some form of fear always has to be there—whether it's a fear of failure, coach's displeasure, embarrassment, or something else.

For me, when I worked for Coach Bill Parcells in New England, I never lost my fear of Coach Parcell's opinion of my work. Whenever he'd walk by the weight room, I'd think, "does he like what I'm doing? Does he think I'm working them too hard or not hard enough? Does he think I'm getting the best out of them?" That fear drove me.

The second step—and you can't quantify when these steps will happen—is a professional respect.

"Boy, that Coach Parker, he's a hard dude. If he says something, you better do it—but he knows his stuff. I'm scared of him, but he knows what he's talking about."

From there, it turns into a personal respect.

"Man, that Coach Parker is tough. You better do the best you can, or he's going to call you out. He knows his stuff, *and* he really believes in me. He really cares about me. I don't want to disappoint Coach Parker."

The fourth (and ultimate) step is an internal shift.

"Man, I like this feeling of doing my best. Coach Parker's got me doing it in the weight room, but now I'm doing it in other areas of my life. I like this feeling of doing my best, and I don't want to let *myself* down."

I started that four-step process with my kids at Indianola, but I have applied it everywhere I coached. Every day, with every athlete, that's what I kept working toward.

The only problem I'd ever have with players is if my expectations for them were higher than theirs were for themselves. My expectations were never coming down, so theirs had to come up to meet mine.

"If you don't want to be the best, *fine*. Don't be." I used to tell my NFL players, "But every time you walk in this weight room, you're going to *give* me your best. If you don't care about being your best, then you're going to fool me because you're going to work like you want to be the best that's ever lived. If that's not really in your heart, *then fake it.*"

There's one thing I'd always tell my kids from the beginning: "Your success is yours, but your failure is mine."

When players found success, I'd be more than willing to stand back in the crowd and lead the cheers. But when a player failed, I wanted every bit of the blame. To me, I owed it to those players to give them my best. Ever since Cindy Courtney, I took these things personally. If a player gave me his best and didn't succeed, that was my fault.

I coached a player at my last job—with the San Francisco 49ers—by the name of Brian Gilmore. Day in and day out, Brian gave me everything he had, but on the last day before the rosters were finalized he got cut. He stopped by my office to thank me for what I'd done for him, and that just opened the floodgates. I was blubbering and crying like a baby. *He's* the one who'd just gotten cut, but he had to console *me*.

I really felt like I'd let him down. I know it wasn't healthy, and I wouldn't recommend it to anybody, but that's the only way I knew how to do it. Eventually, it got to the point where losing hurt worse than winning felt good. That sense of failure, to me, overshadowed any good that might've come from that relationship. That's when I knew it was time to go.

I realized how fortunate I've been, throughout my career, to have worked for quality programs—both in college and the NFL. I've been blessed to have worked alongside great coaches with great players on Super-Bowl-winning teams, but I know there are coaches out there who've done at least as good, if not a lot better, than me, and, for whatever reason, were never afforded the opportunity to work anywhere but a high school, Division II or Division III level.

In the end, all of us are very, very fortunate, and where you coach has no bearing on your self-worth as a coach. What matters is doing the best you can, giving your players your best and always demanding they give it back to you.

———

Good coaches coach the sport; great coaches coach people. We're in the service profession—the kids aren't there for us, we're there for them. Loving the kids is everything—if you really love them, you're going to want the best from them and you're going to demand it every day.

In the end, it's about standing for something as a person. If all players get from you is how to run faster, jump higher, and hit harder, then you've failed. If I was any good, now you know why, and if I wasn't, now you know that too.

Years after I coached that junior high girls' basketball team at Indianola, I met with Cindy Courtney again. I told her how she changed my life and the impact she's had on me to this day, and she said it embarrasses her. She told me I would've been great without her.

"Well Cindy," I responded. "First, I wasn't great. Second, whatever I was, I wouldn't have been it without you."

Luckily, to this day, nobody has ever been able to repeat what Cindy said to me on that chilly, windy November day.

Johnny Parker's Coaching Bio
- 1969-1974 - Indianola Academy, Assistant Football Coach - Finish line for Sprints
- 1974-1977 - University of South Carolina, Head Strength & Conditioning Coach
- 1977-1979 - Indiana University, Head Strength & Conditioning Coach
- 1980 - Louisiana State University, Head Strength & Conditioning Coach
- 1980-1984 - Ole Miss, Head Strength & Conditioning Coach
- 1984-1993 - New York Giants, Head Strength & Conditioning Coach
- 1993-2000 - New England Patriots, Head Strength & Conditioning Coach
- 2002-2003 - Tampa Bay Buccaneers, Head Strength &

Conditioning Coach
• 2005-2008 - San Francisco 49ers, Head Strength & Conditioning Coach

Achievements & Honors
• 1986 - Super Bowl Champions, New York Giants
• 1990 - Super Bowl Champions, New York Giants
• 1994 - Super Bowl Achievement Award - Professional Football Strength and Conditioning Coaches Society
• 2003 - Super Bowl Champions, Tampa Bay Buccaneers

CHAPTER 23

The Jim Peal Story

My steel mill and coal mine roots led me to believe that to become your best, you needed to out-work and out-prepare your opponent. It was early in my teenage years that I realized a stronger, better conditioned athlete had a greater chance of athletic success. In the early 1970s, like my fellow authors, I searched out any strength-related article I could find and tried to decipher what was between the pages.

The body parts that I trained actually became strong. The number of reps I did on our universal gym is still staggering to me. (What I would have given to know about proper leg strength and its correlation to athletic success.) My desire and work ethic helped me walk on at Miami of Ohio, and eventually earn a scholarship. My athletic career was that of a backup offensive lineman; though I did not achieve the success I dreamed of, I am very proud to have competed in and been part of a great program and university.

If I was unable to play football for the rest of my life, my back up plan was to coach football for the rest of my life. That plan changed the month after I was finished playing. I was still working out, just now I was in a humble, renovated university boiler room. Miami's weight room was the freshmen locker room floor. But in that old, reclaimed boiler room I saw something that would change my life's direction; there was an article on the wall about a strength program at Ohio State. I never knew that such a job existed. I wanted to be that person. I wanted to be in athletics, and I wanted to help athletes get stronger.

My career path took me to The University of Evansville as a football graduate assistant. The U of E position paid six hours tuition, a room in the dorm, and an occasional meal. U of E football was a humble starting place; we did not even have our own game field, but it was a good learning experience and a chance to grow as a person. The best part of Evansville was the people I met.

One such person was Doug "King" Salmon, who had just finished his strength graduate assistantship at the University of Tennessee. That season did not go well, I was looking for another place to land, and Tennessee needed a Strength GA. Doug introduced me to Bruno Pauletto, and next thing I knew I was on my way to UT (thanks Doug). What a learning experience UT was. I knew I wanted to be there, but, in many ways, I was not ready to be there, so I tried to rapidly get up to speed and learn as much as possible as quickly as possible. I still remember the lifting conversations with Big Dave Plew, who just wanted to pound the Olympic lifts, and grunted when a player did not get his lift. Ed Coker emphasized the big picture by taking care of the athletes, and Jeff Evans said all you need is one set to failure, i.e. the HIT program. Note: I am not a HIT person, but the HIT programs sure have won a lot of games. Maybe it is the hard work they do.

Compensation in graduate school was $225 a month to live on and one meal a day during the week. My responsibilities were: overseeing the football upper body presses and coordinating the track and tennis team workouts. In many ways I liked the philosophy of a strength coach in charge of a particular lift. As a coach in charge of a particular group, it led to daily individual interactions for both player and coach. The UT squat and lunge halls were really tight on space but a source of pride for the player and coach alike.

In my opinion, Tennessee's athletes were not quite as elite as other SEC programs, but they played the game the way it was meant to be played. We finished fourth in the country that year. The best lesson learned was that you have to get your players to play, the weight room is just one part of the program. Equally as great as working with blessed athletes and future pro football players was the people I met outside the university. I worked out with a number of power lifters who *loved* to lift, at times to a fault, but to see them challenge themselves was special. Highlights of my time in Tennessee was first and foremost the people, then getting my master's, and being part of the first CSCS in Dallas.

After UT, I accepted an assistant job at Kansas State University (KSU), where I was truly blessed to meet a lifelong mentor and friend, Jerry Palmieri. In this profession filled with great people, I am most thankful for Jerry. Compensation was $5000 a year. Jerry went home for lunch, so I got to use his lunch ticket. After eating Ellen's (his wife) cooking, I know why he went home each day.

My responsibilities at KSU were to assist football and oversee baseball and the men's and women's basketball programs. Football struggled mightily, finishing the year 0-10-1. This was a struggle for me as a coach, as I had already given up Tennessee's security and friends. The positive was that our Men's basketball, coached by Lon Kruger, made it to the Elite Eight. The philosophy of KSU's programs is still the basis of my programming today our program. We were a four-day split that emphasized sport specificity and a balanced body to prevent injury. 30 years later, that program will still win you championships and keep your athletes on the field. Jerry went on to win a pair of Super Bowls utilizing those principles.

Today both UT and KSU are BCS schools. The strength facilities were humble then, and are especially humble compared to today's facilities. We made our respective strength programs strong in their preparation. UT had two rooms and hallways where players would "get lost" going from room to room, and KSU had a right angle to the room where you could not see what half the players were doing. Organizing your program was an absolute necessity for success.

After a one-year commitment to KSU, I was offered my first full-time position and head strength job at The Citadel, the military college of South Carolina. I learned many life lessons in my 12 years as their Head Strength Coach, and I am thankful to Charlie Taaffe and Walt Nadzak for the opportunity to have been part of their program. I still consider myself part of The Citadel, though I will never wear The Ring. As I write this, I see where I get my need to be efficient in programming, to make a 75-minute lift into an hour. (I feel that today's strength coaches are doing the opposite, and it drives me crazy.) For the athlete, it was a four-year course in how to manage three major commitments—athletics, military, and a rigorous academic schedule—often on three hours of sleep.

We were strong! The Cadets really challenged themselves. I followed the basic programs we used at KSU: we emphasized the Big Three Lifts, posterior chain, and wore out the lunge hallway. The Citadel teams were never going to back down from a challenge, and that, in many ways, probably won us most of our games. With time being a priority (not to mention a lack of sleep) we never had the luxury of being pretty or moving past the basic movements. The Citadel Strength program was gritty not pretty, lots of hard work and supersets. Our strength program matched the wishbone attack that Charlie Taaffe installed. The wishbone attack was not pretty either, but wow did it win football games. I have never been prouder of a group than I am of Citadel Football. They were occasionally outscored but they were never beaten. It took a hurricane (Hugo 1989) to finally beat them. They gave an impressive effort, but after a month the lingering effects of the hurricane finally got the better of them. I will not disrespect any of the truly great players, people, or assistant coaches by mentioning them here, there are too many and I am sure to forget at least one. It was difficult to leave, and probably the right choice at the time. I started out making $20,000 and free eats at the mess hall and thought I was rich. Our facility was of great size, almost 6000 square feet, but on the second floor of a building that was not designed to have a weight room on its second floor. I am shocked that no one has gone through the floor yet. When we dropped weights, the building shook. Today the room is still the same, but the outdated equipment has received a much needed update.

My wife accepted a job in Indianapolis, so off to Indy we went and for the first time in my life I actually had to work. (Up till that point I had bounced a bar and been a strength coach, which cannot be considered work when you are doing what you love.) I substitute taught and sold weight equipment, both of which are work, especially being a substitute.

After one year of "work," I was blessed to receive a call from Jim Hofher, the head football coach for University at Buffalo, to be his strength coach. I accepted the position. The UB facility was football only but less than 1500 square feet and filled with outdated equipment. We were able to quickly upgrade the weight room with four racks platforms and benches. Of course, I took advantage of the 100-yard hallway outside our door. My starting salary was in the low $30,000s.

UB was in many ways my favorite job, it was the first time I was able to focus solely on one sport and be involved in all the aspects of the program. A few more wins would have made the job even better. UB was transitioning in to the MAC and had some growing pains. Personally, it was great to do things how I wanted, and to focus on football. My basic program remained the same, but changes were starting to creep in. In the millennium (year 2000), strength training was starting to change; there were too many strength "professionals," too many gimmicks, and a devaluing of work. Positives were the emphasis on the total body and the scientific approach to training for the sport's demands. My core work became more than sit-ups and crunches and my core program evolved around body position and how it relates to the individual's needs.

I will always remember where I was, when 9/11 occurred. Our team had loved ones lost. Jim Hofher and our AD, Bob Arkeilpane, did a great job of handling our team and all athletes. I remember immediately going out to get provisions and fill up the gas tank. Times like 9/11 that remind oneself what really matters, and how fortunate we are to be part of a kids' game.

As great a job as UB was and is, my wife was 500 miles away in Indianapolis, and once again I made the correct decision and left a job I loved. I was very fortunate to have quickly found a position at Butler University as a part-time strength coach while personal training on the side. The head strength position opened shortly after that and I became known as the "basketball" strength coach (FYI, Butler is a basketball crazy school) while overseeing all other teams, with the help of just one limited part-time person. What started out as a humble job has evolved into a really great place to be. Butler has moved from the horizon league, to the A10, to the Big East. Barry Collier, our AD, has done a great job overseeing the transitions and upgrading the programs. Brad Stevens probably had something to do with it also. Once again, I will choose not to mention any other specific coach or player out of respect to any person I may omit.

Our final four teams had something in common with the Citadel teams. We were tough and did not back down from any challenge; "the toughest team sets the rules" really applied to us. The other similarity was our weight room commitment. The first final four team had six players bench press over 300 pounds and the second had seven players bench press over 300 pounds. I say those numbers not to elevate the bench press as a basketball movement but as an indicator of effort and strength. Our strength program revolved the Big Three Lifts and posterior chain balance. The successful Citadel and Butler teams had one other element in common, they were not missing games and practices to injury. Parts of injury reduction must be a well-conceived strength program, a commitment to the training room, most importantly having athletes that want to work and compete.

What a great 35 plus years of coaching, with great experiences and memories to last a life time. The memories make it easy to forget the losses both on and off the field. I always tell young strength coaches it is a tough field, and to have a Plan B. I am glad that someone did not tell me that when I was getting started. As rewarding as the field is, I do have concerns about its direction. I feel we are overdoing it by demanding too much time of our teams, often times equating quantity to quality. Our athletes know there is a need for hard work, it is our job to manage that work so that the athlete can still be a *student* athlete. My other concern is the overwhelming number of fitness coaches, strength coaches, personal trainers, nutritionists, etc. that are out there marketing our athletes and influencing society. With a saturated market, people are trying to stand out, and selling hype as opposed to basics and proper work. Ponce de Leon was searching for the fountain of youth back in the 1600s, and in many ways, people are still looking for the magic pill, neglecting their bodies, and trying to take the easy way out.

Lastly, I am definitely the only strength coach to have taken four Rottweilers to four different D1 weight rooms. With my long days, it was also great to have my "sons" with me, and the athletes appreciated having an unbiased friend.

Jim Peal's Coaching Bio
- 1984 - University of Evansville, Graduate Assistant (Football)
- 1985-1986 - University of Tennessee, Graduate Assistant (Strength)
- 1987 - Kansas State University, Assistant Strength Coach
- 1988-1999 - The Citadel, Head Strength Coach
- 1999-2000 - Trak Personal Trainer/Sales Rep Position
- 2001-2003 - University of Buffalo, Head Strength Coach
- 2003-2004 - Butler University, Assistant Strength Coach

- 2004-Present - Butler University, Head Strength Coach

Education
- 1978-1983 - University of Miami (Ohio)
- 1985-1986 - University of Tennessee, Masters in Physical Education

---

COACHES
SERVING
COACHES

WILLIAMS STRENGTH

CHAPTER 24

Williams Strength
The Mike Ramsey & Scott Williams Story

Replay Review

Small decisions and encounters are the overlooked cornerstones of many success stories, not just in the strength and conditioning field. Think about it. When we review our lives, how much of our successes (or failures) can we trace back to a single conversation or chance encounter? Or, in this case, a drive to the airport.

In December 1992, I attended a ski racing camp in Steamboat, Colorado. While there, I met a guy who happened to have a similar flight time home as me and who also happened to need a ride to the airport. During the ride, he explained how his friend had just opened a Play It Again Sports store. Traveling for my then-current computer job was losing its appeal at the time, so I listened closely. I've since begun to question the meaning of the word, "coincidence."

I contacted Play It Again when I returned home and asked about opening a store. How much effort could gathering up some old sports gear and finding a retail space really take?

They told me I needed $120,000—and that was 1992. I told them they were crazy.

Well, I thought to myself. *If you can't join 'em, beat 'em*. I talked a friend into investing $5,000, and, along with $5,000 from my own pocket, we started Replay Sports in Columbia, South Carolina. We scheduled our grand opening for February 1993, and my wife called hundreds of people in the local Trader publication to tell them about the store. Almost everyone sounded interested—not only in the idea, but also in bringing in equipment for us to sell. We were cruising…then opening day arrived.

One person showed up with a handful of equipment – our first and last contributor of the day. *Oops.*

After several months of counting our losses, a man named Scott Williams walked in our door. It was October 1993—over half a year into business—but Scott said he had weight equipment to sell. He built his own equipment and had been selling it in the Trader, but he needed new methods of reaching potential customers.

Leg Press - 1993

After a quick scan of the empty floor space in that retail store, it quickly became apparent—to both of us—that he wasn't the only one with a need.

"Yes, please," I told him.

We had (a bit) more equipment to *display* now, but acquiring the materials was only half the battle. Even after Scott started loading his weight machines into Replay, we trudged through another several months without gaining much customer traction. The end of our lease approached as we fell further and further down into the red.

Then, one Saturday morning, we caught our break. A small group from a nuclear power plant (of all places) walked into the store. They were looking to start an exercise club at work and had received clearance and space to do so, they just needed quality equipment on a budget. We had the solutions—a few pieces in the store and several more for Scott to build. Convention aside, we were in business.

As we finished up that job—installing an entire weight room, including the first-ever Williams Strength Four-Way Tower—we received another inquiry. A coach from a new high school in Greenwood needed equipment, but with a personal touch. He wanted squat benches and weights racks in their school colors. I'll never forget spraying those unfinished benches and stands outside our back door in that blindingly bright purple paint.

However unexpected, those two jobs kept the lights on at Replay Sports. Sure, we couldn't have predicted the path we'd walk down that year, but that's life. Success doesn't require prophecy, just adaptation—willingness to embrace your mistakes, learn from them and keep moving forward.

Maybe some people would've called my response to the airport drive a mistake—especially in that first year of business. If it was, then thank God for mistakes.

Finding Our Niche

In business—or life, in general—it's only a matter of time before you realize what's working. Despite our idealistic or far-fetched intentions, we recognize what's bringing us success, or a lack thereof. When that happens, you have two options: hold onto your pride and continue to latch onto your original vision, or embrace the shift and put your money on the winning horse.

Although maybe I didn't think of squat racks or benches when I envisioned Replay Sports, weight equipment was my Triple Crown winner. We weren't selling hockey skates or baseball mitts, but we installed several high school weight rooms as Scott continued developing new products. As business grew, Scott eventually incorporated his business into Williams Strength Products, Inc. and officially partnered with Replay in 1995.

After our unlikely marriage, we transferred all of Williams' production to the back warehouse of Replay. We were confined to 1,200 square feet and a workforce of Scott and a part-time helper, but that warehouse spat out much more than its perceived capacity. Still, we knew the 1,200-square-foot solution was only temporary. The seams were starting to burst, so we decided to double-down.

First, we upgraded and moved production to a separate warehouse. Powder coating was beginning to establish its presence in the industry, and the expansion allowed us to enhance our systems (and end products) accordingly. Second, we ditched our excess weight. We dropped all other types of sporting goods and focused exclusively on selling fitness products.

Replay Sports became Palmetto Fitness—a name that reflected the commitment to our core business.

Unfortunately, like most businesses in the early 2000s, September 11, 2001 shook more than just our humanity. For several months, we couldn't scoop up more than a handful of customers into our retail store. Although that provided plenty of challenges, it did allow us to centralize our focus even more. Despite the setback in retail

VCU weight room - 2002

traffic, our commercial sales to schools and gyms remained steady. We added outside sales reps to expand into a larger territory. Another dollar down.

We kept the store open for a few more years, but in 2005, we pulled the plug. We moved to our current location in West Columbia and zeroed in on selling commercially and growing the Williams Strength brand. Yes, we were now several ballparks over from the original vision for Replay, but that didn't matter—we'd found our niche.

We wanted to offer the full weight room package—not just equipment—so we created a separate sales company called Total Strength and Speed. We quickly found ourselves dealing all types of equipment and top main brands, while still maintaining the emphasis on Williams Strength as our main line. We added a lathe to knurl the increasingly popular fat bars. We installed a CNC milling machine. We increased our staff to 20 and even purchased a robotic welder. A used sporting goods store had completed its transformation into a full-blown weight equipment manufacturing business.

No one starts life with all the answers. All we can do—before we actually try things and take leaps—is guess, really. We can dream and envision and plan for how things might go, but we can never truly *know*. We can't know, but we can *respond*. As we gain experiences, as we learn, we become more and more adept to make decisions and affect our futures. What makes more sense: to rely on our pre-experience, pre-challenge ambitions or to use our new knowledge and maturity to move confidently into the future?

Riding the Wave

One of the interesting aspects of owning a weight equipment manufacturing business is how many people contact us, on a regular basis, with their "revolutionary idea" for a new product to build, market and sell to the masses. It's not that they're all over-the-top, crazy ideas, either. It's just that, most of the time, they're lack the cost effectiveness or broader appeal to have success in the market.

Still, we listened, and eventually, we found our newest product.

As our business grew, so did our relationships within the industry. From high school coaches to gym owners, if they lived in the area and operated weight equipment, we usually knew their name. One of those names was Joey Batson, the Strength and Conditioning coach at Clemson, with whom, we developed what has now become a staple in almost every weight room and training center—the conditioning sled. Our specific version, The Prowler®, was eventually issued a configuration trademark because of all the copies and modifications of the original sled.

Through that relationship with Joey and Clemson, we found another one of those "great new ideas." We had just outfitted their new West End Zone Weight Room, and David Abernethy, who worked under Joey at the time, asked us to check out this flexible bar that could hold multiple 45-pound plates.

"Thanks, but no thanks," we essentially told David. We were in the steel business, after all—solid, *inflexible* steel.

Still, David persisted, so eventually, we made the trip to Clemson to take a look. David and a couple others took us through several exercises with the bar—it looked impressive, but we weren't convinced. Then we took to the bench and actually got under the bar; only a few reps were necessary to change our minds.

That afternoon, we sat down with David and his business partner/co-inventor Gordon Brown and agreed to help finish the bar's development and bring it to market. When we asked David about the name, he answered with a question:

"The bar moves like a wave—what's the most powerful wave in the ocean?"

He didn't wait for our guesses.

"A tsunami."

Thus, the Level 3 Tsunami Bar® was born. The first bars found their first buyers on May 14, 2012—the University of Missouri and the University of Tennessee at Chattanooga. Again, we didn't see it coming right away, but when the tsunami crossed our waters, we rode that wave.

The success of the 45-pound bar had us thinking—what about smaller, less-developed lifters who wanted to take advantage of this unique technology? I presented the question to Gordon, the "never-stop-developing" inventor (coined by me).

Sitting in my office today is the Level 1 Tsunami Bar as a result of that conversation.

After the initial product launch, we quickly realized we could produce bars with any flex and weight capacity, and, over the next several years, we developed the complete line of Tsunami Bars, ranging from 2.5 to 225 pounds per side.

Since then, doctors published several studies and high school and universities told many success stories about the bar, yet, getting the Tsunami Bar into the popular current hasn't come as naturally as we might've hoped. In an industry that can, at times, hold too tightly to tradition and consistent repetition, the Tsunami goes against the grain. Like us, there have been many coaches and trainers who have, initially, said "not for me" to the bar. Thankfully, for some, that's not the end of the story.

Those who've chosen to give the Tsunami another chance—who actually used the product—now swear by its effectiveness and have witnessed the undeniable results from their athletes.

This isn't a promotion for our product, it's a lesson. Even the most inflexible of people—like Scott and I, with the willingness and openness to "get under the bar"—can be bent in the right direction.

Into the Future

In 2017, we made a decision.

Just as we'd decided to leave retail to focus exclusively on manufacturing and selling commercially, we had another shift in focus—an addition, this time, instead of a subtraction. We asked David Abernethy—who worked with us on the Tsunami Bar at Clemson—to fill our newly created role, Director of Education.

David, as we knew, had great credentials—Director of Strength and Conditioning at Furman University and Master Strength Coach with Collegiate Strength and Conditioning Coaches Association—and he met (and rose above) our standards almost immediately. He instituted our "Coaches Corner" newsletter, where we invite strength coaches from around the industry to write articles and pass wisdom onto other strength professionals. He spearheaded our effort to join the National High School Strength Coaches Association and soon after, helped develop our own strength clinics, which we have hosted in several states.

David played—and continues to play—an essential role in allowing us to give back to the strength community, and he now serves as our full-time Director of Sales and Education.

From a wild idea driving to the airport, to a semi-functional retail business, to a thriving company that has outfitted hundreds of weight rooms around the country, "unexpected" doesn't seem to encapsulate the journey. In my experience, it seems like that's how most stories unfold—circumstantial beginnings, surprising twists and lots of adapting, re-adapting and re-re-adapting.

Hopefully, in telling this story, I've been able to share some insight into a vital component of every strength coach's job. Whether you're a company or an individual, "success"—however you define it—doesn't always take shape from the beginning. It's less about having a perfect plan and more about taking what you're given and shaping into whatever your hands can bend.

If you take anything away from my story, take away these three things:

1. Don't let mistakes define you—the most successful people learn and grow from those difficult seasons and decisions.
2. Look at competition not as a hindrance, but as a reason to continue improving.
3. Welcome advice from mentors, friends and those about whom you care. No one, ever, has all the insight they need.

Into the unknown we go, shaped by our past, flexible in our present, encouraged by our future.

IT'S AN HONOR TO BE INCLUDED IN THIS OUTSTANDING BOOK

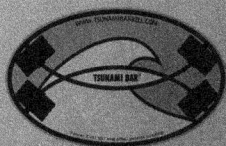

CHAPTER 25

The Russ Riederer Story

In the Beginning

I grew up on a farm in the 1960s, where hard work and exercise were simply a part of life. My father had a genetic handicap, but he was an intelligent man, holding a degree from Kansas State. A college degree was rare in those days, especially in the rural area of Northeast Kansas we called home. He instructed me on how to operate our 200-acre farm and I acted as his legs, doing the tasks he was not physically able to do. God blessed me with an attitude that embraced work as a game or "sport," as I often called it—picking up rocks, baling hay, building fence—I would readily bring my work ethic and competitive spirit to any task. I understood from a very young age that diligence and a strong, conditioned body were the keys to success on the farm. Later, I realized they would be the keys to success throughout my life.

My motto has always been, "Before you can teach it, you should experience it." Not only do I not like asking others to do what I'm not willing to do myself, but I know firsthand that experience is the greatest teacher. That lesson cemented itself as a cornerstone of my coaching and life philosophy. My first experience with hard work and body training were those long days on the farm, but my first experience with formal weight training came courtesy of my best friend in high school, Erik Anderson.

Erik and I became friends in the late 1960s and quickly discovered a mutual interest in training and competition. Erik and I often worked out with our homemade cement-field weights, until one Christmas Erik hit the jackpot — a full set of Olympic weights. Probably the first of their kind in our small town. I can still remember how good that Olympic bar felt in my hands. We would do squats, bench presses, high pulls, and shoulder presses for hours on end. Erik and I loved training so much, but in retrospect, we were definitely overdoing it. With the knowledge I have today, I would advise our younger selves against these too-intense, haphazard regimens. Our enthusiastic weight training, combined with the manual labor we were doing in our everyday lives and the lack of variety in our routines, was a recipe for over-training, but it worked out for both of us. Erik became a state champion wrestler and fielded Division 1 offers. I was competitive in football, basketball, and track and field in high school, and went on to receive a full scholarship to play football at Kansas State University.

When I'm speaking at camps and in combine settings, I routinely tell young athletes that they should be their number one coach. An individual has to set forth his goals and then motivate himself every day to achieve them. As a young man, I lived to become a Division 1 football player. Many coaches at that time were telling players not to lift weights or use resistance training to develop their game, but I wanted to draw my circle wider than the 60 miles that surrounded me in rural Kansas. I was going to follow my instinct and follow the lead of people who were excelling at the highest levels. Here I was, the first kid from my rural high school in small-town Kansas to earn a D1 football scholarship in 30 years, and I wasn't going to squander the opportunity. I had help—and would continue to have help—from many people along the way, but the responsibility for turning my dream into a reality rested on my shoulders.

The Tipping Points

I often call my time as a player for Kansas State University the first tipping point of my career. In those four years as a player for Kansas State, I met incredible people, had unbelievable experiences, and came into my own as both a player and young coach. I was forever trying to motivate my teammates, naturally gravitating toward the coaching role. In fact, I would say I excelled more in that self-appointed coaching position than I did in my playing one.

My first official strength and conditioning coach was Jim Bates, who was our linebacker coach pulling double duty. It was 1975, before most teams had a sole strength and conditioning coach. Bates was a wonderful man who had a long career, 20 years in the NFL. Training with Bates at Kansas State, I realized the variety of training programs available and the nuances and varied purpose of each. Stadium stairs, station agilities, power cleans, squat parties, circuit training—experiencing different conditioning tests helped shape my philosophy. At the same time, my role as a college student also shaped my coaching doctrine. At Kansas State, I took an anatomy and physiology course taught by a memorable professor named Sally Robinson. I was surrounded by high-achieving, hard-working pre-med and pre-nursing students. In the company of these young scholars, I pushed myself to compete at higher levels in the classroom and came to understand that what I was experiencing in the football weight room and what I was learning in the science classroom were inextricably linked.

By the time my college football career came to an end in 1978, I had a clear vision of what I wanted to do with my life. Being an athlete was my life-blood and I wanted to help foster the passion and fire for excellence in others. I was just an ex-player with a love for training others until, one day, Gary Darnell, my position coach at Kansas State, called me over to him. First, he told me that he believed I had a gift for motivating players to work hard and, second, that he had a job for me.

Kansas State was hiring a modern-day strength and conditioning coach, Bill Allerheligen, and I was going to be his assistant. This was the second tipping point. The university that I loved was opening a door to the coaching world and helping me get my first foothold. My new boss was leaving his position as an assistant to Boyd Epley at the University of Nebraska to start the Kansas State program. Boyd Epley, of course, has had a huge impact on the strength and conditioning profession, having built one of the first versions of a modern-day S&C program from the ground up at Nebraska. Bill, in turn, would make a huge impact at Kansas State and on my career.

Bill taught me the values of organization and vision. He gave me a clear view of what it took to build and run a successful strength and conditioning program. Working with Bill at a critical time at the beginning of my career helped me work in this field for a quarter of a century. But in 1981, Bill was ready to advance his career, and he became the head of the strength and conditioning program at Notre Dame. Thanks to all I had learned, and with the help of Jim Dickey and Gary Darnell, I was appointed the head strength and conditioning coach at Kansas State upon Bill's departure.

At the time I became head strength and conditioning coach, Kansas State's football program was struggling. We were having difficulty competing in the old Big 8 and I was charged with helping change the direction of the program with 14 players. Many of the 14 were younger teammates of mine; I knew them to be hard workers who would pursue any challenge they were given. By today's NCAA standards, we would certainly have been in violation of the hour limit rule that programs have today because we trained all the time, even in the early evenings on Friday and Saturday night before the guys took off to hit up Aggieville, the local bar district. Kansas State was changing its mindset about how to grow a winning team and the following season, for the first time in the 100-year history of the school, we made it to a bowl game.

Working at Kansas State, I knew many accomplished, hard-working people. Among them were Gary Spani, the all-time leading tackler for over 20 years and Ring of Honor member of the Kansas City Chiefs, and Paul Coffman, pro-bowler and Green Bay Packer Hall of Fame member. These two NFL standouts had been roommates at Kansas State during their college days and would return to Manhattan each year with several NFL teammates to train for six to eight weeks prior to attending their training camps. They would work out two or three times each day and allowed me to help. Their workouts were legendary, and they helped me formulate the beginning of my philosophy for handling professional athletes. Undoubtedly, they had more influence on me than I had on them. At the time in strength and conditioning, everyone was embracing the big, the strong, the powerful, but this group of players put just as much emphasis on speed enhancement, agility, conditioning, nutrition, and recovery. From supplements, to naps, to massage—they left no stone unturned when conditioning their bodies and preparing for spring training. This experience helped shape my personal total physical conditioning model.

Moving On

As much as I loved my time at Kansas State, if I wanted to reach my goals, I had to prove myself in a different setting—a new school, a new conference, a new part of the country. In 1986, I accepted a job with Purdue University. When I arrived at Purdue, they were undergoing a massive facilities renovation. Getting in on the ground floor of developing a multi-million dollar center for strength and conditioning would be an advantageous experience for me.

Around the time I arrived at Purdue, Bert Hill was at Texas A&M and had been given the school's confidence and financial backing to build a strength and conditioning facility that would be the envy of every college program. Fred Akers arrived at Purdue from Texas, a school that also had a renowned strength and conditioning facility and exceptional coach, Dana LeDuc. LeDuc proved to be an excellent resource as I worked my way through the facilities project and became someone I would often call for advice. During my time at Purdue, I developed relationships with many coaches and trainers who would go on to work in the NFL and become lifelong friends and some of my best workout partners, among them Bill Kollar, Tod Toriscelli, Phil Bennet, Steve Little, and Pete Hoener.

The NFL Calls

My first NFL interview came in January of 1990 with the New York Jets. Not knowing how many chances I would actually have to land an NFL job, I tried to be super-prepared, but I lacked knowledge of the nuances of strength and conditioning in the professional arena. I was also bringing a college mentality to a pro interview, and that wasn't going to cut it, but this interview did open my eyes to the possibility of working in the NFL. The following year, out of the blue, I received a call from the Green Bay Packers. Lindy Infante, the Packer's Head Coach had worked with Dave Redding of the Cleveland Browns. Redding had a great reputation in the strength and conditioning world and gave

Lindy my name along with two others.

When the day of the interview came, I felt nervous going after what I considered a prime NFL job, but I also felt a new confidence that I didn't have the year before in the Jets interview. I knew my coaching philosophy was similar to Redding's, and I knew that style was what Green Bay was after. The interview was going pretty average when Lindy got up and walked me down to the 2000 square foot weight room. At the time, a couple of players were training. I was introduced, we started talking, and soon my suit jacket was off, and I was showing James Campen, the starting center (and current offensive line coach for the Packers) how I liked to teach the power clean. Lindy later told me I got myself hired at that moment.

I coached terrific players that year, some who later became NFL coaches. Unfortunately, we didn't win enough games to keep from being let go by the organization. I had only signed a one-year contract with the Packers, primarily because I was told they had never let a head coach go in Green Bay with years still remaining on their contract. Infante had two years left, but Green Bay decided to go another direction anyway. Some told me I stood a chance to stay, but I was nervous, and for good reason as the entire coaching staff, myself included, was ultimately let go.

The Bears Years

Not 24 hours after our staff had been released in Green Bay, I received an unbelievable phone call. It was Mike Ditka of the Chicago Bears. Ditka wanted me to come to Chicago to interview immediately. It turned out David McGinnis, a long-time friend and workout partner from Kansas State, had told Ditka I was available and Bill Tobin, the general manager, had vouched for my reputation. Four hours after receiving Coach Ditka's call, I arrived in Chicago for my interview.

The interview was short, and I was offered the job, but Coach Ditka said if I left the building without accepting, he would withdraw the offer. I accepted immediately. The Bears had a lot of older players, but they were terrific; many were part of the legendary teams of the mid-'80s. Things at Chicago weren't always easy, but I always had the utmost respect for the players there. I had a directive from the coach, the general manager, and the owner of the Bears about what they wanted to see in the strength and conditioning program. After my first season with the Bears, Coach Ditka and the team decided to part ways, but this time I had asked for and received a three-year contract. For the next six years, I would report to Dave Wannstedt, the new head coach of the Bears.

Previous to his head coaching position in Chicago, Coach Wannstedt had worked with Mike Woicik in Dallas and Buddy Morris at the University of Pittsburgh, two outstanding strength and conditioning coaches. Because of his experiences, Wannstedt had cultivated a tremendous respect for the position of the strength and conditioning coach, but also very high expectations. He wanted changes and had earned the right to demand them. Lucky for me, many of the changes he wanted in the strength and conditioning program were things that I had wanted to implement from my first day with the Bears.

He wanted our team conditioned with the 16-110 model. He wanted a four-day workout model. He wanted to involve consultants in the area of speed development. But, most importantly, he wanted accountability. The NFL of the early '90s was seeing structural growth of its off-season programs, much like college programs had been doing the decade prior. Tony Wise, the highly-regarded offensive line coach from Dallas, always had my best interest at heart. Wise put me in contact with Woicik, Randy Smythe of Speed City, and others who I would turn to for advice and information to improve the program.

Things were rapidly changing in the strength and conditioning arena in the NFL. Woicik was doing incredible things at Dallas, Redding at Kansas City, and Jerry Palmieri at Jacksonville, and the effects of these coaches' programs were translating to wins. The rest of the NFL caught on fast. Quickly, strength and conditioning areas were also becoming centers for nutrition. Met-RX, Advocare, and other shakes were starting to appear—I can remember my desk being covered with powder from various products. Players were consulting the S&C offices for a wide variety of issues, and a new landscape in strength and conditioning was emerging.

When I first arrived at the Bears, I was shocked at the size of the weight room. It was maybe 1,200 square feet. There was no indoor complex. I couldn't believe no one had been injured, but, then again, it was the early '90s and no structured off-seasons were happening in the NFL. Very few players would hang around the entire period from January through June. The Bears, with a push from Dave Wannstedt, Rod Graves, and Mark Hatley, built a new training complex in the late '90s. It felt as if it was designed to feature everything we needed or might ever need in the future. The indoor facility featured a 10,000 square foot weight room, a pool workout area, and a kitchen nutrition area. Everyone involved in the facilities project—myself included—continues to be extremely proud of what we helped create.

After a few years, I had the chance to reunite with Dick Jauron, with whom I had worked at Green Bay, when he became the new head coach of the Bears. Anyone who's ever met Coach Jauron will tell you he is a special person. He trusted everyone to do the job for which they were hired and backed people up when they needed it. He was always labeled a "player's coach," but he was the toughest coach on players I ever worked with. Jauron never questioned a player fine and he pushed all the players to participate in the off-season program.

In 2000, the Bears drafted Brian Urlacher, a linebacker out of New Mexico.

Brian had a stellar college career and an unbelievable combine performance before the draft. Brian had been training with Chip Smith in Atlanta and brought some of those experiences to the Bears' S&C program. He opened my eyes to the notion of embracing people who were specialized in different disciplines and bringing in new faces to help with training. Players get tired of looking at and hearing from the same people day in and day out, and once I admitted that truth to myself, I was able to grow the program and grow as a professional. There are many facets to strength and conditioning, it's impossible to know everything. Any great strength and conditioning program has to rely on qualified specialists to play valued roles in the various phases of the program.

Players began to have workout clauses in their contracts, including Urlacher. His schedule was hectic, so, along with a few other players, we started training in small groups on Saturdays and Sundays to fulfill their workout clauses and for their own performance. I called it "making bank deposits." The small-group atmosphere emboldened the players and intensified the workouts—stairs at Lake Michigan, plyos in the sand, water workouts, speed cleans, bands, chains, boxing. There was so much variety. These workouts were gaining popularity, and other players wanted in. I brought in as many things as I could dream up to find each player's strongest motivated path. In 2001, the Bears went 13-3 with lots of overtime wins and fourth-quarter comebacks. That year, I used a greater variety in training players than I ever had before. I was open to new ideas and techniques, which is something all strength and conditioning coaches should strive to be.

Coming Full Circle

For the 2003-2004 season, the Bears hired Lovie Smith as the new head coach. Bill Kollar, a long-time coaching friend who worked with Lovie in St. Louis put in a phone call and I was retained—another example of why cultivating relationships is key to longevity in the profession. Lovie Smith might be one of the easiest men in the world to respect and admire, and I spent a fun year working under him. He and Assistant Bob Babich, who Brian Urlacher would later choose as his Hall of Fame presenter, made the transition easy. But after the season, I began to think about considering retirement. I remembered the old saying, "Leave on your own terms." I made the decision to retire.

At the time, Lovie told me I was crazy, and he might have been right. But I was ready to take a leap of faith. Many coaches say "Faith, family, and *then* football," and I decided it was time to live it. My wife and I had four young children—now grown—who were the greatest blessings in our lives, and we made the decision to leave Chicago and move our family back to the small Northeast Kansas community of Holton, where I had been raised.

For me, the key to transitioning from life in the NFL to life in a small

Kansas town was to stay active. I began consulting with camps, small colleges, combines, and college football all-star games. I was invited to become a member of one of our community bank's Board of Directors. Once a month I participated in a meeting, and I quickly found how many similarities there are between banking and coaching—certainly more than coaches or bankers might think. I also became involved in functional fitness and cross fit competitions to get my competitive juices flowing. As a 61-year-old athlete, I'm doing snatches, cleans, squats, plyos, sprints, pullups, pushups, and jump rope. I encourage all old strength and conditioning coaches to give it a shot, but, a word of warning, get ready for a helping of humble pie, and always be coachable. My sons coach me now, and, as they say, turnabout is fair play.

My story starts and ends in the same place, the small town in Kansas where I worked the farm and lifted cement-filled weights so many years ago. And, in between, I had the pleasure of living a more fulfilling life than I ever could have imagined as a young boy. I was surrounded by incredible people, helped build successful programs, worked with some of the best coaches and players in the game, and forged unforgettable friendships. As I've said before, my life's motto is, "Before you can teach it, you should experience it." I am humbled by and grateful for all I have had the opportunity to experience.

Epilogue: My Principles

A Russ Riederer-ism is a life rule that has served me well. These "isms" have been crafted over years of experiences, successes, and failures, and are an essential part of my coaching and life philosophy. I'll share them with you here:

- Exercise is the fountain of youth—it just doesn't always taste good.
- Relationships will help build your career more than self-promotion.
- Want to build relationships? Embrace lots of different workout partners.
- You have to live it before you can be a passionate teacher of it.
- The best workout you have ever done is the one you haven't done.
- Many different methods of strength and conditioning have won Super Bowl rings; the common factor is motivation.
- The more you embrace "A different face for every phase," the better strength and conditioning program you will have.
- Show me a S&C coach who's a good golfer and I'll show you a bad S&C coach! (This is mostly just my excuse for not being good at golf.)

Russell H. Riederer's Coaching Bio
- 1975-1978 - Kansas State University, Student Athlete
- 1979-1980 - Kansas State University, Graduate Assistant
- 1981-1986 - Kansas State University, Head Strength and Conditioning Coach
- 1987-1990 - Purdue University, Head Strength and Conditioning Coach
- 1991 - Green Bay Packers, Head Strength and Conditioning Coach
- 1991-2005 - Chicago Bears, Physical Development Coordinator

Achievements & Honors
- Kansas Shrine Bowl Hall of Fame
- Raycom College All-Star Football Advisory Board
- Advocare Advisory Board
- Denison State Bank, Board of Directors
- World Ranked, Functional Fitness Masters Athlete

CHAPTER 26

The Brad Roll Story

I grew up in Houston, Texas, in the 1960s and early 70s.

My mother and father raised me in a faith-oriented, middle-class family. They taught me work ethic, confidence, structure, discipline, and the difference between right and wrong. These virtues were passed down—from my grandparents to my parents, and from my parents to my two younger brothers and me. Everybody else on the block was brought up the same way.

My brothers and I always worked some sort of summer job. We'd mow grass; we'd clean gutters; we all had paper routes as soon as we were old enough to leave the house. We were never given anything. If you wanted something, you worked hard and you earned it.

In the fall, you played football. In the spring, you played basketball. In the summer, you played baseball.

Above all, you treated people with respect. Respect for your parents, teachers, coaches, pastors, and authorities. I still have great memories of those mentors in my life. They implemented all of these institutions, still sacred to me today, that I've tried to pass on to every player I've coached.

I thank God I had people in my life like that, and every day I try to emulate their example in my own life. Because of them, I learned to give 100 percent every day. Because of them, I learned it's not a crime to fail—as long as you get back up. I learned that if you have the work ethic and desire to succeed, you *will* improve and you *will* reach your goals.

That's what I've preached for 40-plus years in this business.

I like to avoid clichés, but for the sake of this chapter I'll use one—strength and conditioning is a young man's game. Outside of this book, you'll be hard-pressed to find any 60-year-old strength coaches still working full-time in this industry.

I've made it a personal goal to never be labeled as "that old strength coach."

Since I started coaching in 1980 at Stephen F. Austin, a number of things about this industry have changed. Equipment has evolved and improved. Education has progressed and become more widely available. Technology has offered new insights into player health, workload and performance.

Throughout my years—especially with the Cleveland Browns in 2013—I've had to reinvent myself a bit in order to stay in this business. As I began to notice the changes, I learned quickly that if I didn't adapt, I was going to get washed up. So I researched the latest developments in sports science. I began to learn and specialize in GPS tracking, internal and external loads.

Underneath all of that—beneath the desire to stay in this business—were the principles I learned as a kid. The work ethic, discipline and structure instilled in me by mother and father have fueled me throughout my career.

Changing Culture, Consistent Motivation: Navigating the Balance of Change and Values

Now I'm not trying to act like Mother Teresa, but my first full-time job—at the University of Louisiana at Lafayette in 1981—covered strength and conditioning for all sports and paid $11,500. I worked as an assistant offensive line coach, broke down film, and even had a recruiting area assigned to me.

During the off-season, my first football session began at 6:00 a.m. Then, from 8:00 a.m. until noon, I'd go out and recruit within a 60-mile radius of Lafayette. When I came back, I had football training groups from 2:00 to 6:00 p.m., and at 6:00 p.m. the Olympic sports had their turn. All of this for $11,500—with maybe 12 official credit hours of strength and conditioning related study.

In 1980, you could major in education. Today, you can major in nutrition, kinesiology, sports medicine, and any sort of strength-and-conditioning-related degree. In 1980, you didn't even have heart rate monitors. Today, if you don't specialize in GPS tracking, internal and external loads, and the different sports sciences, you're behind the pace.

It's not just the resources and equipment that have evolved—it's the technique, and the coaches implementing that technique.

When I first started coaching, a common practice was, "Let's work him out until he doubles over, cramps or throws up." Thankfully, that really dumb, ego-fueled train of thought has revolutionized into things like Onset of Blood Lactate Accumulation (OBLA) training, Max VO2, maintaining heart rates to expand conditioning, and adapting to different training modes. Since we're now more aware of the biology of players and where we want to take them, there's much more of an emphasis on keeping players healthy.

The players, too, aren't from the same mold we saw back in the '80s and even early '90s. When I coached with the Buccaneers in Tampa Bay, I attended my first ever rookie symposium. Sam Wyche asked me to tag along to Atlanta in 1993, so I traveled with our player rep, Mike Sullivan, and spent two days listening to doctors educate players on performance-enhancing drugs, AIDS, and other things like player relationships.

I had no idea that, in 2018, the topics would shift to things like "how to act in a club" or "how to deal with road rage" or "how to respond when you're solicited by a woman." But that's what we do now—that's where we've come.

Unfortunately, for some (not all) players today, yesterday isn't soon enough—whether you're 13, 23, or 33 years old. It's so sad to hear these stories—especially within the last 20 years—of players using PEDs under the promise that "they're going to work" and "they're going to work fast."

At the same time, players are more educated and knowledgeable than they've ever been in the past. In 1980, players never questioned you about sets or reps or loads or quantities, but now, you have to outline the why, where, and how for each exercise a player uses. Players want to know how every exercise will improve their performance, keep them healthy, and extend their career.

As a coach today, I embrace that—and to some degree, I think that's why I've stuck around. Thankfully, I've been able to change and adapt with the times without sacrificing my core beliefs. Now, I might, for instance, explain exercises differently and more in-depth, but the way I motivate players hasn't shifted since that first team at Stephen F. Austin in 1980.

Stephen F. Austin Lumberjacks - 1980

Yes, equipment, players, and education have evolved, but reps, movements, volume, intensity, and the desire to win *have not changed*. I still tell young coaches today not to overthink their exercise programs—a good idea in 1980 can *still* be a good idea today. A lot of exercises that are considered "new" today, I can remember talking about and doing in the '80s.

Take kettle bells, for example. They were all the craze in 2010, 2011, but I saw the Soviets doing kettle bell training in 1983. Another example is CrossFit. There are gyms all over the country talking about "new ways to train," but we were going through those same CrossFit exercises at the University of Miami in the late '80s. A lot of these exercises just ended up going in a big circle.

There's always going to be change—for better or worse—and you have to adapt, but you also only have one set of values. Regardless of new styles or circumstances, I always preach the same thing, to players and to myself: keep working hard, keep pushing yourself to be better, stay disciplined.

Ultimately—amid all of this—it comes down to the players. It's finding players around whom you build your program. Strength coaches don't win football games—players do. If you focus on those relationships with players, you'll begin to see the dominoes fall into place.

Top Player, Top Down: Creating a Successful Program

Some people say if you ever find yourself locked up in prison, on the first day you better find the toughest guy in the yard and try to whip his ass. It's risky, but if you're successful, everyone will stop following *him* and start following *you*.

In football, it's basically the same thing.

Throughout my years, I've consistently found that if you find the best players on the team and convince them to buy into your program, the rest will follow. If you can hit a home run with the top players in each position group, it's going to make things a lot easier across the board.

In my first NFL coaching job—Tampa Bay in 1993—two of those players were Hardy Nickerson and Steve DeBerg. Hardy played linebacker, and Steve was our starting quarterback. The credibility I gained early in my career is, in large part, due to these two men.

From the beginning, these two were the first in the weight room and the last to leave. They were the first ones—on and off the field—to find whatever they could to elevate their games. I feel very blessed to have had the opportunity to coach these two men, to have them believe in me and my program. In one of my most significant career transitions—college to the NFL—Hardy and Steve legitimized my message.

College and the NFL, from a strength and conditioning standpoint, are very different. At the University of Miami—where I coached from 1989-1992—the program was already in place when I arrived. Howard Schnellenberger started it in 1979, and each head coach after him was smart enough to keep that train rolling. They didn't screw up what was already in place, they only made it better.

A lot of times, attention to detail and work ethic aren't passed down from the first generation to the next. Thankfully, this wasn't the case at Miami. All of those qualities were kept, maintained, polished and developed to high standard. I walked into a culture of success in 1989, so all I had to do was keep that train rolling.

In the NFL, things change—especially in your first job. You need that credibility that players like Hardy and Steve gave to me. You're dealing with grown-ass men, and you need to prove to them you can make them more successful.

That's when you target those top players.

If you can set up a program—from warm-up to programming to lifting patterns, body comp analysis and nutrition—that keeps players healthy and in which they can recognize improvement and consistent progress, they'll buy in. They'll believe in you. And if you can motivate those top players to be the first guys in the weight room, the first guys on the field, and the first guys getting a post-workout shake, everyone will follow suit.

Now this is a good starting point, but it's not the whole picture. From that point, in my experience, I've abided by a ratio—15-70-15.

For the majority of programs of which I've been a part, the players can be divided into three categories. Fifteen percent of guys will, regardless, be committed to working hard, bettering themselves and sticking to your program. Another 15 percent won't be committed, won't have that necessary drive. The other 70 percent, though, are the athletes in the middle. They're the athletes to whom, as a strength coach, I tried to dedicate the most focus.

These are the guys in whom you see potential, but for whom you still might have to hide under their car to get them to come into the gym. You might have to put in a little extra effort to help those players realize they have a certain window of competitiveness, and you can help them prolong that window.

When it comes down to it, the players have to make plays on Sunday. On any given practice day, a player has 12 or so team scouts in another room—watching him, measuring his success. If he doesn't make plays on game day, those scouts will find someone better to replace him. If you, as a coach, can convince him that you can help him make plays, you'll have a committed follower.

Beneath all of the talent and exercises and highlight plays, though, there needs to be a drive in your players. There needs to be a competitiveness, a sense of looking over their shoulders, a desire to persevere through adversity. Once that drive is recognized, it's just a matter of access.

Know Your Audience: Building Relationships with Athletes

In 1988, our men's basketball at Kansas University won the national championship. In 1989, our University of Miami football team beat down Alabama to win the national championship. In 1991, at Miami, we completed an undefeated season with a win over Nebraska in the national championship.

On October 3, 1993, I saw my first win as an NFL coach—27-10 over the Detroit Lions in Tampa Stadium. In 1998, I won my first playoff game with the Miami Dolphins. From 1998-2000, those same Dolphins made it to the second round three years in a row.

Looking back, I remember each of these moments distinctly. They're certainly special accomplishments that I'll remember until I'm gone, but as a coach, they're not my proudest.

*1989 Miami Hurricanes - National Champions
with Dennis Erickson.*

*1992 Miami Hurricanes - National Champions
White House Visit.*

In 1986, I was coaching at the University of Louisiana at Lafayette. We were a directional school, so we were limited in that capacity, but that 1986 team had some of the toughest, hardest-working kids I've ever been around. They were average athletes, but from a strength and conditioning standpoint, they worked hard to develop a culture of excellence.

We went 6-5 that year, but those kids played far above their heads. They gave everything they had and listened to everything I said.

At the end of that year, all of the athletes, from every sport, at Louisiana-Lafayette voted on an award. Throughout my career, I've been inducted into the USA Strength and Conditioning Coaches Hall of Fame, the Stephen F. Austin Ring of Honor, among others, but, to this day, winning the 1986 Coach of the Year award at Louisiana-Lafayette is the single greatest, most humbling honor I've ever received.

That meant a lot to me at that point in my career, and it still means a lot to me now. Knowing that I made an impact on those players' lives—that made a big difference.

To me, those are the defining moments. Those "coming to Jesus" workouts at 6 a.m. in the middle of a winter training session or in the 100-degree heat in the summer. Those sessions where you see kids come together and gain respect and love for each other. Those times that you can point back to and say, "This workout led to a better, more consistent culture."

Maybe it's the first time a player benches 300 pounds or finishes a hard conditioning session or sets a personal record. Those are the special moments to me.

I think about Larry Izzo with the Dolphins—an undrafted free agent from Rice who went on to play 14-plus years in the NFL. I think about O.J. Brigance—another undrafted from Rice who came over from the Canadian Football League and ended up winning a Super Bowl with the Ravens in 2000. These were the epitomes of a class act—from their work ethic and desire to excel to all of those intangible qualities that you hope for in a player.

When you see players like that work hard and succeed, that's what really brings satisfaction in this industry. It's not the wins—it's the relationships.

If you can reach him as a person, you can benefit him as a player. That's something I've always believed and, throughout my career, something I've understood more and more.

First, it's understanding the motivation of the *group.* The strength coaches that have been around the longest are the ones who can relate to any athletic personality.

If you're in a group of 10 offensive linemen, all of them will, more or less, have the same group philosophy. But if you're working with 10 running backs or 10 wide receivers or 10 defensive backs, it's a different story. You're dealing with multiple personalities, and if you don't find what makes each of those players tick, you won't be able to move forward.

What motivates them—as a group? Maybe it's fear; maybe it's money; maybe it's women—but in any case, you need to find out what it is. You find that one common denominator among the group, and you dangle it out in front of them like a carrot on a stick.

Then, it's understanding the *individual.* Before you can help an athlete succeed, you first need to understand him on a personal level. *What's going to keep him healthy? What's going to propel his game? Is he an introvert or an extrovert? Does he respond to hollering or encouraging?*

The best coaches in this business are the ones who can identify players' needs and understand their personalities. It's being able to see something in players that maybe other people don't see. It's showing them you care about them—that you're sincere in wanting to help them.

If a player comes to me in confidence with anything—on or off the field—I make it a priority to either help them or direct them to someone that can. Pick any vice you can think of—I've had players talk to me about it in confidence, and it stayed in confidence with me. I don't know if they choose me because of my experience or just because they think I did the same dumb things at some point (which is usually accurate), but I always feel obligated to help them. When the athletes see that sincerity and mutual respect, we're able to have success in the weight room.

If you can reach him as a person, you can benefit him as a player.

As a coach, you want to see these players work hard. You want to see them be successful. Amid all of the personalization and individualization, that stays the same. From rookies to regular starters to veterans, the message stays the same—*don't change who you are.*

There's a message I tell my young players every year: be who you seek.

Look at where you are. Look at how hard you're working. You're making the goals you set for yourself when you played little league football as a kid. You worked your ass off to get to this point, now *don't change*.

Don't change the work ethic that you have right now. Don't change the motivation. Don't change your personality. When the success, the money, the fame comes, don't change that desire to be the first one in the weight room or the last one to leave. Don't let that big second contract change who you are.

Go to the facilities every day. Help in your community. Hold on to that same joy and motivation you had as a kid. Be the same person that you were on the road to get to this point. *Be who you seek.*

Coaching at the University of Tennessee.

I hope that's how players remember me. I hope they remember me as someone who helped prolong their window of time, who helped preserve that joy, motivation and drive instilled in them at a young age.

I believe my success—in part, at least—is due to the fact that I'm *still* that kid riding my bike around Houston in cut-off jean shorts and bare feet, drinking from the garden hose. Although circumstances, people and successes changed around me, I tried my best to stick to those values on which I was raised.

Respect others, work hard, never give up.

I preached that to my players, but I never would've been able to if I didn't believe them myself.

Brad Roll's Coaching Bio

- 1980 - Stephen F. Austin State University, Strength & Conditioning Coach
- 1981-1986 - University of Louisiana-Lafayette, Strength & Conditioning Coach
- 1987-1988 - University of Kansas, Strength & Conditioning Coach
- 1989-1992 - University of Miami, Strength & Conditioning Coach
- 1993-1995 - Tampa Bay Buccaneers, Strength & Conditioning Coach

- 1996-2003 - Miami Dolphins, Strength & Conditioning Coach
- 2004-2005 - Buffalo Bills, Strength & Conditioning Coach
- 2006-2007 - St. Louis Rams, Strength & Conditioning Coach
- 2008-2011 - Oakland Raiders, Strength & Conditioning Coach
- 2012 - University of Southern California, Strength & Conditioning Coach
- 2013 - Cleveland Browns, Strength & Conditioning Coach
- 2014-2015 - University of Miami, Catapult Performance Analyst Football
- 2016 - U.S. Military Academy
- 2016 - University of Tennessee, Catapult/Zebra Performance Analyst
- 2018-Present - University of Tennessee, Director of Men's & Women's Tennis

Achievements & Honors

- 2003 - USA Strength and Conditioning Hall of Fame
- 2005 - Stephen F. Austin State University Ring of Honor
- 2015 - CSCS Certified
- 2015 - CSCCa Legends in The Field
- 2017 - USAW L1 Certified
- National Speed & Explosion Association Certified
- International Sports Science Association Certified
- CPR/Red Cross Certified

Education

- 1979-1980 - Stephen F. Austin State University, B.S. (1979) Ed., M.Ed. (1980)
- 1981-1983 - University of Louisiana-Lafayette, Post Grad Studies Ed.

CHAPTER 27

The Chip Sigmon Story

It was the year 1977, I was a junior at Appalachian State University (an undergraduate mind you) when I got a phone call from ASU head baseball coach Jim Morris. He asked me if I would consider working with his baseball team to set up a strength program during their off-season. I had just won the Mr. North Carolina bodybuilding championships, and word had gotten around that I was into weight training and was even writing up programs for students and student athletes.

You have to realize that weight training wasn't even thought of back then for some athletes, especially for baseball players. Coach Morris was ahead of his time in thinking that if his baseball players got stronger and more explosive, it might improve team performance. To top it off, Coach Morris was going to have his team work with a bodybuilder…God forbid! There was some negative talk, but even then I knew the difference between sports specificity and bodybuilding. Our results were great, even if the equipment was not. The team won the conference championship, finished second in the nation in hitting, and even led the nation in home runs. All this using only an old universal machine and a few free weights in the gymnastics room!

This milestone in my life sealed the deal for me. I now knew what I wanted to be, but how to make a living doing this was another matter. I had a professor ask me what I wanted to do with my PE degree (back then there was no exercise science) and I responded by saying "a strength and conditioning coach" to which he exclaimed, "What's that!" Actually, that's what my concerned future father in law said some 30 years ago, but that's another story.

Since strength and conditioning coaches were basically unheard of, after I graduated from App State in 1978 I took a job back in my hometown of Kannapolis, NC working at my former schools. I was an elementary roaming

PE teacher, an assistant high school football coach, and a head junior high track coach. I even helped out with the A.L. Brown High School weight-training program (which was ahead of its time).

Somehow and someway in 1981, I heard of an opening for an assistant strength coach position at the University of North Carolina, interviewed, and got the job. Mike Marks, former head strength coach at Alabama, was coming to Chapel Hill to head up the strength program. Mike was a great guy—knowledgeable and mild mannered, but he could be intense when needed. That is a key principle I learned that has helped me along the way.

Myself (right) and Jerry Palmieri (left) - 1987

UNC's 2000 square foot weight room was strictly for football. On one side of the room was squat racks, in the middle was platforms and on the other side was bench presses. We had a couple of Nautilus machines in the corner of the room and in a smaller room off to the side. One-day coach Marks ask me and another assistant to put together a new leg press machine we had just gotten in. That other coach was Jerry Palmieri from New Jersey. From then on, it was the North versus the South. For nearly four decades, we have argued like an old married couple but a better friend I could never have.

At one of our first strength and conditioning staff meetings, coach Marks went around the room asking our staff questions about lifts and techniques on certain exercises. I remembered reading in the NSCA journal about "compensatory acceleration" a few months earlier. When Mike ask me about a certain lift, (I cannot remember which one) I nailed it by using that term in my explanation. I learned right then "knowledge is power!" This fueled an important key principle for me: bring a ruthless pursuit of knowledge daily. I don't let a day go by without reading or watching information to make me a better coach and person.

Our staff worked with all teams at Carolina, however the weight room for all other sports was down in the lower section, another term for "basement" at Woolen Gym. Woolen was attached to Carmichael Auditorium, where the basketball teams practiced and played. Again, the equipment was the good ole blue Nautilus machines and free weights. I could tell you stories of Michael Jordan coming down to workout and lift, but what I remember the most even back then in the early '80s was that the bench press, squat, the overhead press, and the cleans were the staple lifts for most of the UNC teams.

I was still at UNC in the summer of 1983 when I made a telephone call back to my baseball friend Jim Morris to see if ASU was ready to hire a strength coach. Amazingly they were! Coach Mack Brown was in his second year as head football coach. One of his assistant coaches, John Palermo, was in charge of the football team's weight training but Mack and the AD were looking for someone to step in and take over as strength coach for not just football, but for all the teams. ASU was indeed ready for the next step, and timing, once again, was everything!

In January of 1984, I headed back to where it all began as ASU'S first strength & conditioning coach. It would just be me, no assistants, and I would be working with all teams. And my salary? I probably didn't tell others then, but it was $00.00 and I got room and board. My home for the next year was a small room under Owens Field House where the officials dressed for game day. It was about 100 square feet with a small bed, a shower and no heat! The North Carolina Mountains are really cold, so after a few weeks, assistant AD, Roachal Laney, brought me a small electric heater. Thank God, as I was beginning to freeze at night! I also received free training table, but many times I would work with the athletes so late that I'd miss the training table times and go to bed hungry.

Our weight room was on the lower floor of Broome-Kirk Gym, about 800 square feet with no windows. It was a combination of two rooms with a wall knocked out in the middle to make up the 800 square feet. One room was comprised of bench presses, incline benches and dumbbells. The other room had two platforms and the rest was for squat racks. There was no music system and I had no office. Since we were in a basement, by the summer I noticed how bad the Olympic Bars were rusting. So, I went to the local hardware store and purchased WD-40 and dehumidifier bags and hung them all over the weight room walls to prevent the rust.

I remember Coach Brown at one of our staff meeting saying, "I hired a strength coach and

ASU weight room - 1984

ASU weight room - 1984

now all we have are pulled hamstrings!" I had the team performing a lot of hip extension work, RDL's for example, but was limited on my knee flexion. I left that meeting, got on the phone to call a friend of mine and somehow talked him into donating two leg curl machines and a stereo system.

Two people at ASU who really gave me a tremendous amount of support were Dr. Harold O'Bryant and Dr. Michael Stone. Now, when I first arrived at App State, I heard that Dr. O'Bryant and others in the exercise science department (Dr. Stone was not there yet) were displeased that they were not included in the hiring process since the strength coach would be working with all teams. Therefore, I knew I needed to get Dr. O'Bryant on board, use his expertise and make him feel a part of the strength program. I made sure I was in his office and then Dr. Stone's when he arrived, weekly if not every day. I always asked them questions, told them about my workouts, and *listened*. Their advice was invaluable. Additionally, the current NSCA president, Dr. Travis Triplett, and my future wife, were both exercise science graduate students. Her insight was a tremendous help.

The decade of the 80s was all about the Jane Fonda aerobics, and Dr. O'Bryant and Dr. Stone were on the opposite end of the spectrum when it came to that type of conditioning for power sports. Boone is very cold in the winter but having an indoor facility for football was out of the question in those days. I had to condition the football team on the balcony of the basketball gym, which was hard concrete! One winter I had a few college co-eds condition the team by performing aerobics in the gymnastic room. Dr. O'Bryant called me into his office and let me have a piece of his mind! "You know your squat strength and power will decrease," he said. I tried to justify my situation to him, but he was right. Soon the entire football team's strength and power went down! A learning moment for sure.

Thankfully, I achieved my goal of proving the need for a fulltime strength coach by year two; every head coach for all Varsity teams took money out of their budget to actually pay me a salary. I can't remember the exact amount but at that point, I felt like it was a million dollars! Needless to say, I had more incentive to work my rear-end off for each of those coaches. A lot of days I would be in the weight room before the sun came up and still there after it went down, never seeing the light of day except to eat. If I got sick, no one knew. Who would take over for me anyway? At one point, I had the flu so bad that I didn't think I could put one foot in front of the other, but it didn't matter. I had to act as if I was okay and keep going. Again, hard work paid off, as year three had our AD, Jim Gardner, petitioning the NC State Legislature to create my official position with a state paid salary. Somewhere around 1986, I officially went fulltime making $21,000. To this day, I remain eternally grateful to ASU for giving me my start, and this award-winning university continues to be one of my favorite places on earth.

As the strength and conditioning program evolved, I started to get some help from the exercise science graduate students. Some much needed help, I might add. You see, in those days, one strength coach worked with *all* sports. With my assistants came help with instruction and the writing up of the many workouts for all athletes from all sports. These individuals played an important role in the success of our entire athletic program. We won two Southern Conference football championships during that time and countless other conference championships in all the other varsity sports. I give my staff a lot of credit for that success during those years. My staff eventually consisted of seven assistants (paid and unpaid). These individuals were the heart and soul of our strength and conditioning program.

Dan Duncan: My first assistant co-published an article with me on the Hack Squat for NSCA journal in 1990, now a successful businessman in Texas.

Kevin Kaga: A successful H.S. S&C coach in SC for over 30 years.

Ben Cook: Went on to be the Head strength coach for the UNC Tar Heels Men's basketball team, now is a NASCAR performance coach.

Anthony Glass: A successful strength & conditioning in his own right. Had stints at Boston College, University of Georgia, and Ohio State University before coming home to be Head Strength coach for Olympic sports at ASU.

Roger Morrison: Has had a successful career in Health and Fitness.

Jennie Mix: My first and only female assistant.

Rick Parker: Now a successful high school principal in Charlotte, NC. For some 25 years, Rick has been my early Saturday morning workout partner. Our brutal leg day is known by many!

Lee Barnes: I would like to share a letter I received a few years ago from Lee. It read, "I am writing you Chip to tell you that I have made a gift to the Appa-

lachian State University Foundation in your honor. The $10,000 dollars cash gift will place your name in the ASU weight room. Your name will be forever etched on the walls of a very important continuing education and training facility." It went on to say, "Coach Sigmon, you instilled confidence in me when you made me a part of your Graduate Assistant coaching staff. As

ASU weight room - 2018

the only undergraduate, you placed responsibility upon me that many would not have. When you left the weight room one day, you told the athletes, 'this is

Coach Barnes; he is Coach Sigmon when I leave and head to the football field. He is in my shoes. Treat him as you would me when I am out the door.' Thank you coach for the important role you played in my experience and development at App State." Lee went on to be a successful business and family man. Now that is what coaching is all about. You never know whom you will influence from one day to the next.

At ASU, I had the privilege to work with five great head coaches between 1984 and 1990 and learned much from each. Coach Mack Brown taught me how important it is to pay attention to details and how each element of the program has to be dealt with on a daily basis. Mack was great and had much wisdom when dealing with athletes and people in general. From that, I knew he would be a great success. From Coach "Sparky" Woods, I learned leadership skills. He would regularly ask his coaches their opinions on situations, and then would make a decision based on the information provided. That leadership led us to two Southern Conference football championships. Coach Jerry Moore taught me humility and graciousness in the good and bad times. (Mostly good times, since he went on to win three National Championships!) Men's basketball coach Tom Apke and women's track coach John Weaver: these two were some of my biggest supporters, taking money out of their own budget to pay me! Above all, these five coaches cared about their players and athletes. They knew when to turn it on and when to put their arms around them. They helped me realize that my job was to teach our athletes to be better men and women both on and off the field.

The year 1990 brought more changes. I left ASU to become a gym manager and part-time strength coach for the Charlotte Hornets of the NBA. The Hornets eventually made me their first full-time strength coach (Thank you Head Coach and GM Allan Bristow for the opportunity) and I traveled with them most of the 11 years I was with the team. "Firsts" are hard and exciting, and working with a professional team was no different. I was always in a "proving myself mode." Our facility went from a small 400 square foot weight room (that I could only get about 3-4 players in at a time) at the Charlotte Grady Cole Center in 1990 to a 2,000 square foot weight room at our brand-new training facility in a Fort Mill, SC in 1994.

My NBA professional strength coaching years also brought me the opportunity to work for some great coaches. Head coaches and former Boston Celtic greats Dave Cowens and Paul Silas were gentle giants off the court but intense in their coaching styles and on the court. Lee Rose, assistant Hornets coach and head basketball coach with the UNC Charlotte 49ers who led them to the Final Four in 1977 is a man I gained much wisdom from.

I had the privilege to work with not only some great athletes but great individuals as well. There are so many, I will name just a few. These five men and women made me a better person as well:

John Settle: All-American running back for ASU and All-Pro for the Atlanta Falcons. Hard work and humility is what John was all about. Never complained, just got the job done!

Dino Hackett: Linebacker ASU, All-Pro for Kansas City Chiefs. Dino was one of our Captains. Whenever we had a team meal, Dino waited until everyone was seated and eating before he made his way up to be served. Humility and leadership.

Alonzo Mourning: Charlotte Hornets NBA. The Hall of Fame center was one of the most intense and relentless human beings on the court, but off the court one of the nicest individuals I know, a true gentleman.

Dawn Staley: Charlotte Sting WNBA, Head Women's Basketball Coach USC, National Champions 2017. A solid individual. In just watching Dawn on and off the court, I saw just what a champion is all about. She made every day count.

Tony Bennett: Charlotte Hornets NBA, Head Basketball Coach, UVA. I knew Tony would follow his dad's footsteps. Tony knew his basketball, a relentless worker, devoted to his craft and pays attention to the details. I learned from Tony character and integrity and it shows in his coaching at UVA. A man of great faith and still an influence on me to this day, plus a great friend.

Many philosophies have influenced me but here are Principles that I adhere to daily:

• Bring the energy and your A-Game every single day.
• Have a relentless and ruthless pursuit of knowledge every day.
• Know when to be calm and when to be intense.
• Have a sense of urgency every day.

In the 1980s, strength coaches were in the background, starting programs, fighting for what we believed in every day, working with all teams, and making the most of inadequate facilities. Even with that, I wouldn't have changed a thing. Every sacrifice was worth it and honed my character. Strength coaches have a tremendous influence on their athletes. I still get calls and notes from past players and athletes thanking me for helping them become what they are today. The rewards never end! Today, strength coaches are in the forefront, a major part of each team. Years of well-run, science-based programs all over the country have solidified the strength coach influence. I love watching and learning from these young great coaches of today. They bring so much knowledge, passion and energy to the collegiate and professional sports, and I love it!

I have always said, "I have failed more than I have succeeded, but with those failures have come great wisdom." In addition, through all of my victories, defeats and struggles in life, I would be nothing and would not be "still standing" without the Lord by my side. I thank Him each day.

To the Three Ladies of my life: My wife Michelle and my daughters, Claire and Sydney, beautiful inside and out.

Chip Sigmon's Coaching Bio

- 1978-1982 - Kannapolis City Schools, High School Teacher, Football and Track Coach
- 1982-1984 - UNC Chapel Hill, Assistant Strength & Conditioning Coach
- 1984-1990 - Appalachian State University, Head Strength & Conditioning Coach
- 1990-2011 - Charlotte Hornets, NBA, Head Strength & Conditioning Coach
- 1997-2011 - Charlotte Sting, WNBA, Head Strength & Conditioning Coach
- 2001-2011 - OrthoCarolina Sports Performance
- 2011-Present - Sigmon Sports Performance / Wellness Coordinator, Europa Sports Products

Professional Certifications

- NSCA*D
- RSCC*E
- CISSN (International Society of Sports Nutrition)
- USAW

Published Books

- Author: *52 Week Basketball Training*, Human Kinetics Publisher
- Co-author/Contributor: *NBA Power Conditioning*, Human Kinetics Publisher
- Authored articles for *NSCA Journal*, *Training & Conditioning*, and various other strength & conditioning plus nutritional journals.

CHAPTER 28

The Jerry Simmons Story

Growing up in Southwest Kansas on a 5,000-acre farm, along with my father's passing when I was 15, instilled a hard work ethic that has been the backbone of my career. With his last words to me, my father told me to "depend on yourself to get things done, not others," and reminded me that "you are no better than anyone else, but just as good as anyone." I have used those words to inspire myself and go after jobs in my career. Someone is going to get that job, why not me?

My first coaching job was at Fort Hays State University (FHSU), where I had played football in 1977. As a Graduate Assistant Linebacker and Assistant Strength Coach, while getting my master's, I coached and also bartended at night to bring in enough money for rent. Jerry Cullen, the Defensive Coordinator/Strength Coach, was my first mentor and someone from whom I learned a tremendous amount. At the end of my second year as a GA, the coaching staff was fired, leaving me wondering what the future held. During the Head Coach search, the new semester had started, and I decided to go ahead and start the off-season program on my own. This proved to be a good decision. When the new coach was hired, he retained me as the LB and Strength Coach at $4,000 a year. Needless to say, I still had to keep my bartending job.

While coaching the next year, 1978, it become clear to me that I wanted to get out of X's and O's and concentrate on the strength and conditioning. During the spring of 1979 I started to look in a new direction as a Strength Coach. I knew this would mean starting over, but I was determined to make it happen. When a graduate assistant position became available at Clemson, one of the top programs in the country, in late spring of 1979, I went after it. I was able to convince George Dostal, the Clemson Head Strength Coach, to give me an interview even though he had already settled on someone else. I got the job, with the pay at $62 every two weeks and meals on the training table.

I could only make this happen because of my fiancé and future wife Rebecca, who worked to help support us during this time. We also shared an apartment with another couple. Life was good.

I spent one year at Clemson before getting my first major college head coaching job at Rice University in 1980. I had met Ray Alborn, the head football coach at Rice, when their team came to Clemson for the first game of the 1979 season. They worked out at our facility, and while talking with Coach Alborn I found out that they did not have a full-time strength coach at that time; the defensive line coach was also the Strength Coach and that they were trying to create a position.

I kept in contact with him during the season about the new position. During the off season of 1980, I interviewed with Wake Forest and was offered the job, but I wanted to coach at Rice.

I immediately called Coach Alborn to see if they were going to be able to get the new position funded, buying a couple days before I needed to give Wake an answer. He asked what salary was offered and when I told him $9,000 he said he would pay it out of his salary. So we headed to Rice with a hand shake agreement, no contract.

Upon arriving at Rice University, I was not prepared for the small and ill equipped weight room facilities compared the Clemson facility that I had just left. There was much to be done. Rebecca and I personally painted the room, changed the equipment color, and created a better layout for workouts. We wanted to bring a new look to the strength program and build some excitement for the team. With no budget and very little money for necessities or new equipment, I convinced Coach Alborn and the Athletic Director to let me organize an alumni football game at the end of spring practice where we offered game film of the ex-players playing days. This raised $2,000 for the weight room budget. We had done the same thing at Ft. Hays; it was one of the things that were done in the early days to raise extra money needed for budgets. Along with my work as the Head Strength Coach, I was also the nutritionist and in charge of the training table, something that would continue throughout my college and NFL career.

Staying in line with my dream of someday coaching in the National Football League (NFL) I contacted any scout or NFL coach I could. In 1981, the newly formed United States Football League (USFL) was starting. Long-time NFL head coach George Allen was the new coach at the Chicago Blitz, and they were holding a try out in Houston. I went to the University of Houston, where try-outs were being held and waited for an opportunity to talk with Coach Allen and see if there would be an opportunity available with the Blitz. I was able to speak with him as he walked off the field on his way to the airport, so I introduced myself and inquired about a strength coaching position.

I found out in our brief visit that he was interested in a strength coach (fitness coach as he called it) but there wasn't money in the budget for one. He was working on some things with the city of Chicago for an after-school program at the facility that could fund a strength position for both. He asked me to stay in touch with him. Three weeks later, I called about the position and mentioned that I was going to be in Chicago the next Sunday to see if we could meet. I flew out that Sunday with only a six-hour time span to meet and then fly back to be at work on Monday at Rice. During our meeting, he asked what business I had in Chicago. I told him there was no business and I had taken the chance to be able to meet with him about the possibility of a job.

I found out there were no funds from the Chicago Blitz, only the City of Chicago would be paying my salary. With Rebecca pregnant with our first child, Joe, we were going to live in a classroom. She would cook for the players and I was going to get another job at a gym at night to make ends meet. When the person in charge of the after-school program found out that they were going to be the sole source of my salary, they refused to hire me. I was very disappointed but obviously the good Lord was watching over us.

A few months later, I was networking with NFL Strength Coaches to get to know them and learning about the different programs they were using. Al Vermeil, who was the Strength Coach at the San Francisco 49ers and I had spoken a number of times. One day, I had called to speak with Al and was told that he resigned that morning, which was a shock as we were scheduled to talk that day. I was given his number, and I called him to see what had happened. As we talked, he asked me if I was interested in his old position and promised me that he would recommend me to coach Bill Walsh. I then received a call from Mike McCormack, the GM, about an interview with Coach Walsh. The next week, Mr. McCormack called to let me know they had hired Jerry Attaway from University of Southern California and had recommended me to Ted Tolner, the new head coach at USC.

Although I was disappointed about the 49er job, I became excited about the opportunity to talk to Coach Tolner. Not knowing anyone at USC, I diligently and persistently called him about the job. There was a National Strength Convention in Los Angeles the spring of 1983, and there I interviewed with Coach Tolner and Athletic Director Dr. Dick Perry. While interviewing with Dr. Perry we realized we had many things in common from my FHSU days and we both know some of the same people. He had also played for one of my coaches at Fort Hays 20 years earlier, and his first coaching job he worked as a basketball coach at Hays High. Leaving the meeting, I felt confident about the job.

Finally, after all of my schooling, experiences, hard work and networking, I obtained a job with one of the most prestigious and successful college football programs. I was now the Head Strength coach at USC, a team I had watched growing up on New Year's Day playing in the Rose Bowl, it seemed yearly.

On arriving at USC in the summer 1983, I was astonished that the facilities were so meager. There was only a 1,200 square foot weight room used for all sports, not just football. I was hired as a football strength coach, but had told

USC weight room - 1983

Dr. Perry in the interview that I wanted to coach all sports not just football. Based on the experience I had at Clemson, I knew working with all sports would pay off.

The first year at USC, we did circuit training with teams starting at 5:45 am in 45-minute sessions per team, with football lifting in the afternoons. Since the summer Olympics were coming the next year in 1984 and USC's campus was to be the Olympic Village, I was told any thought about a new facility would not be possible. I had to be creative to make the facility work and keep pushing for a new weight room.

In the fourth game of the 1983 season, we traveled to play the University of South Carolina. My good friend Keith Kephart was their Strength Coach, and his facility was phenomenal. At Southern Cal, Boosters, V.I.P.'s, etc. all traveled on the team plane. It was a great opportunity for them to see a first class weight room and Coach Kephart was happy to show them around.--

It was a tough loss, 34-14, but ended up working in my favor. On the airplane ride home, I was asked to come to the back of the plane and speak to boosters and other USC officials on what exactly I was looking for in a new facility. They wanted me to have plans together by the next week for an architect to draw up for a new training facility. If this was going to happen it had to be started by December 1, 1983 and completed by June 1, 1984, in time for the Olympics. With the help of the USC family of boosters, who donated construction crews, HVAC, flooring, and other things needed to build the new facility, we were able to open the doors on June 1st with a new, fully-equipped training facility. To fund the new equipment, a letter was sent to all Cardinal and Gold boosters, advertising that a gold plate with their name would be placed on a piece of equipment for $ 2,500 each. All equipment had gold plates.

The next four years were a dream experience for me: coaching great athletes, both male and female, winning Championships, coaching in two Rose Bowls, along with other bowls, and the addition of Jennifer and Jordon to our family.

The Southern Cal strength clinic was also born and turned into a very successful clinic, with over 300 attendees and speakers from the PAC-10, NFL and across the country. Although I loved USC and the college experience, I still had a burning desire to coach in the NFL.

A position opened at the New England Patriots. Not knowing anyone there, I cold called with hopes of talking to Coach Raymond Berry. With a little persuasion of his assistant I was able to speak with him, and I got an interview and my first NFL job in the spring of 1988.

The three years in New England were the toughest of my career. Having three head coaches in three years, a 1-15 record for the 1990 season, and a team in turmoil, I needed to make a change.

In February of 1991 Bill Belichick had just been hired by the Cleveland Browns and Steve Crosby, who had been with us at New England, was hired as the running back coach. He became my contact to Coach Belichick for the strength coach position. Since I was under contract with New England, Coach Belichick would not call and ask for permission to talk to me; instead I would have to ask the Patriots for permission. This turned out to be a very tough situation. The President of the Patriots was not happy about my request to interview with Cleveland but gave me permission.

A few days later, I interviewed with Coach Belichick and was told he had two more candidates to interview and would not be making a decision that day. Returning to New England, I was given two days for a decision. On the second day the general manager at New England called for me to come to his office.

As I was getting ready to go up to the office, I received the call from Coach Belichick offering me the job. In March of 1991, off to Cleveland we went.

During my years in Cleveland, I felt Bill, with his demanding style, made all of us the best we could be. Our fourth year, we made the playoffs, winning one game. The 1995 season, we felt

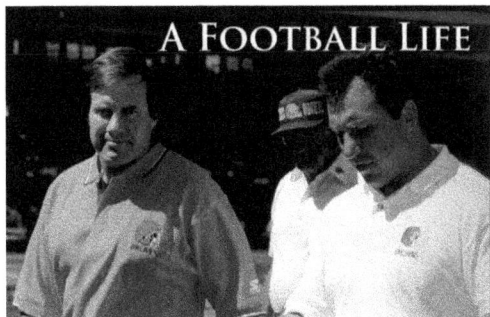

Cleveland Browns - 1994

we would be a contender for the Super Bowl. But before the fourth game of that season, we found out the team was going to move to Baltimore, and we didn't win another game that season until the last home game against Cincinnati. When the season ended, all our jobs and future were up in the air, and on Valentine's Day 1996 we were fired. After the meeting, I went back to my office to pack and received a call from Mr. Model, the owner, asking me to stay and move to Baltimore.

We started the 1996 off-season program in Cleveland, not knowing exactly when the move was to happen but to be ready to move at any time. I received a call on a Tuesday in early March that the organization would be moving to Baltimore that Thursday. After Thursday's workout we loaded up the weight room and off to Baltimore we went, working out of the old Baltimore Colts training facility. We restarted the off-season workouts three days later on Monday. The weight room was one-tenth the size of Cleveland's, so we used two racquetball courts as a part of the weight room.

The next three years were spent rebuilding the team while playing in the previously abandoned Memorial stadium while the new stadium was being built. In 1999, Mr. Model was making another head coach change. Not sure who the new coach would be, and after an interview with George Seifert, the new coach at Carolina Panthers, we moved to Charlotte.

Once again, after two seasons, there was a change at head coach and John Fox was hired. I was asked to stay on. With Coach Fox we played in two NFC championship games and Super Bowl XXXVIII. After the 2008 season, we received a new two-year contract but were told by Jerry Richardson, the owner, it would be our last regardless of how well we did. He felt we had been there too long and were making too much money to fit in his business plan any longer. So in January 2011 my time at Carolina Panthers was over. I was very grateful for my years there, as it allowed my kids to finish school. I took the next two years off from coaching to decide what would be next while working at the Dowd YMCA.

In the spring of 2012, Lance Stucky, who was an intern with me at Carolina, called. He was working at Fort Bragg training Third Special Forces, Green Berets and asked if I had interest in training some of the greatest Americans we have in this country. In March of 2013 I received a call from Ray Bear, the Director of Human Performance, about coming to work with them. Because of my daughter Jen's sacrifice for her country as an MP and a prison guard during her deployment in Bagdad, I felt the calling for me to do something also. This has been the most fulfilling job of my career. To witness the sacrifices made on a daily basis by these soldiers and their families for our way of life is very humbling.

I have been very blessed these 35 years of coaching to have coached All-Americans, All-Pro's and now Special Forces. The biggest blessing I have is my children and their success: Joe a private Chef for numerous NFL players, Jen for her sacrifices, and Jordon the Head Strength Coach at the University of Nevada.

Training Principles

Entire books have been written about training philosophies that include strength, power, agility, conditioning, etc., so I'm going to give you a brief overview of mine.

My philosophy relies on the premise that a strong and stable foundation is vital in order to perform efficient and effective movements. I prefer free weight compound movements that require the involvement of core and stabilizer muscles as opposed to machines, which eliminate them. Once this foundation is

Thor 3 weight room, Fort Bragg - 2018

built, the other focus areas I listed above are achieved much easier.

I would be making a big mistake to not mention that nutrition is key. The level of an athlete's understanding of proper nutrition and hydration can make or break a program. Do not skip over this area.

Finally, mental toughness is an area that I have always stressed, but since I have been working with Special Forces I have greatly increased my focus on it. We are capable of things far beyond what we think. With mental toughness training, barriers can be broken down and the sky is the limit.

Jerry Simmons's Coaching Bio

- 1977-1979 - Fort Hays State University, Linebackers Coach, Strength & Conditioning
- 1979-1980 - Clemson University, Graduate Assistant & Strength & Conditioning
- 1980-1983 - Rice University, Head Strength & Conditioning Coach
- 1983-1988 - University of Southern California, Head Strength & Conditioning Coach
- 1984 - Olympic Site Director
- 1988-1991 - New England Patriots, Head Strength & Conditioning Coach
- 1991-1996 - Cleveland Browns, Head Strength & Conditioning Coach
- 1996-1999 - Baltimore Ravens, Head Strength & Conditioning Coach
- 1999-2011 - Carolina Panthers, Head Strength & Conditioning Coach
- 2013-Present - Thor 3- 3rd Special Forces Ft. Bragg, N.C., Ray Bear Human Performance Coordinator, Tactical Strength and Conditioning Specialist

Achievements & Honors
- 3rd Special Forces Dedication Achievement Award
- 1984 - NSCA Regional Director of the Year Award
- 1988-2011 - NFL Strength Coaches Association
- 1988-2011 - American Football Coaches Association
- 2003 - Samson Professional Football Strength Coach of the Year Award
- 2004 - Professional Football Strength & Conditioning Coach of the Year Award
- 2013 - YMCA Rose Award

Professional Certifications
- 2012 - NSCA-CSCS

CHAPTER 29

The Meg Stone Story

I never set out to be a strength and conditioning coach. If truth were told, I did not know what a strength and conditioning coach was, or what they did, until I arrived in the USA on January 9, 1980. Having competed in two Olympic Games, Moscow (1980) and Los Angeles (1984), I remember driving back to Tucson from the Los Angeles Olympics to join the University of Arizona Wildcats Football Team to begin their pre-season camp at Cochise College next to the Mexican border.

In April of 1984 I was approached by Larry Smith, the Head Football Coach of the Arizona Wildcats, in Tucson Arizona. He had requested a meeting. I guessed he wanted to find out what this woman with the 550-pound squat, 350-pound bench and 352-pound power clean could contribute to his football team. Larry Smith being a "Michigan man," I was sure that he was apprehensive about having a woman work with "his boys." Fortunately for me, Larry was married to Cheryl Smith, no shrinking violet, and was well aware of what a woman with a strong personality was capable of. I think in no small way, I have Cheryl to thank for initially being hired.

I was offered the job for several reasons: I was cheap to hire, I was a woman, I was stronger than most of the team, and I am also pretty sure another candidate had been offered the job and turned it down. I hesitated to take the job, as I was set on becoming a track and field coach, but I was hooked when Coach Smith told me I would be the first women to hold such a position. My starting salary was $8,000 lower than the previous strength coach, but I realized I was an unknown, unproven quantity and I had no bargaining power. My starting salary was a whopping $20,000 per year, a fortune for someone who had been living on an athletic scholarship.

Having been offered this job, I remember thinking, "How am I going to approach the training program?" I decided to focus in on the very best athletes in the program without neglecting any sport, or position on the football team. A walk-on would be given as much support and attention as the starting quarter back. This became a pretty important approach, as Chuck Cecil was the first walk-on I encountered. Later he played for the Green Bay Packers and has had a variety of coaching position in the NFL. Presently, he is back in Tucson working with the football program.

My approach was two-fold: power cleans, squats and bench press would be the core of the program, and every athlete, regardless of sport, deserved full attention from our strength and conditioning staff. Every effort would be made to make sure every team was covered with what they needed from the strength and conditioning staff.

The first year on the job, the Strength and Conditioning program was run by myself, and the Head Athletic Trainer was Sue Hillman. Sue was an extremely competent Athletic Trainer; although Sue and I were never close friends, I am sure we recognized each other's professional abilities. So, as one Texas newspaper stated, these programs were run by a "pair of women."

I was aware that a balance was needed in our department. It was important that we hire a male assistant, and I was very fortunate as the years went on, to hire some of the best people/coaches I could ever wish to work with in Dan Burk, Dwight Daub, Darryl Eto.

When hiring an assistant, loyalty was paramount, first to the program and then to me as a female coach. I was aware that if I chose the wrong person, it would be very easy for someone who lacked good character to undermine our program with the football coaching staff. So I made sure the person hired was of good character first and knowledgeable second, a philosophical approach that has served me well in every job I have had.

The years working with football were a challenge I really enjoyed, and I must say I miss the intensity of football game day. The previous strength and conditioning staff had been machine orientated, particularly focusing on the old-style Hammer equipment. My approach was, as previously mentioned, free weight orientated, so some negotiations had to happen with the players during this transition. I taught the power clean and the derivatives the first year. We would hang on to the hip sled machines, etc., and then the second year, once trust was established, I could then get rid of the hip sleds (keeping one for injury issues) and convert everyone over to the squat in the second year. This approach appeared to be successful.

Early in my tenure, I had the good fortune to work with several extremely talented athletes in several sports. In football, as previously mentioned, Chuck Cecil, as well as the tremendously talented twins Chris and Kevin Singleton. In Basketball, we had a very well-recognized, nationally-ranked team with Sean

Elliot, Steve Kerr, Jud Buechler, and Harvey Mason, etc., all who have gone on to their own fields of interest and been tremendously successful.

A good talking point of the program during my stay at the U of A is that we never lost to Arizona State (our in-state rivals) the whole of my tenure at Arizona, although we did draw one year. I was most fortunate to participate in the Sun Bowl, John Hancock Bowl, Aloha Bowl (twice), and the last bowl game during my tenure was the Fiesta Bowl. The final year of my tenor was also the year of the nationally-acclaimed Desert Swarm defense. With many of the players on that team gaining national recognition, such as the Outland Trophy winner for the best defensive player nationally, going to Rob Waldrop.

One of my favorite teams to work with, because of the professional approach of the coach, was Women's Softball, from whom I am fortunate enough to have two D1 National Championship rings, thanks to Coach Mike Candrea.

The first time I attended NSCA national convention in 1985, I had a meeting with Boyd Epley, and I have never forgotten the piece of advice I received from him, "Never totally depend on the funding you get from your athletic department." He was exactly right, my budget was sparse.

The weight room facility was approximately 8,000 square feet, with an extensive, hard rubberized flooring that was easily marked off with eight-foot, square platform areas, and so we developed six platforms, five squat racks, six flat benches, four inclines, and had an extensive dumbbell area. I believe, for the time, it was a reasonable weight room.

Many people have asked me, "Were you aware of being a trail blazer for women?" I really did not think of myself in that way, my thoughts were all on the nuances of the job; my focus was on the training programs for the various sports I was responsible for, the particular needs of the athletes under my charge, and the facility and staff needs for the program to run well. I think three factors allowed me to be successful in the S&C position. Firstly, I was older than most athletes competing in the NCAA; I had been grandfathered in when the AIAW merged with the NCAA. Secondly, I had a diploma in physical education, and anatomy and physiology. And finally, I had been mentored by two of the most outstanding coach mentors in the UK: Frank Dick who had coached me and introduced me to track and field 1972, and remains a mentor to this day, and Carlton Johnson, the Director of Coaches Education for the UK during the '70s and '80s. I was lucky to have this background when I was hired at the University of Arizona. Only after several years did I think of the role I played for female coaches. I believe I was given a chance and did the best I could with that chance. Lesson learned: the chance is only 10%, the 90% is what you do with it.

One of the major challenges I faced was the transition of the coaching staff at Arizona. During my third year as Head Strength and Conditioning Coach,

Coach Smith took the job at the University of Southern California and went on to coach that team to a National Championship performance. A new Coaching Staff arrived from Hawaii, and suddenly our football team became slow, weak and ill-disciplined. If you think this is sarcasm, you're right! Miraculously, within three months, the team became strong, quick, and organized, and I came to realize this was the operating procedure of all new coaching staffs anywhere in collegiate football.

When the new Head Coach, Dick Tomey, arrived, I believe he was very skeptical about a female in the weight room, and I believe the AD Cedric Dempsey's words to him were, "It's been working for three years. No need to change now." The traditional, hard-nose football guy was the kind of strength coach most football coaches valued, and that was not my motivational style. I believe that motivation and intensity come from within, and caring, technical coaching can bring out that intensity in an athlete who really wants to win.

When the of six years with Dick Tomey began, his first approach to me was to give me seventeen letters which had arrived from applicants for my job. His statement to me was, "I will leave you to answer these." Which I did, and I was most grateful for the way he handled that situation. My job was never advertised; other coaches assumed I would be out of a job with the coaching staff change. I also realized at this time how tenuous a job this was, I remembered a statement I have heard several times, "You are not a coach worth your salt if you have not been fired several times." I have been very fortunate to have been part of sports for close to forty year and never have experience being fired.

I had many differences of opinions regarding the training for football, but research into evidence-based practices supported my position. The most noticeable difference of opinion centered on the running program. I felt the program was excessive, and after a season with excessive ACL issues (completely due to fatigue), my gut feeling proved accurate. This led me to remember that rest and recovery are just as important as the training program itself, and must be incorporated within the training program, yes, even for football. What has concerned me most, and still does, about working with football is the insane notion that driving athletes into complete exhaustion through badly designed training regimes will make the team mentally tough. Think on this: too many young athletes ended up in the hospital, or worse, died.

My last years with Arizona football and the Desert Swarm defense ended my tenure. The Fiesta Bowl in Phoenix was my last game, and the team gave me the game ball, which I treasure to this day. I had hired Darryl Eto as the speed development coach, and Dan Wirth to assist me with Football. The team and the department were in good hands, and it was time for a change.

Texas Tech

In 1992 and 1993, I slowly came to the realization that the only university I had ever experienced was the University of Arizona. I had an overwhelming desire to experience new challenges. This desire, along with an acute sense of having reached the limit of what I could accomplish as a wildcat, led me to consider moving on. I guess I started to look to my future and ask myself, "What will I been doing when I am 55-60? What would my future be?" After nine and a half years in Tucson, it was time to look elsewhere.

In 1993, I received a call from Bob Bockrath, the previous associate athletic director at the U of A. He had moved to Texas Tech University in Lubbock, West Texas as the Athletic Director. Bob was looking to replace Joe Juraszek, a well establish and first-class strength coach who had taken the strength and conditioning position with the Dallas Cowboys. Bob asked me if I had any suggestion for a replacement, I thought about it for some time and realized this would be a great I opportunity for me to expand my knowledge of Intercollegiate Athletics.

Texas Tech was all I hoped it would be; it introduced to me a whole different culture particularly working with football. As everyone knows, West Texas football is legendary. The first week on campus, I was introduced to the beef coach, the watermelon coach, and the car coach, and on the training table I had my first introduction, by one of the players, to mountain oysters. During my interview, the person who had to give their approval for my hire was Spike Dykes, the Head Football coach. This was not an easy thing for him to do, as many of the alumni, as I later learned, had threatened to withdraw their funding if the university hired a woman for the program.

I spent two and a half wonderful years in Lubbock. The coaches were extremely supportive and the athletes were respectful and hard working. I can honestly say it was a pleasure to work with a great group of people, particularly my assistants Sid Bright, Darren Honeycutt, and Lynn Stosell, and athletes such as Zach Thomas. The last game I attended representing Texas Tech was their first ever appearance in the Cotton Bowl in 1995.

Several years earlier, I met Dr. Mike Stone shortly after moving to Texas Tech. We made the decision to get married, and so in 1995 I moved up to Boone, North Carolina. Again, a story in the making, I was earning a massive $55,000, and over $60,000 with the bowl bonus. I decided to move to Appalachian State University, where I was offered a consultancy position earning $4,000 per year. I moved, and within two weeks a position came up in Track and Field, and John Weaver, the Head Coach, offered me the position. I was working full-time again, and with a good salary. Talk about taking a chance and it paying off!

Favorite Quotes

"The opposite of right is not wrong, it's left. The job of the coach is not to criticize, but to redirect."

"The truth is like a lion, you do not need to defend it, turn it loose and it defends itself."

"Experience is tough, you get the test before you get the lesson."

I have no idea who to attribute these saying to but none the less they are impactful. The most important motivational quote for our Center of Excellence and Olympic Training Site:

"We are what we repeatedly do, excellence, therefore, is not an act, but a habit" -Aristotle

---

Meg Stone's Coaching Bio
- BA, MA, OLY, NSCA-E, NSCA FELLOW
- 1999 - Moved to Scotland to take the Position of National Coach for Scotland
- 2000 - Scottish Institute of Sport, High-Performance Coach
- 2002 - Carmichael Training Systems, Colorado Springs, CO, Coached for the U.S. Paralympic Team
- 2003 - US Olympic Committee, Colorado Springs, CO, Coaching Manager
- 2005 - East Tennessee State University, Assistant Track and Field Coach
- 2009 - Director at Center of Excellence for Sport Science and Coach Education (CESSCE)
- 2012 - Added the Director of the US Olympic Training Site and CESSCE

Achievements & Honors
- 1993 - Level 1 Club Coaches Certification, U.S. Weightlifting
- 2003 - USA Strength and Conditioning Coaches Hall of Fame
- 2007 - Legend in the Field Award – Collegiate Strength Coaches Association.
- 2009 - Lifetime Achievement Award –National Strength and Conditioning Association

- 2013 - Registered Strength and Conditioning Coach Emeritus
- 2016 - Named as a member of the Pac – 12 All-Century Team

CHAPTER 30

The Rich Tuten Story

I began my career as the Assistant Strength and Conditioning Coach at the University of Florida. My former Head Football Coach at Clemson University, Charlie Pell, offered me the job during the summer of 1980. I had played Football at Clemson under Coach Pell in 1977 and 1978. During that time, Coach Pell allowed me to take charge of the lifting and running programs the players were working out with during the '77 and '78 summer-school sessions. Making up lifting and running programs was easy for me, and Coach Pell would always ask me how the players were doing, and I think that's how he knew that I could do the job at Florida.

The weight room at Florida was an old wrestling room converted into a weight room, with no air-conditioning. With a donation from Dave Thomas, owner and founder of Wendy's, whose daughter attended the University of Florida, the room was equipped with a complete line of Nautilus machines and some free weights.

I was the assistant to the Head Strength Coach from August 1980 to April 1981, when he left to be the Head Strength Coach at Auburn. Coach Pell promoted me to Head Strength Coach in April 1981, and that's when my career really started. I was able to hire an assistant and the two of us worked with over 150 football players for the next two years. Strength Programs were easy to design back then because they had to be based on the type of equipment we had since budgets were non-existent. The running programs were also a little different back then. A big reason for that was the lack of places or fields to run on. We weren't allowed to run on the football fields because no one wanted us to tear them up, and the track was reserved for the track teams. So we did more distance running than interval sprints or shuttles my first two years.

In the summer of 1983, after the end zone was renovated we moved into the new, south end of the stadium and added a new equipment room, training room, two locker rooms, and a new weight room. We increased the square footage from 2,000 to 6,000 and added new and different machines and free weights. At the time, it was considered one of the top weight rooms in the country.

I was also allowed to hire two more assistants, increasing the staff to four, but the number of players was pushing close to 200! During the winter workout months, called the off-season program, it would take us twelve hours to work all the players out by splitting them into groups based on their class schedules. By this time, we were lifting for an hour and running for an hour.

The 1984 team was a very special group. To me it was very rewarding because for the first and only time in my career, the whole offensive line could bench press over 400 pounds! Back then, that was huge. Lomas Brown, a great left tackle in college and the NFL, was the last to do it, and he did it the Thursday before we played Auburn and Bo Jackson. We beat them pretty good.

We won the school's first SEC Championship in 1984, which was also very special for the program, but the NCAA took it away from us. They had already fired the head coach who gave me my first job, God rest his soul, but the school promoted Galen Hall as Head Coach after we came home to a huge crowd after winning our last conference game and SEC title. At that point, this was the most exciting time in my career.

I have great memories of the players I worked with my first eight years. One player that I'm most proud of was Louis Oliver. Louis walked on at Florida as a skinny DB at 6 feet and 1 inch and 170 pounds, and ran a 4.61 forty. He was one of the most determined players I ever had the pleasure to work with. I had to make him leave the weight room at the end of the day. When he left Florida, he weighed 222 pounds, ran a 4.38 forty, and was a first-round draft pick by the Miami Dolphins!

This is funny story about the leading rusher in the history of the NFL, Emmitt Smith, when he was a freshman at Florida in the summer of 1987. Most of the upper classmen went to both sessions of summer school, and the freshman would attend the second session. Well, Emmitt showed up a day early and wanted to work out with the older guys. It just so happened we were pulling Sleds 100 yards that day on the stadium field. I told him that if he started, I would not let him quit! He spent his first night in Gainesville, FL in the infirmary, getting IV's. The coach that recruited him said he had to go to the infirmary and re-recruit him. Emmitt and I still laugh about it, and he says Dancing with the Stars was harder.

All was going well until the summer of 1988, when my best friend in coaching was hired at the University of North Carolina by Mack Brown and called me to see if I would be interested in working as the Strength Coach there. I was offered a nice raise as well. Due to some strange circumstances that took place during the talks with the administration at Florida, I decided to accept the job and was hired in June 1988.

I cannot say enough good about the players I worked with at the University of North Carolina. We were not very good my first two years there, but these players were the most dedicated and determined I've ever had the privilege to work with as a team. One of the reasons I was asked to go back to Florida was because they were physically beat by Mississippi State during the regular season that year and it just so happened my last game at North Carolina was the 1992 Peach Bowl and we beat Mississippi State! I left the next day to return to Florida! I was at the University of North Carolina five years and returned to Florida in January 1993.

I arrived in Gainesville, FL on January 2, 1993. The players at that time were all over the place. There were a lot of great players, but they were not playing together as a team. I met with them for the first time on January 5th for five minutes to go over my plan and requirements regarding attendance. I thought showing them how I run my program would be better than explaining it to them. I simply said, "Get dressed, and meet me on row 32 in the stadium in 15 minutes." The 1993 Off-Season was about to begin! The next eight months was an unbelievable bonding process. I was the bad guy and they reacted just like I had hoped they would: me against them. By August, they had become a team!

During the two years I was there, we won the SEC Championship and were pushing to win the National Championship, which they won after I left in 1996. Those two years, '93 and '94, were the most challenging and rewarding years of my career. Twenty-five years later I'm still in contact with most of those incredible players.

Another funny story I remember is about a great player we had, Kevin Carter. Kevin was a Defensive End, six feet, six inches and 275 pounds, and he ran the 40-yard dash in 4.49 on his pro day. He was the sixth pick of the NFL draft, but he should have been the first. The Head Coach at that time wanted the fall conditioning test to be a mile and a half run on the track (six laps). I tried to tell him that I don't teach or coach players how to run slow, but he wanted to run with the QB's and WR's, and he's the boss, so we ran six boring laps around the track! Well, Kevin was not very good at running distances. Most explosive players are not! So, to train Kevin and a few other players how to run a mile and a half in 12 minutes, I would take them on three-mile runs twice a week. Kevin would like to stop occasionally, so I had to carry rocks in my pocket and I would throw them at him whenever he stopped. After all the training for the mile and half run, Kevin did not pass the conditioning test! He had to repeat the test the next morning at 6 a.m., and 20 players volunteered to help him. I spread the players out around the track every 200 yards and they physically pushed Kevin in the back around the track for six laps. Finally, he passed! What a team effort! When I was coaching with the Denver Broncos and played his NFL team, we would talk and laugh about his running times.

I received a phone call in February 1995 from the new Head Coach of the Denver Broncos, Mike Shannahan. We had coached together for four years ('80 to'83), and I was offered the job as the Head Strength and Conditioning Coach. I started working there in March 1995.

The first player I met was John Elway. He came into the weight room to ask me about my program. He hadn't cared much for the programs before me and was very interested in knowing what I had planned. When I explained to him that I do not use power movements in my programs, he was sold! His back-up at Denver, Gary Kubiak, hurt his back doing power cleans and had to have surgery to repair the damage. Gary later became the head coach at the Houston Oilers and the Denver Broncos and has at least three Super Bowl rings that I know of.

The most impressive player I've ever worked with was Harold Hasselback of the Denver Broncos. Harold was what the players would call a freak. He was six feet, six inches, and 290 pounds, and was one of the best workout players I've ever seen or heard of in 32 years of coaching. He could out run any player on the team. Even the wide receivers and defensive backs did not want to run with him during the conditioning run because he could make all of them look bad. As far as the weight room goes, he had no contest. I spotted him on the incline bench, and he pressed 405 pounds nine times! Unbelievable! I was the first college player in NCAA history to bench press 500 pounds in 1977, but that lift really blew my mind. He started at Defensive End in Super Bowls '97 and '98 and *won*!

During my 17 years coaching in Denver, '97 and '98 were very special. In '97 we made the playoffs and beat Jacksonville at home in the first round, and then beat Kansas City at their place in the second round (they beat us during the regular season at their place) which put us in the AFC Championship game at Pittsburgh (who also beat us at their place during regular season).

The winner of this game goes to the Super Bowl. And what a great game it was! In the last minute of the game, we needed a first down to run the clock down and win the game. It was third down and seven yards to go. A play was sent in from the sidelines, but Elway decided to make up his own play! He told Tight End Shannon Sharpe to go to the first down line, turn around, and catch the ball! John hit him in the chest with the ball and Shannon caught it. First down, game over. We won, and we were going on to the Super Bowl!

After the game, I met with a coach from Pittsburgh, a very good friend of mine, Ron Zook, who later became the Head Coach at The University of Florida. He had his two daughters with him on the field after the game and they were crying, and I told them they would enjoy Hawaii. (At that time, the losing coaches from the AFC and NFC Championship Games would coach the pro bowl in Hawaii). He ended up not taking them!

On the plane ride home after the game, I don't think anyone sat down the whole trip. Everyone was so excited, smoking cigars, and having a great time. When we landed we were met by our families and friends at the airport and we also had buses waiting to take us to the stadium where there were about 50,000 fans. It was late, and it was cold, but no one cared!

Super Bowl XXXII, Green Bay, San Diego, CA. We were 11 points under dog! They had won the Super Bowl the year before, and we knew it was going to be the toughest game we played all year. We won that game on the last play of the game also (on defense this time). John Mobley (LB) knocked down a ball thrown to their Tight End for a first down, and we won the game.

I can still remember turning around after that play and looking up in the stands for my two sons, Will and Matt. They had already come down to the wall, waiting for me to lift them over and onto the field. They have a lot of memories from the seventeen years we were in Denver.

I had a wonderful 32-year career and was able to work with three great programs and thousands of athletes, some who were the best in the world at what they did! Not just football, but all sports. When I was at Florida, we had over 20 sports, and we had an assistant strength coach for each sport who provided individual programs for each athlete. When I was at North Carolina, we had 26 sports, over 400 athletes, and we provided each sport with their own individual program and all 26 sports used the same 8,000 square foot weight room.

When I was asked by a young person what they needed to do to get into the field of Strength and Conditioning, my first piece of advice was to take a course in Anatomy and Nutritional courses either in college or online if you have to. You need to be able to understand the language for both and be able to communicate with the athletic trainers and the person in charge of nutrition, meals, and hydration. Also, if you are having trouble finding a place to start your career, do what the best assistant I ever hired did when I was in Denver. He volunteered for a whole year and worked from 5:00 a.m. to 6:30 p.m. without pay, even with a wife and two kids! That's the kind of passion that makes a great coach, because he doesn't watch or care about the clock, money, or title, just making sure the job gets done! I hired him the next year at $100,000 salary! He's now a Head Strength Coach at a major university.

An interesting and funny story about my playing days at Clemson University (75-78) was my last game, the 1978 Gator Bowl. We were playing Ohio State and the great Woody Hayes! In the fourth quarter, we were ahead 17-15 with less than two minutes to play. Ohio State was driving down the field against our defense and the Quarterback, Art Schlichter, was 19 of 19 throwing the ball. The Clemson coaches decided to send in a fresh defensive line to rush the Quarterback on third down. My replacement at Nose Guard (we lined up over the center) was Charlie Bauman, who was also my roommate. For some reason, Charlie hit the center and ran to the right side of the field, right where the QB had thrown the ball and Charlie intercepted the pass. He was pushed out of bounds and Coach Hayes ran up behind him, grabbed him from behind, punched him in the throat, and tried to hit him again, but was stopped by his own players. We won the game and Coach Hayes got fired the next day. Charlie says to this day, a day doesn't go by when he doesn't get asked about that game, and he lives in Ohio!

Rich Tuten's Coaching Bio
- 1980-1981 - University of Florida, Assistant Strength and Conditioning Coach, Graduate Assistant Football Coach
- 1981-1988 - University of Florida, Head Strength and Conditioning Coach
- 1988-1993 - University of North Carolina, Athletic Director of Strength and Conditioning
- 1993-1995 - University of Florida, Administrative Director Strength and Conditioning Coach
- 1995-2012 - Denver Broncos Football Club, Head Strength and Conditioning Coach

Achievements & Honors
- 1981-1994 - Coached in 7 Collegiate Bowl Games
- 1997-Present - Coached in 8 NFL Playoff Games
- 1997, 1998, 2006 - Coached in 3 AFC Championship Games
- 1998-1999 – Two-time NFL Strength Coach of the Year
- 1998-1999 – Two-time Super Bowl Champion
- 1998-1999 - Coached in two Super Bowls
- 2006 - Coached in Pro Bowl

Education
- 1979 - Clemson University, Bachelor in Therapeutic Recreation

CHAPTER 31

The Steve Watterson Story

Everybody Starts Some Where

In 1975, I went to the University of Rhode Island to study Oceanography, but changed course my sophomore year when I applied for a position on a research vessel and got red-flagged because of the severe amblyopia in my right eye. Kim Bissonnette, a respected FIJI brother (Phi Gamma Delta) suggested that I visit URI's Training Room, where he worked. The next day I met Head Trainer Tom Dolan, who allowed me to observe as athletes came in to rehab and got prepared for practice. Tom told me there was a position available if I was interested. He had a dry sense of humor, "It's hard work, long hours, with cheap pay; how can you beat that?" Plus, I'd have access to the football weight room.

Prior to college, I had never lifted weights. Bob Sewall, a great friend from high school, got me started after my freshman year in college. We'd meet at the Newport YMCA and train during the summers. Two days after our first work-out, Bob introduced me to D.O.M.S. (Delayed On-set of Muscle Soreness). I was so sore I could hardly move. All Bob said was, "Let's go! The best thing to do is work out again!" He was right.

It would take 30 years to repay Bob for getting me started in my future career. His son Bobby Sewall Jr. played football at Brown University graduating in 2010. He was overlooked in the draft even though he was All-Ivy 3 times. I was able to convince our personnel dept. to sign Bobby as an NFL free agent with the Tennessee Titans.

Junior year, I worked under Tom Dolan with the URI football team. At the end of the season he asked if I would be interested in working an NFL football training camp. He still had connections from when he worked as an Assistant Trainer with the St. Louis Cardinals. I was stoked! A few months later I got an offer from the Philadelphia Eagles. Tom called and said, "Work hard and have fun!"

Hard Work Does Pay-off

Working hard had never been an issue for me. My parents instilled that in us at an early age. My dad worked as a machinist. The minute he got home from work, he would jump into some project around the house. My mom taught school, and she was very intelligent (class valedictorian in high school and college). The running joke in the family is we got our work ethic from our dad and our smarts from our mom. I have four siblings. The oldest is my brother Bill. As a Captain in the U.S. Marine Corps, he was awarded a Bronze Star during his service in Vietnam. He retired to become a much beloved teacher. My three sisters, Mary, Nancy and Jane, are all career nurses. They exemplify the term 'caregiver'. Being around any one of them made you want to be a better person.

From Swimming with Dolphins to Working with Eagles

A lot can change in a year. I was studying animals in the ocean and then twelve months later I'm flying to Philadelphia to work with Eagles. I reported to training camp on July 5th, 1978. This would be a historic year for the Eagles: Vince Papale, a high school teacher at age 30, made the team (as in the block-buster movie 'Invincible'); the Eagles made the Playoffs thanks to Herman Edwards' Scoop n' Score play known forever as 'The Miracle in the Meadowlands'; and The '78 Eagles Training Camp catapulted my career in the NFL. (Okay, maybe the last one didn't make history.) But for me, that summer I got to meet and work with my lifetime mentor, Ron O'Neill.

Ron was the Eagles' Assistant Athletic Trainer. He was incredibly smart and had a great rapport with the players. I spent as much time as possible learning from him as he rehabbed injured players, administered treatments, recorded Cybex test results, and sometimes even worked out with the players.

In 1978, only a handful of NFL teams had full-time strength coaches: Clyde Emrich with the Chicago Bears, Alvin Roy with the San Diego Chargers, Bob Ward with the Dallas Cowboys, Lou Riecke with the Pittsburgh Steelers, and Kim Wood with the Cincinnati Bengals. Stan Jones with the Buffalo Bills was the D-Line Coach as well as Strength Coach. For 10 years, Ron O'Neill had the responsibility of designing and implementing the Strength and Conditioning program for the Philadelphia Eagles.

The Most Influential Yet 'Unknown' Man in NFL Strength and Conditioning

That summer I watched Ron O'Neill chart players body weights, implement conditioning tests, warm players up before practice, and then between these responsibilities he wrote the players workouts and supervised the weight room. In my mind, Ron O'Neill should be added to the list of Pioneers who elevated the Strength and Conditioning Profession in the NFL.

In 1984, I got a call from O'Neill. He'd just taken the positon as the Head Trainer for the Patriots and wanted to know if I would like to take his position with the Eagles. I returned to the Eagles for two years. A few of the players were still on the team from when I was an intern, including Ron Jaworski, Wilbert Montgomery, and Jerry Sisemore, but the most influential man I would get to work with was Strength Coach Tim Jorgenson. He had worked at LSU and Alabama before arriving at the Eagles. In the spring of '84, we lived together in the deep abyss of Veterans Stadium fending off cats, rats and cockroaches. It was during my time with Tim that I truly learned the intricacies of how to build a comprehensive training program for the players. After two years in Philly, Tim left for the Falcons and I headed to Houston.

In March of '86 I got a call from Milt Jackson. He'd left the Eagles to join Jerry Glanville's staff with the Houston Oilers. Glanville had cleaned house, including their Strength Coach, and Milt had recommended that Jerry bring me in for an interview. When Glanville called, I said six words and I thought I'd ruined the interview:

"Hey Bo, this is Coach Jerry Glanville. You interested in comin' down and talkin' to me 'bout being my Strength Coach?"

I responded, "Yes sir, that would be awesome!"

Immediately I hear, "Aw, hell no! Are you a Yankee?" There's a slight pause and then I hear others chuckling in the background. "Well, c'mon down anyway. The only reason I'm letting you interview is because Milt says you're pretty good with injuries. My secretary Linda Lou will make arrangements to fly you in tomorrow." Click.

I was scrambling to get materials together for the interview. A player I'd been rehabbing, Jody Schulz, leaned in my office and said, "Let me give you a little advice. I wouldn't go down there looking 'preppie' or wearing deck-shoes. You're going to Texas; I'd find a pair of boots."

I packed up approximately 50 pounds of files, binders, and books containing every workout program and Rehabilitation protocol I'd ever collected. I left Veteran's Stadium and headed home. My flight departed at 6 a.m., so I needed to stop and pick up the boots on the way home. No problem, there's a Sears on my way home. I was in luck – they had a nice pair of tan, size 10, square nosed Dingos. Things were going my way!

My trip to Houston went smoothly. Once at the Oiler's offices, I was brought into a conference room where I spread out my impressive array of books, binders, and folders. A few of the Coaches came in and began introducing themselves and then in walked Coach Glanville. He wore a black shirt, black jeans, black belt with a giant shiny belt buckle and black pointy cowboy boots. NFL Films had cameras in the room to document Jerry's interview process, but most were pointed at me. As Jerry started towards the other end of the table, he suddenly realized where the cameras are pointed, he looked at me and said; "Hell no! Switch!" Then told the NFL cameraman, "This guy doesn't need to be in the picture; I probably won't even hire him."

As I gathered up my stuff to change seats—bam! A true nightmare unfolded! It was like the strike-of-midnight at Times Square. Binders opened up, folders went flying, throwing papers everywhere. Everyone was dying of laughter, but I was just dying. Coach Glanville bent down to pick up one of my folders and screamed. "Stop the presses! Oh my! What the heck are those on your feet?" I didn't even get a chance to answer when he grabbed my leg and put my foot up on the table and asked Floyd Reese, "Are those concrete boots? You know, boots you wear when you're pouring concrete? Don't you have a pair, Floyd?"

Floyd responded, "Heck No! I've never had anything like those on MY feet!" (Floyd Reese was Jerry's Linebackers Coach).

I could hardly breathe when the questions started to fly. The staff grilled me for two hours. Glanville only wanted to know three things: what were the best exercises to get the players' triceps bigger, could I get the players to hunt like dogs, and did I like Jerry Jeff Walker?

I got the job. To this day, Jerry says the reason he hired me was because he felt sorry for me having to wear those boots.

A Change in Identity

First thing I did was evaluate each player. I took body measurements, weighed them, and measured their body fat. I interviewed each player while they stood in front of the mirror wearing only their shorts. I asked each to estimate their max for Squat, Clean, Snatch, and Bench. I was stunned that so many didn't know their scores and that so many had never heard of a Snatch, never mind done them. At the end of the first week they all agreed on one thing— never before had they done so many triceps exercises!

Coach Glanville believed a team must have an identity. He gave players nicknames. For example, our star special teams player, Steve Tasker was 5'10" and weighed 184 pounds, so his nickname was "Mini-Brute." In the weight room, the nickname "Sizemaster" had to be earned. Every week guys competed in a designated lift such as weighted dips or benching 315 pounds for reps. The winner got to wear a weight-belt with "SIZEMASTER" written in magic marker. Even though the workouts were long and hard, we also made it fun.

I wouldn't have made it through that first year without the support of a few key players; that's especially true for Warren Moon. For a quarterback he was incredibly strong: benching 330 pounds, power cleaning 275 pounds, and squatting 365 pounds. Those first weeks I pushed the players hard. Workouts lasted three to four hours. Several players grumbled about the workload. Our General Manager, Ladd Herzeg told me that a dozen players came up to his office, complaining the workouts were too much and

Tennessee Titans - if you want them to do it right, show them.

too long and to get rid of me. But Ladd said not to worry; he told Warren about the complaints, but Warren said he loved the workouts and it was just what the team needed.

The players' 24-Day Strike in 1987 was a challenge for every NFL Strength Coach. After two regular-season games, the players held a strike. Teams only had a few days to build a roster of replacement players, evaluate, train and prepare them to compete. I found myself training some guys that had never played in college, someone pulled off of a construction site, and even a guard at the state prison. The movie "The Replacements" wasn't that far from the truth.

'87 was the first of seven straight years in the playoffs. When Glanville left in '89, Jack Pardee took over. Jack was one of Coach Paul Bryants' "junction boys." He played 15 years in the NFL. His favorite saying was, "You're a professional... work like one!"

After starting 1-9 in '94, Jeff Fisher became the Head Coach. He'd played for the Chicago Bears and worked for Buddy Ryan at the Eagles. For 17 years I was honored to work with him both at the Oilers and Titans. The lessons I learned from Coach Fisher were invaluable to me. He was a master of navigating through incredible turmoil. A great example is how in 2000 he guided the Titans to play in Superbowl XXXIV just after moving the team twice in a three-year period.

For almost twenty years I was a one-man-gang running the team's strength program until 1996, when Sammy Cribb asked if he could intern to gain college credit. He did an excellent job and continued to work part time until '04. Jeff suggested hiring a full-time assistant in 2004 and I knew exactly who to hire, Jason Novak. I worked with his Dad, long-time NFL Coach, Frank Novak. I'd train Jason when he was in school. Jason developed a passion for the strength profession and chose it as his field of study at Stephen F. Austin, continuing on to get his master's from Baylor. He brought fresh ideas and new methods to train the players, and Jason's contributions dramatically improved our program.

His presence was missed long after he left in 2015 to head-up the program at Central Michigan University.

In 2006, Coach Fisher added Assistant Head Coach to my title. Although I was truly honored, I would have given up the title if I could have relinquished two other roles which I despised. "'Get-Back' Coach" is truly the most unenviable job on the sideline. Trying to keep the players back was hard enough but keeping the Coaches off the field—even worse. "The Turk" is the other role I despised. When we'd release a player, I had to find that player and tell them to "Bring your playbook and go see Coach Fisher." At the end of Camp players would stay far away from me. It was the worst job ever.

One of the greatest days in my career was witnessing the promotion of Mike Munchak to Head Coach of the Titans. Mike played for the Oilers from '82 to '93 with a nine-time selection to the Pro Bowl. He joined the Oilers coaching staff in 1994. In 2011, Munchak replaced Fisher. From when I joined the Oilers in '86 Mike had become one of my closest friends.

Mike hired several ex-teammates from his playing days to work as coaches. During an early morning workout, I looked around and realized I was training six of my ex-players, who are now coaches: Frank Bush, Jerry Gray, Steve Brown, Marcus Robertson, Bruce Matthews, and Mike Munchak. These were not only great players, but they were really good men. Many of them attended a weekly Bible study lead by Bruce Matthews.

When Coach Whisenhunt was hired, that may have been the first time I truly thought my job was in jeopardy. I'd heard Ken was bringing 'his guy' to take over as Strength Coach, so I didn't think he was considering me for his staff.

Pay Attention, Young Coaches

As I left for work the next day, my wife sensed that I was not in a great mood and said, "Sweetheart, Coach Whisenhunt does not know you, so when he calls you in to talk, you can choose to either walk into his office with a sour attitude and give him justification to not retain you, or you can change your attitude, walk into his office, and explain how you design and implement your workouts for each player and show him the passion you've always had in doing your job… Who knows what will happen?"

I met with Coach Whisenhunt and explained the details of my workouts. I remember there being a pause when I was done, then Ken saying, "That's impressive. I'll tell Ruston I'd like you to stay." I was ecstatic. Over the years, working with different Head Coaches, I've learned that each has unique qualities that separate them the others. With Ken, I quickly discovered that it was about results. You could build a relationship with him, but only after he knew he could trust you. Working for him was simple: work the players hard, hold them accountable, and stay on schedule.

Mid-season 2015, Mike Mularkey took over the helm. Mike had played nine years as tight end and Coached 23 years in the NFL. Mike embodied both loyalty and preparedness. Coach Mularkey was unquestionably loyal to Coach Whisenhunt but also well prepared to take over as Head Coach. Having previously been a Head Coach, Mike had a plan of action. First thing up— change the culture. He emphasized 'accountability' to team, to community and especially to your teammates. His qualities as a great man came through as Head Coach. Mike and his wife Betsy were great examples on how to live out the mantra of "God, Family, Work" even while working in the fast-paced, high-stress world of the NFL.

Tennessee Titans - Friday training with Head Coach, Mike Mularkey, and Tight Ends.

A Secret to Success is to 'Win at Home'

"I win!" Those are the first words my family would hear me utter upon coming home from a game, regardless of the outcome. That usually signaled a race to greet me at the door between my beautiful wife Heidi and whichever children were home. I am the proud father of six children (Kelsea, Brock, Cole, Bergen, Caden, and Dottie) and I said these words because I wanted them to know they were my top priority in this life and remind them how blessed we were.

So on April 6, 2018, when I heard "We win!" as I walked in the front door and saw Heidi and the kids barreling down to give me a hug, no two words

My Family - the reason I worked so hard for 34 years in the NFL.

could have been more welcoming, especially knowing that this would be the last time I would return home employed as the Assistant Head Coach/Strength & Conditioning Coordinator of the Tennessee Titans. I had worked with the Titans/Oilers Organization for 32 years. (It's reportedly the NFL record for consecutive years with the same Team as an Assistant Coach.)

Only Heidi, and my incredible assistants, Tom Kanavy and Taylor Porter, had any idea that I was considering retirement. I had recently had a fourth surgery on my elbow. My grip strength had diminished, and I doubted my ability to properly teach technique or safely spot players when lifting—I guess you could say the decision was *out of my hands*!

Over the years, I'd undergone 14 surgeries. Three were on the same day (both knees and a shoulder reconstruction), and yet I never missed a day of work. Before surgery, I'd go to work and lay out the player's workouts, and I was always back at the office the next morning to train the players. To some this may seem unbelievable, to others ridiculous, but for me it was just a result of how I was raised. My dad ingrained in me the importance of having 'a strong work ethic.' I can remember him saying, "There'll always be someone bigger, stronger, and smarter than you, but it's your choice to let someone outwork you!"

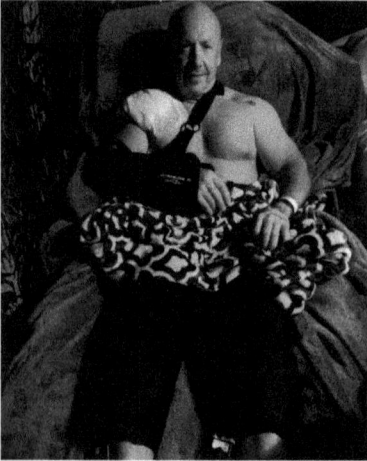

Don't try this at home! Triple surgery, then back to work the next morning.

My decision to retire was difficult, but to continue in my role as the Strength and Conditioning Coach for the Titans would have been even more difficult. Matthew 26:41 says it all; "The spirit is willing but the flesh is weak." Whenever asked, "How much longer do you want to Coach in the NFL?" My answer was always the same, "When the very best that the players deserve was more than the best I could give – it would be time to go!" It was time.

I was at ease about my decision for two reasons. It was re-affirmed through prayer that it was the right decision and I had full confidence in the two men replacing me, Tom Kanavy and Taylor Porter.

In 2016, I had an opportunity to hire a second assistant. I asked Tom to search for the brightest young coach available, someone with unique skills. Tom proposed Taylor Porter. I was incredibly impressed with his past work experiences (including three other NFL Teams), and his knowledge in nutrition and extensive work with GPS tracking. I truly appreciated the positive attitude and incredible work ethic he brought to the weight room each day.

Tom Kanavy would take over as the Head Strength and Conditioning Coach. When I hired Tom in 2015, I fulfilled a promise to hire one of my highly qualified peers who had NFL experience. Tom had an incredible resume, having worked for almost 20 years in the league as both an Assistance and Head Strength Coach. I could not have chosen a better person to have worked with my last three years…or a better Coach to replace me.

It is because of men like Tom and Taylor, that I have absolute confidence in the future of the Strength and Conditioning profession.

Steve Watterson's Coaching Bio
- 1980-1984 - Amphitheater High School, Head Athletic Trainer/ Instructor
- 1984-1986 - Philadelphia Eagles, Assistant Athletic Trainer
- 1986-2018 (Retired) - Tennessee Titans (Houston Oilers), Assistant Head Coach/Strength & Conditioning Coordinator

Achievements & Honors
- 1974 - Newport 18 Under Tennis Champion
- Judicial Board, University of Rhode Island, Bob Weisenger, Chairperson
- Intramural Sports Council, University of Rhode Island
- 1978-1979 - Athletic Advisory Committee, University of Rhode Island
- 1991 - Professional Strength Coach of the Year, Selected by The Presidents Council on Physical Education and Sport & USA Sports Fitness
- 1992 - Golden Foot Award, Presented by the American Academy of Podiatry and Sports Medicine
- 2003 - Presidents Award, Professional Football Strength and Conditioning Coaches Association
- 2015 - University of Rhode Island Distinguished Graduate Award

Inventions
- L.A.M. - Limb Accurate Measurements: a patented measuring device designed to evaluate circumference changes in the extremities
- W.I.E.R.D. - Watterson Internal and External Rotation Device: a device designed to rehabilitate the shoulder in all functional patterns

CHAPTER 32

The Dave Williams Story

"Life is about the places you go, the people you meet, and the decisions you make."

I was born and raised in South Charleston, West Virginia. My parents separated the summer before my senior year in high school. That summer I spent much of my time working out with my friend, Robin Bodkin. We lifted weights and ran. We really didn't know how to write up a workout and our coaches didn't either in the early '60s. We just went from one exercise to another until we were exhausted.

We both went into our senior year hoping to earn a college scholarship. That actually happened to Robin. He played defensive tackle for Duke. But on the second day of practice, I broke my ankle badly. Temporarily crushed and discouraged, I was determined to rehab and come back and play. I ended up playing in seven games but couldn't sprint full speed until the last three.

With no scholarship, I decided to attend Fairmont State College, where I earned a BS in biology and physical education. During my senior year at Fairmont, I was captain of the football team that won the NAIA National Championship in 1967. I also had the honor of being selected as a first team Associated Press Small College All-American defensive lineman. In the last regular season game, I re-injured my ankle. It was swollen and black and hurt more than it did when it broke in high school. I taped it up and went through two weeks of practice and a playoff game. Then we went on to beat Eastern Washington for the championship.

In May of 1969, I graduated with honors and my college coach offered me a graduate assistant position. It began with working in the weight room with incoming freshmen players. I quickly discovered that this was something I could

265

see myself doing. On July 23rd, I received two letters in the same mail. One was an acceptance to attend graduate school at West Virginia University and the other was from Uncle Sam. That was a Monday. On Saturday I got married and left for basic training one week later. In 1970, I was stationed in South Korea, where I spent the next twelve months. While there, I played football for the Seventh Infantry Division and later helped run the division athletic facility and the base weight room.

Before entering the strength and conditioning profession, I spent six years teaching and coaching at public and Christian schools. In 1979 I had an interesting job as the fitness director at the Roanoke Athletic Club instructing members while they were using the new Nautilus Circuit.

A big turning point for me came in the spring of 1980 when I attended a National Strength and Conditioning Association (NSCA) clinic held at the University of North Carolina. It was an awesome day for me, and I set my goal to become a college strength and conditioning coach. I contacted the coaches who had been at the UNC clinic and visited Steve Bliss at Ohio State and Dan Riley at Penn State. I asked them all the same question, "What do I need to do to become a college strength coach?" They all said the same thing. I needed to go back to school, get my Master's, and work in a winning program—someplace like Alabama, which had just won two national championships in a row. I decided to visit the athletic director, Al Worthington, at Liberty Baptist College (now Liberty University). Combining Christian education with strength and conditioning seemed like the perfect profession for me. The athletic director told me that the school was too small to afford a full-time strength and conditioning coach and, besides, I needed more experience. He gave me the same advice as the other coaches. I thanked him and told him, "I'll do it, and I will be back." I was willing to work and sacrifice. It could not have happened if my wife had not been on board with the idea. She had my back and encouraged me all the way.

In 1980, I became a graduate assistant at the University of Alabama and volunteered as an assistant to Mike Marks working with the football team coached by Paul "Bear" Bryant. In the spring, my GI Bill ran out, my grad assistant position was over, and my wife's teaching contract was up. I put my application in at Kroger and continued to sell my rare blood plasma for $25 every two weeks.

My wife and I decided that I needed to step out in faith and take what little money we had and go to the NSCA National Convention in Dallas, Texas. I planned to sleep in my car and eat two meals a day at McDonalds. Mike Marks was kind enough to share his hotel room with me and even bought me dinner one night. It was at this convention that Mike Flynt announced that he was leaving Texas A&M University. I went back to Alabama and mailed my resume immediately. Several days later, I received a call from the A&M athletic director inviting me to come in for an interview. When I went to A&M, my forearm was badly bruised from giving blood. I had to wear a long-sleeved shirt to cover the bruise. I didn't want anyone thinking the bruise was from drug use. They selected me, the coach from Liberty High School and Timberlake Christian School, and I felt truly blessed. My experience working with the University of Alabama program and Mike Marks really paid off.

While I was at Alabama and at Texas A&M, I attended seminars at the National Strength Research Center at Auburn University four years in a row. They presented results of research with athletes from various sports using periodization models for sets, reps, and intensity. I followed much of their advice in the following years.

The weight room at A&M was bigger than the one at Alabama, but still can't compare to what either school has today. There were six very light weight power racks with four benches, four inclined benches, a long rack of dumbbells, two racks of pre-loaded barbells, and Olympic bars with a lot of bumper plates. There was a full Nautilus circuit painted Aggie maroon. The floor was actually the turf from the old football field which had a thick layer of rubber under it. I immediately had plywood platforms installed which greatly improved our power clean technique.

After coaching at A&M for over two years, I still had the desire to coach at a Christian university. I shared this with a pastor friend of mine named Wes Bigelow. He said, "I have three questions for you. Did God lead you here to Texas A&M?" I answered, "Yes." Wes said, "Have you done what he has led you here to do?" I thought of so many athletes and coaches that I knew God wanted me to share my faith with. I said, "No, I haven't." Question three was, "Have you been here with one bag packed and ready to go since you got here?" That question hit me hard. I knew that we had never come to Texas to stay but to get the experience needed to go to Liberty. I remember Wes telling me that I could forget about Liberty until I unpacked my bags and did the work God brought me there to do. I then told God I wanted his blessing at A&M. I mentally unpacked my bags and worked like I was never going anywhere else. Workouts were going well and the FCA and Bible study groups were going strong. Less than four months later I received a call from Liberty. They had hired a new football coach, Morgan Hout.

I became the first full-time strength coach at Liberty in June of 1984. That's where I spent the next thirty-three years.

When I first started working with football at Liberty, we had two good lifting platforms, three iron stairs for squats, and two benches with some other junk in a former classroom. Before Christmas, I took out a personal loan for $3,000 to buy used equipment from a gym that had gone out of business. Still, some

LU Weight Room Athletic Center - 1987

LU Football Operations Center - 2018

of our athletes said their high school weight rooms were better. For three years, we had to make do with what we had, and the players made unusual gains in spite of the facilities. I told them that gravity works the same here as in any Alabama or A&M weight room. Attitude is what makes the biggest difference. That weight room was a tough sell on recruiting visits. Then Dr. Falwell caught the vision, found the donor, and built an 8,000 square foot weight room, a training room, locker rooms, and offices. I thought I was thinking big when I asked for and got $200,000 for equipment. You could buy a lot of equipment in 1986 for that amount of money.

As exciting and amazing as it was to be working in "Big Time" athletics at Alabama and Texas A&M, I had missed the intimacy of working in a smaller school and the genuine Christian environment. Developing this new program was exciting, and I believed that I could make a difference if it was God's will.

The final version of the new weight room had two levels. Downstairs had a rubber floor with fourteen inlayed platforms and fourteen heavy duty power racks with plateholders for the iron plates and bumper plates. On the second level there were three circuits of different machines. Eventually we got rid of a lot of the machines and added more power racks and platforms.

As time went by, this weight room was demolished to make room for a new visitor's center. Football now has a huge weight room at the stadium, and all the other sports work out of the three additional new weight rooms which are outfitted with the latest equipment. The student body has an awesome fitness center and club sports have their own weight room.

One basic philosophy or attitude for life that I felt was important to teach was humility. I know that seems at first to be the opposite of the signs we see in many weight rooms, but when I became the head strength coach at Liberty, I wanted the athletes to embrace the idea that our school was different in a positive way. Dr. Falwell, the founder and chancellor of the school, said, "If it's Christian, it ought to be better." One of the first things I did was to put up a sign that said "Humility" not "Pride." I understand team pride, but I wanted to emphasize working to help your teammates be the best they can be. Each recruiting weekend, I asked the prospective player if they saw the big pride sign. Then I told them to turn around and look up. There was HUMIL-ITY painted eighteen inches high in red. They always seemed surprised. I taught my athletes the difference between having humility and being humbled.

Humility sign in the Hancock weight room.

Humility is not thinking less of yourself but thinking of yourself less and others more. Being humbled is a proud man being embarrassed. So, roll up your sleeves and go to work helping someone else get better today.

One of my most basic philosophies is "T-T-T-T: Take Time To Teach." The best coaches are good teachers who continually teach and review proper techniques on all core lifts, especially the Olympic lifts. I like to use "technique warm up sets" for all Olympic lifts. For example: pull to knees, pull to shrug, high pull, power clean. I would often show a short two to five-minute video of great lifting technique and regularly had live demonstrations. We often let players "volunteer" to demonstrate as all watched. I have always believed that if a good athlete can see another good athlete properly perform a lift, jump, sprint, or agility drill, he will be able to imitate it. One year, the head coach, Sam Rutigliano, put the four T's on the back of everyone's T-shirt. It turned out that "Take time to teach" was his basic philosophy also.

I had read about Soviet weight lifters using 'weight releasers' for eccentric overload. I began to incorporate weight releasers that I made into my personal workouts and discussed them with other coaches.

In the early '90s, Johnny Parker was the strength coach for the New York Giants. He hosted a seminar on speed-strength training with the Russian weight lifting coach Gregory Goldstein. Bill Gillespie and I invited other coaches such as LeBaron Caruthers, Mike Gentry, Eric Lawrence (former Liberty assistant strength coach), Richard Sorin, and UVA coaches to pitch in. Coach Goldstein talked about the Soviet philosophies of training and demonstrated many unique lifts. His ideas were revolutionary for the profession, and we were blown away by his knowledge and expertise.

Another interesting advancement was the study in the value of position-specific strength for athletic development and injury prevention. I began to study the rate of force development from velocity-based training using tendo units. These units made a huge difference in my athletes and how they moved. I became a big believer in band resistance and assistance training; teaching acceleration, deceleration, and quick changes in direction. My focus advanced over the years to be more about injury prevention and mobility/stability for my athletes.

I loved coaching women's basketball, volley ball, and softball. They were willing to do what I asked them to do and had great attitudes. Being on winning teams didn't hurt, either. One of the best experiences of my life was in 2014 when Coach Cary Green invited me to travel with the women's basketball team to Israel. He is an awesome coach and a great friend. We spent one week touring historical sites and one week in a basketball tournament with other teams from the Middle East and Europe. I really enjoyed working with the "Lady Flames."

During the thirty-three years of coaching at Liberty, I have enjoyed great freedom and joy. It was such a gift to be able to stop and pray with a player or team about a need or a situation, to begin with a prayer for help, safety, and blessing and ending with a prayer of thanks. Learning to depend on God for everything and seeing how He provides and changes lives, including mine has been incredibly fulfilling.

A special thanks goes out to Mike Marks for going out on a limb and talking Coach Bryant into letting me be a volunteer strength coach at Alabama. He gave me a chance and it really paid off. I will always be grateful. Thank you, my friend.

Special thanks to Morgan Hout, former head football coach at Liberty, for hiring me as the first full-time strength coach in 1984. He was one of my biggest supporters and still is. In 1989, Coach Hout led the Flames to their best turn around season, from two wins and nine losses to eight wins and three losses.

Another special thanks goes to Bill Gillespie for being such a loyal friend and assistant when I came to Liberty. Thank you for coming back to Liberty from the Seattle Sea Hawks to take my place after the first of my five major back surgeries. It has been a pleasure to see how you've grown and developed as a fantastic strength coach.

Bill Gillespie in the classroom weight room - 1985

Of course, Dr. Jerry Falwell Sr. was a wonderful influence and cheerleader through the years. His son, Dr. Jerry Falwell Jr., has been an encouragement and blessing. Thank you both more than I can say.

Others that I have learned from are Al Vermeil, Vern Gambetta, Dale Baskett, Randy Smythe, Dick Hartzell, Doc Kreis, Johnny Parker, Al Miller, George Dostal, Steve Bliss, Dan Riley, LeBaron Caruthers, Louis Simmons, Boyd Epley, Dave Schmitz, Bert Hill, Mike Gentry, Chip Sigmon, Jeff Connors, Clyde Wright, Charles Anderson, Neal Bryant, and Barry Rice, Ellie Rollins, and Jeff Boschman.

Dr. Falwell and myself in the Liberty weight room - 1985

To all of the guys who worked alongside me at Texas A&M and Liberty University, thank you all. You made my job so much easier and more enjoyable.

And a special thank you to my relatively patient wife.

Some final thoughts and advice:

- Develop a hunger for knowledge in the area that you are passionate about.
- Visit other coaches and compare training ideas.
- Invite experts in speed development, flexibility, and mobility to come and do clinics with your staff and athletes.
- Do the exercises and drills yourself to see if they really work. Then tweak them.
- Don't be afraid to try something different—Louis Simmons is like that. Kindred spirit.

Books I Recommend
- *Weight Training* by Michael Stone and Harold O'Bryant
- *Scientific Principles and Methods of Strength Fitness* by J. P. O'Shea
- *Power: a Scientific Approach* by Fred Hatfield
- *Speed – Strength Training for Football* by E.J. "Doc" Kreis
- *Sports Illustrated Strength Training* by John Garhammer
- *Explosive Lifting for Sports* by Harvey Newton

Dave Williams's Coaching Bio
- 1968-1971 - Served in the U. S. Army
- 1971-1973 - Liberty High School, Science Teacher and Assistant Football Coach

- 1973-1978 - Timberlake Christian School, Teacher and Coach
- 1978-1979 - Longwood Avenue Christian School, Administrator
- 1979-1980 - Roanoke Athletic Club, Fitness director
- 1980-1981 - University of Alabama, Graduate Assistant Strength Coach
- 1981-1984 - Texas A&M University, Head Strength Coach
- 1984-2006 - Liberty University (formerly Lynchburg Baptist College), Head Strength Coach
- 2006-2017 (Retired) - Liberty University, Associate Strength Coach

Achievements & Honors

- 2002 - Inducted into the Fairmont State University Athletic Hall of Fame
- 2007 - CSCCA certification
- 2008 - Master Strength Coach Award
- 2013 - Liberty University Flamespy Support Staff of the Year Award
- 2017 - Liberty University Flamespy Cornerstone Award
- 2017 - Inducted into the Liberty University Athletic Hall of Fame

Education

- 1964-1968 - Fairmont State College (currently Fairmont State University), B.S. in Biology and Physical Education
- 1980-1981 - University of Alabama, M.A. in Physical Education (Exercise Physiology)

CHAPTER 33

The Mike Woicik Story

Back in the early '80s, I had a small apartment in Syracuse, New York. It wasn't much—it had one bedroom and a few pieces of old furniture—but it's all I needed.

In 1980, I became Syracuse University's first head strength and conditioning coach. I oversaw all sports as the head strength coach and served as the assistant track coach for all field events, both men and women. I worked 10 months and earned $12,000 each year.

A few years earlier, I had been competing in track at Boston College and studying to become a physical education teacher and high school football coach. Now, I was at Syracuse, on the ground level of a fairly new industry, living in that little apartment, eating mac and cheese 12 nights in a row.

I had other food that I'd put in my cupboards—cereal, crackers and other boxed meals—but most of the time, the rats reached them before me. I had a solution, though—traps. The rats may have taken the battle, but the war was mine.

I still remember lying in bed at night, reading, and hearing that sweet sound: *WHACK!*

Those were some great years.

———

I've put 39 years into this business. In a fairly volatile job market, I've never been out of work more than a few months.

I've worked with some of the greatest players and winningest coaches in NFL history. I've trained Michael Irvin, Troy Aikman, Emmitt Smith, Tom Brady, and several others who I've seen develop from young rookies to current and future Hall-of-Famers. I've coached alongside Jimmy Johnson, Mike Ditka, and Bill Belichick. I own six Super Bowl rings.

For most people, these things will define my career. For those who don't know me, these may be the things that define my life.

From the outside looking in, people look for these things—especially in professional sports—to distinguish athletes, coaches and management. When we're looking for a quick conclusion, it's easier to use stats and figures than to discover techniques, determine motivation, and judge character. It's much easier to ask (and answer), "Did you win games?" than "Did you help your players grow?"

Not to say these things are bad—those Super Bowls were great moments, for sure—but I've chosen not to let the "outside-in" define me, as a coach or as a man. For me, it's always been about what I can control, and I can't control what comes in from the outside. Plus, if I've learned anything in these 39 years, it's that strength coaches don't win football games. Strength coaches don't create superstars. Strength coaches don't win Super Bowls.

If I still believed those things, you probably wouldn't be reading this chapter.

Inside-out Success

In my first seven years in Dallas, we won 77 of 112 games. We made the playoffs six of seven years and won three Super Bowls (1992, 1993, 1995). In my 11 years with New England, we went 126-50, won 16 of 16 regular season games in 2007 and claimed four more AFC Championships and three more Super Bowls (2001, 2003, 2004). Those are the years people talk about.

In New Orleans—during my three-year stint from 1997-1999 with Coach Mike Ditka—we won just 15 of 48 games, including only three wins in my final season. We never finished better than third in the NFC West. Those are the years I like to talk about.

In many ways, I look at my time in New Orleans as some of the best work I've done in the NFL to date. No, we weren't winning, but our guys still worked hard in the off-season and saw tangible results. The lack of winning didn't define that time period for me; rather, it's what we accomplished *in spite* of that lack of winning.

When you're in the middle of a 3-13, it's much harder to keep guys working hard and maintaining motivation in the gym. When there's no light at the end of the tunnel, you don't have that carrot to dangle, so to speak, in front of your athletes that 15 or so other coaches in the playoff hunt might have.

So, you can understand why seeing measured improvement in players after a 3-13 season can still keep me satisfied despite finishing last in our division. In my mind, that's what defined a successful strength coach.

From the outside, people assume that if your team's winning, you're doing a good job, and if they're not, you're not.

In Dallas, after we won those three Super Bowls, I received phone call after phone call. Coaches wanted to visit our facilities from all over the country. They wanted to see what special things we were doing to create success. In New Orleans, doing the same exercises under the same philosophy, hardly anyone called because we didn't have that on-field success.

Some coaches might look at the wins, the losses, and the phone calls and wonder, "What am I doing wrong?" For me, it's about your source of satisfaction. If your satisfaction comes from the outside—the media, fans, pundits, etc.—you might do a good job but still be disappointed. But in my experience, if you focus on what you can control, you can find success outside of your circumstances.

By God's grace, I've been blessed with "outside-in" success, but I've chosen to find my satisfaction elsewhere. For me, it's always about doing everything I can to help the players with whom I'm working—to create effective training plans, to motivate athletes to work hard and to see tangible improvements. And if that means we win more games, then even better.

The Super Bowls were definitely great moments in my career, but to me, my proudest moments came when I saw a practice guy make the roster, or a roster guy earn regular starts, or a starter become a Pro Bowler. Take Michael Irvin, for example.

Michael was entering his third year in the League when I arrived in Dallas in 1990. In those previous two years, the Cowboys had only seen four total wins, and although Michael was on pace for 1,000-plus yards in 1989, a torn right ACL in Week Six against the 49ers ended his season on the injured reserve. Even though he'd been a high first round draft choice and still had plenty of potential, the future of his health began to surface some doubts.

When I got to Dallas after Michael underwent major knee surgery, there was a question of, "Is Michael going to make it?" So, to see him come back from that even stronger and eventually continue on to a Hall-of-Fame career, that was pretty special. That was a pretty satisfying thing to watch unfold.

Again, don't get me wrong, the wins were great; but throughout my career, it was the moments like Michael returning from that serious injury or players telling me I helped them improve that brought me true satisfaction. Those were the high points for me.

After all, even if I did my job perfectly, the Super Bowls were never guaranteed.

Team (not individual) Success

Back when I coached track at Springfield, I had a method.

I'd run track back at Boston College, but since I was still pretty new to coaching it, I decided to use the resources—specifically, the people—around me. I took it event by event. If I was coaching a pole-vaulter, I'd call up the best pole vault coach in the country and ask for his training, his methodology, and his philosophy. Same went for triple jump, shot put, hurdles, and all of these events I was still learning how to coach.

I certainly found information that way, but sometimes I discovered that teams were successful in spite of their event or strength coach. A good team or athlete didn't always have a good coach.

Take the triple jump, for example. When I called up the best triple jump coach I could find, I was underwhelmed. He gave me all of their information, and I realized, "Boy, this really isn't anything special." Upon further investigation, I discovered he wasn't necessarily a good coach; he just recruited talented, foreign triple jumpers. These athletes had reached a high level before they even came to America.

In my experience, too, I've discovered the inverse to also be true—good strength coaches don't always translate to good teams. Take my years in New Orleans, for instance. Like I said, I consider that period to be some of my best work, yet we never won more than six games in a season.

Coaches who say, "I am the reason"—whether positive or negative—are missing the big picture. Yes, I've always felt that strength coaches—as well as any other coach—can have a positive impact on a team, but coaches don't win ball games—*players do*. When you have good players, you have a good chance to win. When you have good coaches, the same is true. Neither one is exclusively responsible.

For instance, yes, I've been incredibly blessed to have been a part of many successful seasons with several successful programs, but it'd be foolish of me to take personal credit for those winning seasons or Super Bowls. I've had the privilege of working with some outstanding mentors, outstanding coaching staffs and outstanding players. Certainly, I've been influenced by a number of individuals.

I think about Boyd Epley, one of the pioneers of strength and conditioning. When I came into college coaching, he sent me his manual; he talked to me on the phone. I was just a young kid who was just getting started, and Boyd gave me a lot to push me along.

I think about Remi Korchemny from the Soviet Union, who, to me, was one of the most brilliant speed training coaches in the world. I don't think he'd even remember me, but when I was a young coach working with sprinters, I'd listen to clinics at New York University where Remi spoke. He was hard to understand at times—because of his heavy Russian accent—but he gave me plenty of information. I sent him my off-season running programs, and he gave me feedback and running drills—drills that we still do to this day.

I think about Johnny Parker, who—prior to his New York Giants smashing my Cowboys in my first NFL game—walked across the field to welcome me to the League. I think about Rusty Jones, who spent so much time talking through training and nutrition with me. I think about Louie Simmons, Al Miller, Dave Redding, and a number of others who've been very helpful along the way.

I think about Jimmy Johnson, who gave me my first NFL coaching job. He wasn't an expert at strength and conditioning, but he placed an emphasis on it and helped give me traction and credibility. The same goes for Dick McPherson, Bill Belichick, Mike Ditka, and Jason Garrett. I've been really lucky to have been connected to such quality head coaches.

And of course, it doesn't end there. I wouldn't be writing this if it weren't for the Michael Irvins, the Emmitt Smiths, the Tom Bradys, the Daryl Johnstons, the Troy Aikmans, the Teddy Bruschis, the Jason Wittens, the Jaylon Smiths. Some players work to make themselves better. Other players—like the guys I mentioned and multiple others—drag 10 people along with them.

Although I'm grateful to have worked with these athletes—and many from early in their careers—I'd never say that I "made" them or that I am *the reason* these players became great. Certainly, it's easier to raise these guys as pups, but their success didn't come from me—it came from within them.

I may have helped them along the way, but I didn't go to the gym for them. I didn't lift the weights or jump in the morning hot tub or see the chiropractor for them. It takes much more than a good strength coach to do that.

Drive for Success

In my opinion, I still think I'm a tough strength coach. I'm still demanding. I still require excellence, hard work, and perseverance. If you talk to the players I coach now, they'll tell you the same thing.

If you talk to the players I coached in the '80s and '90s, though, they'll probably tell you I've gone completely soft.

When I was younger, I yelled, screamed, and cursed in the weight room. Some people look at that as a sign of a good strength coach, but as time's gone on, I've realized that's not as effective as I once thought—especially at an NFL level.

In college, you're dealing with 100 players—maybe 40 of who are regular contributors and have motivation to be their best. Even at a Division-I level, you still have a bunch of guys who are more interested in degrees or women or partying. To get some of those guys to work—since they're younger and less mature—you have to be more forceful. But the script changes in the NFL.

In the NFL, you're dealing with adults. You're working with grown men. Sure, maybe some of your rookies still act a bit like college kids, but for the most part, these players *want* to be better. They *want* to have more success. They *want* to continue earning a paycheck, to eventually become a starter or a Pro Bowler or a Hall-of-Famer.

There's an internal motivation—whether it's money or Super Bowl rings or just a love of the game—that becomes much more important than yelling or cursing. In the NFL, it becomes less about motivating players and more about understanding *their own* motivation and showing them that you care.

One of the greatest inspirations I've ever witnessed is Jaylon Smith. Jaylon, who played linebacker at Notre Dame, suffered a catastrophic knee injury in the Fiesta Bowl at the end of his junior—and final—season. He tore both his ACL and LCL and dropped from a projected top-five draft choice to the second round, where we got him with the 34th overall pick.

Talk about adversity—this kid had a torn ACL, peroneal nerve damage, drop foot. After the injury, his foot would just flap down.

Despite all of that, he showed up every day with a smile on his face. He put in all the work and more, and he's come all the way back. He's overcome the odds completely, and in 2017, he finished second on the team in tackles. Every year, he continues to improve, he continues to invest more time. He shows up in March before the off-season program even starts.

It's unfortunate, but you'll see plenty of athletes experience similar injuries and never return to the game. But for Jaylon, it became very clear early on that wasn't going to be his story.

Some people play for the paycheck. Some play for the status. Jaylon Smith plays because he loves the game of football. Not that any of these motivations are better or worse than the others, but, because that's where Jaylon's motivation lied, it was very important for him to get that game back when he lost it. To me, that's why he could overcome the odds. That's why he could continue to show up every day with that contagious smile.

In my experience, every NFL player has some sort of deep motivation—whether it's money, fame, success, or a love of the game. It's that internal desire from which players can draw in order to push themselves to be great. It's the root of their success (or lack thereof).

That's why a strength coach can't win football games. As strong as my desire might be to make athletes better, unless I can understand their motivation and come alongside them in that, I'll never have any impact at all. Unless I can align my desire for success with theirs, we'll never move forward.

And that was my ultimate motivation—to help those players. That's how I defined my success. It wasn't the wins. It wasn't the Super Bowls. It wasn't even the 30-plus years in this business. It's knowing I helped these players work hard, persevere, never give up, be consistent, and not to let others determine their ceilings. It's knowing I helped these players on the field, and hopefully, beyond it.

I look back on those days in the small, rat-infested apartment with fondness. If I'm being honest, those were some of the greatest, happiest days of my life.

No, I didn't have more than a survivable salary or any NFL experience at that point, but unless you've been in the storm, you don't appreciate the sunshine. Those days shaped me into who I am today. They developed the character, work ethic and perseverance I relied upon for the rest of my career.

Back then, it was mission impossible—I could never end the day and feel like I accomplished what I wanted—but I still felt, every day, like I'd given everything. When I'd return home from the weight room—sometimes well into the night, I could look in the mirror and confidently tell myself I'd done my best. Looking back, I know that was true.

I believe God gives us all a purpose in this life, and that was mine. This has been mine. This is mine. Maybe I didn't do it exactly how He wanted me to, but I know I tried my best and I (hopefully) helped others along the way. That's all I could've asked for.

I didn't need the six extra rings or the 16-win season or the praise from other people. I just needed a dozen boxes of mac and cheese, some mousetraps, and the satisfaction of helping at least one athlete along in his journey. To me, that's all success ever was.

Mike Woicik's Coaching Bio

- 1978-1980 - Springfield College, Graduate Assistant - Track and Field, Weight Room
- 1980-1989 - Syracuse University, Strength and Conditioning Coach
- 1990-1996 - Dallas Cowboys, Strength and Conditioning Coach
- 1997-1999 - New Orleans Saints, Head of Strength and Conditioning Program
- 2000-2010 - New England Patriots, Head of Strength and Conditioning Program
- 2011-Present - Dallas Cowboys, Strength and Conditioning Coordinator

Achievements & Honors

- 39 years of Strength and Conditioning experience, including 29 years in the NFL
- Claimed six Super Bowl Championships in 29 NFL seasons (three with the Dallas Cowboys and three with the New England

Patriots)
• Five-time Professional Football Strength and Conditioning
Society's Coach of the Year (1992, 2004, 2010, 2014, 2016)

Education
• Boston College, Bachelor's Degree in History
• Springfield College, Master's in Physical Education

CHAPTER 34

The Kevin Yoxall Story

The following is an excerpt I wrote for *43 Lessons to Legacy* in honor of one of my former players at Auburn, Philip Lutzenkirchen, who died tragically on June 29, 2014:

I am truly blessed to have been a strength and conditioning coach for the past 30-plus years. Every day of my career, I have witnessed countless displays of incredible physical strength by female and male student athletes. The level of physical stress that student athletes encounter every training day and in actual competitions is difficult to express to those who have not lived an athlete's life at some point. I found that, for many athletes, developing physical strength is not that difficult if the right amount of effort and consistency is used properly each training session. With the correct conditioning plan, athletes will gradually strengthen the skills they need to perform in their respective sports.

While physical strength is an important characteristic of a student-athlete, mental and spiritual strength through one's will, character and/ or faith are all necessary elements for success as well. Developing mental and spiritual strength requires as much, if not more, effort and dedication as developing physical strength, and those gains must be desired and sought constantly. These gains can only be found through firm and unwavering faith that God walks with every one of us each and every day. The effort to gain physical, mental AND spiritual strength will never come without negative feedback or reaction from others, making it easy for many to give up. However, if the desire to build a foundation of physical, mental and spiritual strength is expressed by enough individuals they will come together and become an overwhelming and unstoppable force.

———

In 1983, I was a special education teacher. Yes, I was *also* a competitive collegiate powerlifter and Olympic weightlifter and even finished fifth at the National Collegiate Powerlifting Championships that year, but still, I had graduated from East Texas State University with a degree in special education.

When I would tell people about my then-profession, they were always complimentary. They'd tell me what a "special person it took" to teach special ed. They'd talk about the great amount of patience I must possess. Don't get me wrong, I was always grateful for the compliments, but I just did it and enjoyed it. It was as simple as that. I knew what I wanted to be doing, and I loved doing it.

That's the same mindset I had when my wife, Nancy—a TCU alum—and I headed down to Fort Worth for a Horned Frogs football game in 1987. Having heard examples of the strength and conditioning occupation in professional sports, I had started to form my own ideas of combining my love for education with my love for strength training at the high school level, but at the end of the day, I still thought special education was my path. Even when my friend Robbie Robinson—the head strength coach at TCU at the time—offered me an open graduate assistant position in his weight room. Even when I took the job.

I took that GA position with TCU in a different era of strength and conditioning. From TCU (1987-1992) to Minnesota (1993-1996) to UCLA (1996-1999) to Auburn (1999-2012) to Rice (2013-2016), I've seen this industry change, shift, transition, and everything in between. The facilities, the staff sizes, the exercise menus—not a lot is the same from 1987.

Frankly, neither am I.

Change: The Effects of Industry Development

In all honesty, when I walked into that 1,200 square-foot weight room at TCU, I was in awe.

Keep in mind, this wasn't 1,200 square feet for one football team. It was one weight room for 16 TCU sports. Four squat racks, four benches, four platforms, two coaches and 1,200 square feet for sixteen different sets of athletes. But I was content. I was just thrilled to have this opportunity.

Then I started traveling.

See, for college football strength coaches, all of our work is done before the Friday of each game. While the rest of the team runs through final preparations, the strength coaches would either, at home games, be giving tours of our weight room to other coaches or, on the road, touring a facility ourselves.

When you're walking through facilities like Bert Hill's 23,000 square-foot weight room at Texas A&M, suddenly 1,200 doesn't seem like such a large number.

Now, looking back at 1989, it does seem a bit crazy—the amount of sports for the facility and staff size. Today, you'd be hard-pressed to find a quality football program in the country without ample floor space dedicated exclusively to strength and conditioning. Back then, though, I didn't think anything of it. That's just how things were.

You didn't have football, basketball, or track-only strength coaches like you do now. You didn't have double-digit staffs. You had yourself, (usually) an assistant of some sort, and a whole lot of work. That led to a number of different consequences.

Take specialization, for example.

Today, exercise menus are so large and varied, and—in my opinion—a bit convoluted. Each basic exercise now has an unbelievable amount of alternate movements from which coaches can choose. In the '80s and early '90s, our staffs were spread so thin that we couldn't have much variety, especially early on. We determined what lifts and movements were going to make our athletes better, and we focused on perfecting those.

I think we try to get so particular in what we're doing today that, in some cases, we teach athletes to get pretty good at certain things while we could be *perfecting* a smaller number of exercises. I think it's far more beneficial to help athletes become *great* at using proper technique for tried and true techniques than navigating through an overly specialized menu.

For me, it's important to get a quantitative result, from consistent exercises, to know that an athlete is improving at his or her sport. I've always found the best way to accomplish that is by keeping it simple—focusing on the essentials of strength, power, flexibility, conditioning and speed, and promoting exercises that enhance all of those things.

Maybe that's just an old strength coach's opinion, but I think most of my colleagues in this book would agree with me. We saw what worked back in the '70s, '80s and '90s. So much has changed—and a lot of it, for the better. We're just trying not to forget the 40-year-old pieces of wisdom that are still valuable today.

Nevertheless, it's a different time.

Now, when I see these young coaches working their first jobs with one or two sports and large staffs, the older coaches and I can't help but laugh a little bit. From multiple standpoints—resources, facilities, education, communication—the industry has changed significantly. No more coaches assigned to 10 or more sports with less than $15,000 salary. Still, I'm grateful for my starting point.

It just meant plenty of trial and error.

Trial and Error: Building My Philosophy

In 1992, I left TCU for the University of Minnesota. After locking into one sport (football) for a number of years, UCLA offered me the position of overall head strength and conditioning coach. I went from 16 sports at TCU to one at Minnesota to 21 at UCLA.

I always tell people UCLA shaped me into a better strength coach than any other place simply because of the variety of world-class athletes. To give you a point of reference, at the 1996 Summer Olympics in Atlanta, there were 40 former or then-current UCLA student-athletes competing for the United States and a number of other countries.

If my exercises weren't already firm after implementing consistent programs across 16 sports at TCU, they certainly solidified at UCLA. Sure, the gymnasts weren't doing identical exercises to our offensive linemen, but what I consistently found was that a few core exercises remained the same. If I could keep exercises simple while still focusing on improving necessary skills, that's the direction I took.

This is how it was for most of my philosophy—I had to figure it out as I went along. I used what I'd been given and did my best to make it work. Then I tracked the results, made changes if necessary and moved on. Sometimes, we saw a lot of success; sometimes, we saw things we needed to change. Over time, my philosophy gradually took its shape.

Today, my philosophy is guided by a number of sound principles that help enhance a student-athlete's performance, prevent injury, and aid in the hastening of the rehab process. Three words summarize my thoughts and beliefs regarding the overall, successful training of the student-athlete: "work, hard work."

I've always believed that—in order to achieve success in a training program—you must have a high level of intensity and a discipline that is carried throughout an entire training cycle. Student-athletes must be challenged physically and mentally during every cycle and outwork their future opponents in every training session. Through hard work, dedication and effort, student-athletes should develop a high level of confidence, enabling them to dominate their opponents—both physically and mentally.

Also, because of the uniqueness of conditioning, I've always placed a premium on that side of the equation. Regardless of our plan in the weight room, my kids were going to get their conditioning work done. I never wanted to be that team on the field that couldn't finish right.

No one knew this better than the student-athletes I coached at the University of Minnesota. On a fairly regular basis, I ran those kids through 40 50-yard sprints in a single workout.

Looking back, I wouldn't even go near that today. Even with my emphasis on conditioning, I still had plenty to learn—and plenty I did learn—through experimentation and correction. It's funny, today I have kids from the Minnesota days on Facebook that will see how my programs have changed and ask, "Yox, what happened?" I always tell them the same thing.

"Well, I'm a lot smarter now."

Today, conditioning and athleticism remain key priorities with the overall, year-round fitness of student-athletes holding the top spot. All athletes must be trained to maintain a high level of physical fitness, even during low-level training periods. Constant development of total body power, flexibility, explosiveness, speed, and strength must be strived for every training session.

I've learned all of this through many experiments and over several decades in the industry. Of course, none of this arose exclusively from my *own* mind.

Relationships: Uniqueness of the People in this Industry

I met Mike Gentry on a cold phone call.

It was the early 2000s. Mike was the head strength coach at Virginia Tech at the time, and I was at Auburn, wanting to learn from one of the greats in our industry. I gave Mike a call and asked if I could come visit, and of course he was immediately on board.

Since it was the early 2000s—and I couldn't book a room at any hotel on my smartphone—I asked Mike if he had any recommendations for accommodation near campus. Now, Mike didn't know me from Adam at that point, but I'll never forget what he said to me:

"Coach, you're not staying in any hotel. You're staying at my house."

Eighteen years down the road, we're the closest of friends.

There's something especially unique about relationships within this industry. As strength coaches, we're tasked with having to get these athletes to do difficult things—things they often don't want to do. That creates a mutual respect, and I think, as a result, we're always trying to help each other out.

Also, in an era without the Internet, if you had a question, it was much more common to make a phone call to another coach than to watch a DVD or browse the web. Not to say there isn't communication now, but back then, that's basically all we had—each other.

In the summer of 1988, I earned my first strength and conditioning certification from the National Strength and Conditioning Association (NSCA), an organization started by Boyd Epley. Along with the NSCA, I also earned my second strength and conditioning certification from the College Strength and Conditioning Coaches Association (CSCCA), started by Chuck Stiggins from BYU in the early 2000s.

I had the privilege of being one of the 30 or so founding members of the

CSCCA, served on the board of directors for many years and also received the honor of being selected as a CSCCA Master Strength and Conditioning Coach in 2002. Obtaining these nationally accredited certifications and distinctions from two respected organizations is something I believe to be very important, especially in this day and age, and my involvement with both the NSCA and CSCCA has also provided another avenue for me to connect with other strength coaches.

Back in the late '80s and early '90s, I still remember attending NSCA conventions that gave tours of facilities like Al Miller's with the Broncos. In fact, when Al worked in Atlanta with the Falcons—and I was at Auburn—I'd make the two-hour trip to see Al at least twice a year. I gained some very valuable insight watching him train kids. The same goes for Johnny Parker when he was in New England with Bill Parcells, and Mike Woicik with the Cowboys.

In some way, shape, or form, I consider each coach associated with this book to be a personal mentor. I won't go through and try to name every name—I know I wouldn't do everyone justice—but I've been blessed to work with incredible people throughout my career. All of these unique relationships have shaped me, and hopefully I've also been able to help others along the way.

Like the coaches with whom I've worked, I have to give credit where it's due. Now this may be biased, but in my opinion, I've had the privilege of training some of the hardest working student-athletes—male and female—in the country. I always enjoyed working with young people—not just because it keeps me young, but also because of the unique relationships I built with *them* over the years.

I had a former quarterback at Minnesota who, well after his football career, sent me a letter.

The letter, in great detail, explained how he'd recently run a marathon and the difficult process he'd endured to get to that point. He had pushed himself through months of strenuous training to prepare for this marathon, all the while thinking of his workouts back during his time in Minnesota. He credited those conditioning sessions for his success in the marathon.

I think this is a great example of how a strength coach's job creates unique relationships with athletes. As coaches, we have to spend plenty of time explaining why each movement, each rep is necessary. But, when the athletes come out on the other side, there's this new level of trust and depth to the relationship.

Beneath all of that—before the day with players and coaches began and after it ended—was my support system.

I couldn't write this chapter without praising my wonderful and beautiful wife, Nancy. She didn't marry a strength coach back in the summer of 1986, after all. She married a special ed teacher. For the most part, our married life started out pretty "normal." After I took the job at TCU, though, "normal" turned into 16-hour days, pressure to win ballgames, and Nancy thinking someone was breaking into the house if I returned home *before* 6 p.m.

Nancy has been unwaveringly supportive, incomprehensibly patient and has done an excellent job raising our two kids—Collin and Marlee—who both attended TCU and happen to also be awesome. I could not be prouder of the fine adults they have become. In fact, Marlee, who majored in kinesiology, also earned her certification through the NSCA, as a personal trainer. It makes me extremely proud to know Marlee makes her living in the same industry.

Instead of filling them with my stories, I probably could've used these pages to list everyone who's benefitted me in my career and my journey. From athletic directors to strength coaches to non-football sport coaches to families, I've always worked for, worked with, coached, and lived alongside incredible people. All of my many staff members throughout these years have done an absolutely incredible job—not only for me, but for their assigned sports as well. I am the man and the strength coach I am today because of them.

Every day, I wake up knowing I love what I do for a living. Even when I roll out of bed before the sun to get in an early workout, I know it's worth it because of these relationships. Sure, this business has changed plenty since the '70s and '80s, but, because of these people, I've changed right along with it.

——

Because of Los Angeles housing prices, when I coached at UCLA, my wife and I couldn't afford insurance on two vehicles. Thankfully, we lived close enough to campus where I could bike into work every morning. By coincidence, the rest of my staff lived within my same general area, so when they heard about my ride, they followed suit.

Because of different schedules, we never rode in together, but we always found a way to bike home in a pack. We'd pack up our things, close down the weight room, and ride off in a two-wheeled fleet. It quickly became a nightly tradition.

My house always marked the first stop on the home tour, and on most Fridays (when we didn't have Saturday games or training sessions), after a long week of training student-athletes, I'd turn to everybody on the ride home and make a suggestion. Let's stop, order some pizza, pick up some beers and sit around for a while at my place.

We'd talk about anything that came up—family, life, sports—and, a lot of the time, that's where we'd discuss different techniques and training methods. That's where those relationships, that accrued knowledge, where it all came from. It was the same as in the weight room, just in a much more relaxed setting.

Though I'm grateful for where I've come, I miss those Friday nights—that staff with whom to wrestle though ideas and in whom to confide. Still, even without that on a regular basis, I try to make do with what I'm given.

At CSCCA conventions, for instance—and you can verify this with the other coaches—there are known to be "gatherings" in my hotel with upwards of 40 to 50 of my closest friends and a handful of adult beverages. And, just like the days in our UCLA home, we'll talk family, discuss training technique and reminisce about stories just like these.

Some things never change, I guess.

Kevin Yoxall's Coaching Bio

- 1987-1989 - Texas Christian University, Graduate Assistant Strength and Conditioning Coach
- 1989-1993 - Texas Christian University, Head Strength and Conditioning Coach
- 1993-1996 - University of Minnesota, Head Football Strength and Conditioning Coach
- 1996-1999 - University of California - Los Angeles, Head Strength and Conditioning Coach
- 1999-2012 - Auburn University, Head Strength and Conditioning Coach
- 2013 - Strake Jesuit College Preparatory of Houston, Head Strength and Conditioning Coach
- 2014-2016 - Rice University, Head Strength and Conditioning Coach
- 2016-2017 - East Central Independent School District, Head Strength and Conditioning Coach
- 2017-Present - Midway Independent School District, Head Strength and Conditioning Coach

Achievements & Honors

National High School Strength and Conditioning Coaches Association
- 2017-Present - National Strength and Conditioning Coaches Association Member

National Strength and Conditioning Coaches Association
- 1983-Present - National Strength and Conditioning Coaches Association Member
- 1988-Present - Certified Strength and Conditioning Specialist
- 1998 - PAC 10 Strength and Conditioning Coach of the Year
- 1998 - Nominated for National Collegiate Strength and Conditioning Professional of the Year

Collegiate Strength and Conditioning Coaches Association
- Charter Member Collegiate Strength and Conditioning Coaches Association
- 2001-Present - Collegiate Strength and Conditioning Coaches Association Member
- 2001-Present - Certified Collegiate Strength and Conditioning Coach
- 2002 - Nominated for Master Strength and Conditioning Coach
- 2002 - Received Master Strength and Conditioning Coach Distinction
- 2004-2016 - Elected to Board of Directors Collegiate Strength and Conditioning Coaches Association
- 2010-2016 - Elected to Vice President of The Collegiate Strength and Conditioning Coaches Association

Professional Football Strength and Conditioning Coaches Society
- 2005 - Selected National Collegiate Strength and Conditioning Coach of the Year

USA Strength and Conditioning Coaches Hall of Fame
- 2006 - Selected to Collegiate Category of USA Strength and Conditioning Coaches Hall of Fame

American Football Monthly/Samson's Strength Coach of the Year
- 2008 - Selected to Collegiate Division IA Category of Samson's Strength and Conditioning Coach of the Year

Education
- 1983 - East Texas State University, Bachelor of Science, Major in Special Education, Minor in Physical Education
- 1989 - Texas Christian University, Master of Science in Physical Education

CHAPTER 35

Woodway
by Sam Washburn

Woodway has worked with many strength and condition coaches over the years, including coaches in this book. Their demands and goals for us, as an equipment manufacturer, were an extension of their vision for the blossoming profession of strength and conditioning. To execute their vision, heighten the performance of players, and bring the profession to the forefront, they needed equipment that could match their demands. Woodway worked with them to figure out what that would look like, how it would be achieved, and ultimately, delivered products that were fail proof.

In the mid-'80s, Doug Bayerlein, president and owner of Woodway, Inc., envisioned a coming fitness boom based off the advice and knowledge of his brother-in-law, Chris Wilson. Fitness clubs were growing, and equipment was being developed by manufacturers. However, treadmill products were notoriously bad, both uncomfortable and prone to breaking. Looking to branch his manufacturing capabilities into areas that could be controlled from cradle to grave, Mr. Bayerlein sought out various improvements on the traditional treadmill. Intending to redesign the traditional conveyor belt treadmill, what Mr. Bayerlein and Chris Wilson found was a medical treadmill company founded in 1974 in Germany—Woodway.

The key differentiator of the treadmills Woodway built—even at this early stage—was slat belt technology. The tank-like belt composed of individual slats allowed for more shock absorption which meant less joint impact, decreased muscle fatigue, and by extension, better biomechanics because there was less tendency to alter one's gait. Not only did the belt of these treadmills look like a tank, they were built like a tank. The belt was carried along a ball bearing transportation system which alleviated the forces of mechanical wear by reducing friction. This reduced friction allowed for simple, non-technical maintenance, fewer repairs, and a longer overall treadmill life. In a desire to bring this medical treadmill technology to the American market, Mr. Bayerlein applied for a U.S. manufacturing license. In 1988, the license was granted to Mr. Bayerlein to begin manufacturing this style of treadmill in Waukesha, WI. Today, that facility is the global headquarters and distribution center for all Woodway treadmills. Very quickly, Mr. Bayerlein and the other three employees of Woodway understood the durability and technology of this treadmill could be applied to performance athletics, strength, and conditioning.

It took a year to build the first treadmill. Woodway tested the proof of concept with their own in-house athlete, former NFL player Donald Kindt Jr., better known as Deke. It was believed Woodway had a treadmill that could live up to the ideals set forth by the burgeoning company. After building a few more treadmills the following year, Woodway began hauling them around the country and meeting with strength and conditioning coaches to assess what the treadmills could do for them and how Woodway could cater to the needs of the coaches, build a treadmill to fit those needs, and innovate upon it.

"We would go to their facilities to see how they were using competitors' treadmills. We would see crazy stuff, for instance the coaches would line up the whole team behind a couple of treadmills and crank up the speed to unrealistically high speeds and then have the athletes, literally, jump onto the treadmill," says Vance Emons, the sole remaining engineer from the very early days of Woodway. "They would run as fast as they could for as long as possible and then, again literally, jump off the treadmill. The issue was that no treadmill could hold up to this atmosphere. The athletes couldn't sustain that high of speed very long and the treadmills they were using couldn't sustain that level of use and abuse."

In 1991, John Gamble, the strength coach for University of Virginia, asked if Woodway could build a treadmill that would "hold up" in his environment. Every other treadmill he had tried failed within month of work. Gamble promised, "If you can build a treadmill that lasts a month, I'll buy two." Woodway reinforced their existing treadmill offer and drove it to UVA. The treadmill met and exceeded Gamble's request. "The technology behind the running surface was second to none. It was so sturdy that I felt our athletes could go all out without risking damage or injury." John Gamble ultimately bought many treadmills, and he also became a spokesperson for Woodway, stating, "Quality and craftsmanship make this treadmill the Rolls Royce of the industry."

Despite great words of endorsement and a product that functioned well, Woodway still had to overcome its share of trials and errors as growing company. Hauling treadmills around in a van—and at times sleeping in the van—was a time consuming and arduous process. One salesman commented, "It is actually a comfortable surface to sleep on too!" Weeks and months would slide off the calendar as the small sales team moved around the country from facility to facility, learning the needs of the coaches and comprehending the training cycle of the various athletic seasons—witnessing the effects of their treadmill's success and failures.

"These guys are training the biggest, strongest, fastest athletes in the world—and they want them to get bigger, stronger and faster. They want to push the limits. We had failures in these conditions," says Emons. "The strength and conditioning coaches would literally yell at us over the phone, yelling was how many of them operated. But we didn't take it personal. It was their job on the line when our product failed - it meant money was wasted, players unable to train, or worse, an injury could occur." Emons continues, "Mr. Bayerlein would personally promise the coaches that Woodway would build the treadmills needed. He would personally take the phone calls when equipment broke, letting the coaches yell and vent at him, assuring them we stood behind our products and would not just fix it, but make it better."

Building the relationships with the strength and conditioning coaches meant that Woodway sales and engineers saw exactly how products were being used, in ways they could not envision without being present. By extension Woodway became pioneers in developing their product in conjunction with the community they were selling into—it was the coach who advised, consented, and gave the ultimate stamp of approval on the product.

Fernando Montez, of the Cleveland Indians, would incline the treadmill and control the speed up and down for his players at set intervals to simulate running the base paths or quick sprints to a fly ball in the outfield. This early form of interval training caused Woodway to develop the Odyssey treadmill, a precursor to their Curve product that allows for HIIT training. Set at a permanent incline, the belt of the Odyssey was free spinning. Players could do a seven second sprint at max speed and then jump off; they had reached base or fielded the play in a simulated environment. Deke, by this time having moved from product tester to main spokesperson/salesman, remembers that Montez also wanted a way to keep his players on treadmills for longer, to build better aerobic capacity. "We built a treadmill with a TV," Deke says, "Coach Montez had a tower of VHS tapes that his players could watch while running and it worked—no one else had coupled television and a treadmill at that point."

The development of new products became reiterative during this golden period of strength and conditioning, for both coaches and Woodway. It was somewhat like an arms race—a coach would have an idea, Woodway would build it, then another coach, trying to find a competitive advantage for his team or realizing a missed opportunity, would tell Woodway to take what they did and tweak it.

For example, the Odyssey treadmill went from just a manual treadmill at a steady state incline to a manual treadmill with resistance—also known as the Force. Emons states that, "Coaches were having their athletes drag parachutes, pull sleds and tires, or even chains, across their practice fields—those are elements of training as old as gladiatorial events. The issue was, this required a large field or track, and what if it was raining or storming outside? No one was using covered training grounds at the time." The Force treadmill replaced all those implements that needed to be dragged or pushed, and the large space needed, by compacting the exercise into a single manual treadmill. By adding attachment points and a harness that was variably resisted, coaches could do resisted sprints anytime, any day. "The coaches loved it, athletes hated it—it become affectionately known as "The Vomit Tread'" says Emons, "We even added load cells so that coaches could measure the power output of the athletes."

The more experience and knowledge that strength and conditioning coaches gained the, better the professional field became, and athletes got bigger, stronger and faster. Woodway feels they had a hand in helping coaches and athletes get there. It also meant the arms race for new products became bigger and larger. Woodway treadmills weren't big enough anymore, so products such as the Pro, Pro XL, and ELG needed to be developed. Products were reinforced and enlarged—oversize treadmills that had faster speeds, greater inclines, declines, jump plates for getting on/off, and side controls were built. "When you're over-speed training," Deke says, "don't worry about buttons for speed and incline—leave that to coaches—you need [athletes] to be able to jump on, hit their target speed, and jump off quickly and safely. So, we developed treadmills that could do exactly that."

Working at the edge of physical boundaries comes with inherent risks, such as the potential for an athlete to lose their footing and fly off a treadmill, so Woodway built overhead gantries and suspension devices to prevent falls. The off-weighting systems also meant that players could rehab at reduced loads, further preventing injury and allowing them to stay in some semblance of shape during these reduced work periods. In doing so, Woodway saw additional market opportunities and took a step back into their German roots by building rehab and physical therapy-specific treadmills. Meanwhile, the golden era for computer development was also occurring during the mid-'90s. As computers miniaturized, capturing player data and metrics could be done directly from the treadmill motherboard. Early email and internet reduced the distance between Woodway sales staff and coaches. Strength coaches wrote periodization and data gathering software for us to develop for on-device use, allowing simple exportation to spreadsheet software. Today, Woodway treadmills can be built with a touch-screen interface. The ProSmart software has 30 years of strength and conditioning development contained within its on-device computer coding. The responsive programming can tell the user their target speed, when to move into a recovery zone, when to push the boundaries—artificial intelligence meeting fitness intelligence.

No level of intelligence, however, can replace the desire of the strength and conditioning coaches of the golden era. Collectively, there was a commitment to pushing the boundaries and developing new techniques and methodologies to leverage every bit of the human body possible in the pursuit of peak athletic performance. The brain trust that was borne out of this era is irreplaceable, both to the strength and coaching community, but also to Woodway. Our products stand on the shoulders of all these coaches who envisioned what a treadmill could do. They took a device historically used for torture and helped Woodway develop it into a device that liberated training from run-of-the-mill to state-of-the-art. Over the years, Woodway has aimed to remain performance dedicated, because their company wouldn't have achieved their successes without this period of trial and error, failure and defeat, success and triumph. The Woodway aim is not to tell you how to train, but to let you tell Woodway (and their treadmills) how you want to train. Woodway has carried this belief through the development of other products, the Blade hockey treadmill, the Carver skiing treadmill, the Boost off-weighting treadmill, the Curve manual series, and the flagship 4Front series. Every product built and developed in conjunction with the experts in strength and conditioning, who Woodway has been so lucky to work with for over 30 years.

CHAPTER 36

Sport Science & Strength & Conditioning

The Michael H. Stone Story

I went to college primarily for two reasons—I was interested in science, particularly biology, and I had a background and interest in sports. My interest was especially centered in trying to understand all I could about strength-power training and athletic performance. I honestly had a hard time understanding why, as popular as sport was, that more importance was not placed on "Sport and Science"

Although I had done some research in my master's degree and PhD that impacted sport, none was really directed specifically toward improving sport performance. And indeed, when I started searching the scientific (and coaching) literature, it was quite clear that very little sport performance research was available, and most of what was available was aimed at aerobic/endurance activity. Indeed, at the time, strength training was even frowned upon in the academic world, and the amount of time I had been exposed to any information about strength training amounted to about two to three lectures in my entire master's and PhD programs. However, it was during my PhD that I started corresponding with John Garhammer, who was also trying to integrate sport with science. We were strongly encouraged by my PhD mentor Dr. Ron Byrd, one of the few scientists that had actually done any research dealing with strength training.

After finishing my PhD at FSU (1977), I took a job at LSU as the first paid Head S&C coach and also taught in the Physical Education Department (exercise physiology) with the stipulation that I would slowly move toward more time in academics. I hired Kyle Pierce (now at LSU-Shreveport) as my gradu-ate assistant while he worked on a doctorate. It was also during this time that Harold O'Bryant became a PhD student at LSU. I had little previous experi-ence as a coach, and although LSU had done some pioneering work in strength training for athletes (Marty Broussard, Dr. Francis Drury, Alvin Roy), it quickly became apparent to both Kyle and I that very little was known about the best methods of training athletes. At LSU, we provided women athletes with some of the first opportunities and guidance they had on S&C and carried out one of the very first studies on women athletes and strength training (Moulds et al. 1979). While at LSU, Kyle, Harold and I began some of the first work on single versus multiple sets, machines and free weights, and periodization/program-ming, including the idea of block periodization (BP). Harold O'Bryant's disser-tation (and his other published work) is still one of the best sources for informa-tion on early ideas of periodization programming for strength-training.

Kyle and I moved to Auburn (where Kyle finished his doctorate) in 1980 as a part of the National Strength Research Center (NSRC). The NSRC was funded by Diversified Products (Opelika, AL) and was conceptualized by Terry Todd. The NSRC provided a training area for lifters and brought together several scientists that had interests in this area, including Dr. John Garhammer and myself. John, as the lead, and I (along with several graduate students), served as the basketball strength coaches while we were there. Again, this provided considerable insight into the various problems associated with training athletes in a collegiate environment.

It was during this time, at an early NSCA meeting, that I met Meg Ritchie, Olympian, NCAA record holder, first female Head S&C coach and much more—who eventually became Meg Stone and my best friend. No doubt she has done more to help me understand the need for sport science and coach education than anyone.

Kyle went on to S&C coaching positions at Tulane, LSU, and became part of the faculty; currently he is a professor at LSU-Shreveport, where he has produces many of the best weightlifters in the USA, as well as young, up-and-coming coaches and sport scientists, does considerable work for the Interna-tional Weightlifting Federation, and is presently serving as the national coach for Ghana.

While at Auburn, we were able to conduct more research dealing with the effects of strength training on endurance and strength-endurance variables. We began to gain a much greater understanding of the components that should make up the Accumulation Phase of BP and provided more information concerning the influence of resistance training volume on body composition and maximum strength. We also continued to develop ideas about the overall programming for BP. To my knowledge, the first study dealing with BP programming and strength gains was published while we were at Auburn (Stone et al. 1980).

Moving on to Appalachian State University in 1988 once again allowing me to work with Dr. Harold O'Bryant. Harold may be the most unappreciated scientist and teacher I've ever known. He was very meticulous, and if he carried out a study it took a while, but you would always know it was done right. It was also at ASU that I Met Chip Sigmon and his wife-to-be, Michelle. Chip was the Head S&C coach, and, as most S&C coaches in those days, vastly unappreciated and underpaid. As a result of interaction with Chip, we were able, with his help, to begin providing students as S&C interns and continue research with actual athletes. Chip went on to be the head S&C coach of the Charlotte Hornets, and currently he and Michelle are in private business but still consult on a regular basis with professional and collegiate athletes and coaches.

One of my first students at ASU was Travis Triplett. Travis went on to earn a PhD, became an excellent scientist, and is presently (in 2018) the first woman to be NSCA president. In 1992, Greg Haff became my student at ASU, later he earned a PhD, became one of the leading sport scientist in the world, and became NSCA president. During this time, Harold and I collaborated with Kyle, John Garhammer, as well other colleagues such as Dr. Any Fry, on a variety of projects. At ASU, we again studied the effects of multiple versus one set to failure (a very popular but erroneous idea at the time), began studies on several ergogenic aids including creatine, began to better understand the importance of fatigue management, and most importantly, continued periodization programming research.

When Meg took the position of Head Athletics Coach for Sport Scotland in early 1999, we moved to Edinburgh, and I became Professor and Chair of Sport at Edinburgh University. We moved to Colorado Springs in December 2001, where I became Head of Sport Physiology for the USOC and Meg became a coaching manager (coach's education). However, I wanted to get into a position where I could concentrate on research and Meg wanted to get back to coaching and really concentrate on coach's education.

Interestingly, while at the USOC, Meg and her colleague Kathy Sellars completed a rather damning study of coach's education and sport science in the USA. Basically, most coaches are very poorly prepared to be coaches. In 2005 we moved to Johnson City and East Tennessee State University, where I am a professor and Laboratory Director and Meg is the Director of the Center of Excellence for Sport Science and Coach Education and the Head of the ETSU Olympic Training Site. Along with our colleague Mike Ramsey, we have created a rather unique graduate program which combines direct work with sports and academic pursuits. During the time between ASU and the present we, along with our colleagues and students, we continued to study various aspects of strength-power production including cluster training, accentuated eccentric loading, and effects on endurance activities, but in particular we continued research dealing with periodization programming.

During this period of time (from roughly 1978 to the present), while there have been some great strides in sport science and strength and conditioning, there are many aspects that have not really changed. S&C coaches are still undervalued, and in some cases underpaid. Although some schools and professional teams are hiring "Sport Scientists and High Performance Directors," they are greatly undervalued and often ignored and many of them are very poorly trained to be sport scientists. Without a doubt, coaches are unfortunately still, for the most part, poorly educated to be coaches (Hornsby et al. 2018).

References

Moulds, B., Carter, D.R., Coleman, J. and Stone, M.H. Physical responses of a women's basketball team to a pre season conditioning program. In (J. Terauds, ed.) *Science in Sports*, Academic Publishers, Del Mar, California, pp.203-210, 1979.

Hornsby G., Gleason B., Wathen D., Deweese B., Stone M., Pierce K., Wagle J., Szymanski D.J., Stone. M.H. *Servant or Service? The Problem and a Conceptual Solution*, Journal of Intercollegiate Sports 10(2): 228-243, 2017.

Stone, M.H., O'Bryant, H. and Garhammer, J. A hypothetical model for strength training. *Journal of Sports Medicine and Physical Fitness*, 21: 342 351, 1981

———

The Travis Triplett Story

N. Travis Triplett, First Female President of the NSCA, Former Director of Strength Centers at University of Wisconsin-La Crosse, Exercise Physiologist

My story begins with an anatomy class in the newly-formed degree program in Health and Sport Science at Wake Forest University in 1984. About that same time, I took a weight training class for one of my physical education credits and was hooked. My high school weight room was very small and not used much by the girls' sports teams, so I had almost no prior experience with lifting weights. I was always interested in the human body, enjoyed participating in track, and realized I that loved to lift weights. I could see all the positive effects in my body and vowed to continue to lift throughout my lifetime.

Being able to study exercise science was a new option nationwide, and exercise science degree programs were springing up, having recently separated out of physical education programs, where they were originally a concentration within the physical education degree. These new degree programs took many forms, and some emphasized sport and athletic performance more than others. Some even had "sport science" in the name, like my program, but it was quite different from the sport science we know today. Much of the early focus of exercise/sport science degree programs was on endurance activities and endurance athletes. To be able to study strength-power athletes or strength and conditioning in general was a rarity. There were very few academics who identified as being primarily strength-and-conditioning-focused in their teaching and research, so when it came time for me to seek out a master's degree program, I fortunately had to look no further than my own backyard, to Appalachian State University.

I had stumbled across "Weight Training: A Scientific Approach" while in my bachelor's degree, and realized that one of the authors (Dr. Harold O'Bryant) worked at Appalachian State, which was in the town where I grew up. I applied only to Appalachian State and was able to gain admission and secure a graduate assistantship in the exercise physiology labs there starting in the fall of 1987. The first year was spent taking exercise science core classes and teaching undergraduate exercise physiology labs, as well as helping other faculty and students with their research. Dr. Mike Stone (the other author) even came to town and gave a guest lecture in one of the graduate classes. Shortly after, Dr. Stone took a position at Appalachian State, which was really a turning point in my training and had a tremendous impact on my career.

The second year of a master's degree is typically spent taking more specialized classes and conducting thesis research. Dr. Stone taught several of the classes I took and became my master's thesis mentor. I remember feeling a little lost about what to study. There were so many interesting topics in strength and conditioning and so few studies had been done, so it became difficult to narrow down a topic. However, Dr. Stone guided me through the process to a successful completion. Another attribute of Dr. Stone was his willingness and interest in discussing all things strength and conditioning. My fellow students and I learned just as much outside of class—chatting while lifting with Dr. Stone in the Athlete weight room (where Chip Sigmon was the Head Strength and Conditioning coach) or while going out for lunch to the local buffets—as we did in class. Doc Stone, as we called him, insisted we all learn and become proficient in the weightlifting movements, and within two to three years of finishing my master's degree I earned both the NSCA CSCS and USAW Club Coach certifications.

Dr. Stone also helped my career tremendously by encouraging and supporting me to take a one-year research assistant position in the Sports Physiology labs at the US Olympic Training Center in Colorado Springs in 1989. It was there I was able to see true Sport Science—using science to advance the training and performance of athletes. We tested hundreds of athletes, mostly developmental, but were able to see how the Sports Physiologists who were on staff communicated with the sport coaches about how to take the information we obtained and use it to guide training. All of my prior experience had been on the academic side of sport science, studying athletic performance in order to understand the function of the human body, with the eventual goal of finding some useful information for practitioners. This experience showed me the final application of the science to actual sport performance and training.

After my year-long experience was over, I went to Penn State to study with Dr. William Kraemer for a PhD. I was back into the science side of things for the next eight years, around five years for my PhD degree and around three years for a post-doctoral research fellowship in Australia with Rob Newton, a biomechanist who was known for his work with power performance and power training. I branched out into working with resistance training in the older adult but retained my interest in working with athletes and in athletic performance. After my post-doctoral fellowship was complete, I took my first university position as a faculty member in the Exercise and Sport Science program at the University of Wisconsin-La Crosse (a Division III school), but also as the Director of Strength and Conditioning for the entire campus. Not only did I have responsibilities with the Campus Recreation side of strength and conditioning, but the Athletic weight room also fell under my purview. I had a great staff who did more of the direct athlete interactions and who were sport coaches themselves, and we had a concentration in strength and conditioning within our Exercise and Sport Science degree program, so much of our time was spent training the next generation of strength and conditioning professionals, many of whom have gone on to careers in both collegiate and professional sports. It was a tremendous learning experience for me to see strength and conditioning from an applied side, and I have carried that knowledge gained into my current position as the Director of the Strength and Conditioning concentrations in the Exercise Science degree program here at Appalachian State, where I have been a faculty member for the last 15 years.

I am optimistic that the broader fields of Strength and Conditioning and Sport Science will continue to evolve and grow. The influence of technology on both fields has been tremendous, and the ability to quantify training and performance has increased exponentially in the last 15 years. I remember measuring vertical jump using chalk and a chalkboard with some markings on it mounted to the wall. Now we have force plates and portable units that attach to the athlete and record not only vertical displacement but force, velocity, power, and rate of force development. The earliest form of computer-based motion analysis utilized video cameras filming on black backgrounds and now we have sensors on the various limbs that send a signal to a box in the next room or on the sideline. There is really more data than we know what to do with, so the challenge now is taking huge datasets and distilling the numbers into something useful for the coach. A new role within Sport Science is data analytics, so future professionals will need skillsets never before used for strength and conditioning. From a more global perspective, strides are being made by the NSCA and other professional associations in strength and conditioning to elevate the role of the strength and conditioning professional and the sport scientist. Change can be slow but by learning from the past and continuing to push ahead to the future, we will get there.

www.ingramcontent.com/pod-product-compliance
Lightning Source LLC
Chambersburg PA
CBHW052031090426
42739CB00010B/1868